THE SECRET BEHIND COMMUNISM

ABOUT THE AUTHOR

Former member of the House of Representatives in Louisiana, Dr. David Duke, is unique. He earned a PhD in history and is a world famous political figure.

Dr. Duke lecturing in the Mayakovsky Museum near infamous Lubayanka Prison

"What is the point of studying and understanding history," he says, "if we don't learn enough from it to prevent a repeat of its horrors."

In Russia and Ukraine Dr. Duke researched the foundations of communism and its Red Terror. His book reveals the force behind them that still endangers the world, and it also throws light on the common origins of Communism and Zionism, and how many features of Communism now flourish in Zionism and Israel.

Duke was a politically incorrect young man. He says what he thinks, popular or not. His views have evolved, but the media never forgives criticism against the Zionist extremists who so powerfully influence it.

He opposes any sort of racism or ethnic supremacism, including that of the hyper-racist tribalism that runs Zionist Israel, and that also influences global media, governments and finance. He believes that every people on Earth has the right to be free and independent; to preserve its heritage and diversity as a unique expression of humanity; that no people has the right to oppress or exploit others.

It is ironic that the Ziomedia voices that excoriate this non-violent man are the same who revere people like Menachem Begin. Only in an upside down world could an unrepentant, Zionist terrorist who murdered and ethnically cleansed Palestinians, be honored with a Nobel Peace Prize.

Dr. Duke, a courageous, non-violent voice for peace against the Zionist-driven wars of our time, finds no media redemption. He has, however, found redemption from voters and respect from millions of the truly open-minded.

David Duke went on from his controversial younger days to win four elections. He won the New Hampshire Democratic Primary for Vice President of the United States in 1988 with over 60 percent of the vote (the same election Al Gore won in 1996). He won election to the House of Representatives in Louisiana in 1989. In 1991 Duke defeated the sitting Governor of Louisiana (Buddy Roemer) for the Republican nomination. Duke was elected Chairman of the Republican Executive Committee (1996-2000) in the largest Republican district of Louisiana.

David Duke has a doctorate in History and has lectured at over two hundred universities on four continents. He has appeared in major televised debates and programs, including three appearances on the leading American political program, *Meet the Press*. He has appeared on over 1,000 programs in America, Europe and 20 other nations. Dr. Duke's videos earn a 90 percent positive rating from tens of millions of viewers. He has penned four books: *My Awakening, Jewish Supremacism, The Secret Behind Communism* and *The Zionist Conspiracy*.

DR. DAVID DUKE

Visiting a memorial commemorating the genocide in the nation of Ukraine. Dr. Duke has spent years in Russia and Eastern Europe researching the origins of Communism and The Red Terror.

THE SECRET BEHIND COMMUNISM

THE ETHNIC ORIGINS OF THE RUSSIAN REVOLUTION & THE GREATEST HOLOCAUST IN THE HISTORY OF MANKIND

THE FACT THAT THE WORLD IS SO IGNORANT AND UNCARING ABOUT THIS ENORMOUS CRIME IS PROOF THAT THE GLOBAL MEDIA IS IN THE HANDS OF THE PERPETRATORS.

-- **ALEKSANDR SOLZHENITSYN**

DR. DAVID DUKE

WITH RESEARCH AND WRITINGS ALSO FROM
ALEKSANDR SOLZHENITSYN, FRANK BRITTON AND OTHER SCHOLARS

THE SECRET BEHIND COMMUNISM

THE ETHNIC ORIGINS OF THE RUSSIAN REVOLUTION AND THE GREATEST
HOLOCAUST IN THE HISTORY OF MANKIND

FREE SPEECH PRESS
MANDEVILLE, LA

COPYRIGHT © 2013 BY DAVID DUKE

ISBN: 978-1-892796-01-1

AUTHOR'S CONTACT
WWW.DAVIDDUKE.COM

DEDICATION:

TO THE MEMORY OF A MAN WHO COMBINED GENIUS WITH COURAGE.
FOR HIM, THE STRUGGLE FOR HUMAN RIGHTS AND VALUES IS MORE THAN
A MATTER OF PRINCIPLE, IT IS THE MEANING OF LIFE ITSELF.

ALEKSANDR SOLZHENITSYN

Table of Contents

Introduction

"You must understand. The leading Bolsheviks who took over Russia were not Russians. They hated Russians. They hated Christians. Driven by ethnic hatred they tortured and slaughtered millions of Russians without a shred of human remorse.

The October Revolution was not what you call in America the 'Russian Revolution.'

It was an invasion and conquest over the Russian people.

More of my countrymen suffered horrific crimes at their bloodstained hands than any people or nation ever suffered in the entirety of human history.

It cannot be overstated. Bolshevism committed the greatest human slaughter of all time.

The fact that most of the world is ignorant and uncaring about this enormous crime is proof that the global media is in the hands of the perpetrators."[1]

-- Aleksandr Solzhenitsyn

These were startling words, spoken to me by the famous Russian writer and philosopher Aleksandr Solzhenitsyn when I had the privilege of meeting him in Moscow in 2002.

His words made me fully realize the fact that most of the people of the world know little about the tribalist entity which created and drove the Communist juggernaut that took over Russia. They also know frightfully little about the greatest slaughters in history, the genocide of tens of millions of people that was spawned by deep ethnic hatred.

For so many people, even for some of those who have studied the "Russian Revolution" in history courses in universities around the world, this is "The Secret Behind Communism." This secret, even though plain to see if one just looks closely, is rarely spoken about in either the mainstream press or in mainstream academia.

The revolution occurred in Russia, and although a percentage of Russians participated in it, it was not a "Russian Revolution." It was led by an alienated, non-Russian, Jewish ethnic minority that hated Russia, Russians, and the Tsar for their alleged anti-Semitism. As will be documented in this book, their fellow tribalists around the world financed, and their shock troops executed the brutal takeover of the Russian government. Upon achieving total power, their deep, psychopathic, racist hatred became manifest in the greatest human slaughter of all time.

Any historian who has studied modern Communism from its ideological origins in Karl Marx and Moses Hess, through the mass dispossession, forced starvations, and Gulags of the twentieth century, is aware that Communists are the real world champions of mass murder. There is no historical dispute that Communist regimes killed many times more innocents than any other government in history, including Hitler's Germany.

But unlike thousands of even lowly soldiers of Germany, the Red Terror murderers of millions have not been hunted down across the face of the Earth. They have not faced trial for their horrific crimes against humanity. Perhaps even more importantly they have never faced the court of popular revulsion. Why? It is because these Communist perpetrators have been shielded by their tribal brethren who now identify with Zionism who have an inordinate influence on media, academia, and governments.

The deaths in just one of the many Communist killing fields totaled 5 to 8 million. Men, women and children of the Ukraine were starved, killed, imprisoned, and worked to death in what is called the Holodomor. It is a death toll equal to or even greater than the numbers in what now is called the "Holocaust."

Today, most people through mass media and government commemoration, are aware of and empathize with the victims of the Holocaust, but 99 percent of humanity are completely unaware of the Ukrainian Holodomor.

The world has been inundated with both fictional and non-fictional dramas about the sufferings of Jews and Jewish children, such as Anne Frank, in the war. However, the great masses have not been led to shed tears for the little girls of Ukrainian and

Why Do the Hollywood Bosses Ignore the Largest Holocaust in Human History?

Russian heritage who suffered and died. They are unknown, unremembered and unmourned in the media of today. People are unconscious and cut off from empathy for the millions murdered by the Bolsheviks in Russia, even if they have a vague knowledge of millions suffering under Communism. Very few people have an emotional attachment to the victims of the Communists because Hollywood and the media have done nothing to instill any concern for them, in contrast to their unending dirge of "The "Holocaust. "

In the Hollywood media of movies and television, in broadcasting and major publishing, every adult has absorbed thousands of hours of what is called "The Holocaust." It is the trademarked, jealous god which demands no other gods before it.

When I met Aleksandr Solzhenitsyn (1918-2008), he had just published his last work, called *Two Hundred Years Together*

THIS LITTLE GIRL WAS STARVED TO DEATH IN THE INTENTIONAL ETHNIC GENOCIDE OF THE UKRAINIAN PEOPLE...

YOU DON'T KNOW HER NAME.
YOU DON'T KNOW HER STORY.

THE SAME HOLLYWOOD THAT BRINGS YOU THE "HOLOCAUST" ALMOST EVERY DAY OF YOUR LIFE -- SHOWS YOU NOTHING ABOUT THE LARGEST GENOCIDE IN THE HISTORY OF MANKIND.

WHY?

(2001). It was about the Jewish experience in Russia, and contained three chapters devoted to discussing the Jewish role in the revolutionary genocide and secret police purges of Soviet Russia after the Bolshevik Revolution of October 1917.

I waited for ten years in vain for the book to be published in English. It remains unpublished to this day. Of course. The secret behind Communism must remain a secret to most of the public.

Solzhenitsyn knew that he would be condemned for daring to point out the secret, but he went ahead nonetheless, telling me that it was his duty to tell the truth so that the world would know. He paid the price. Although his book was a runaway bestseller in Russia, this last important book by the Nobel Prize-winning author has never been published in English. So the largest audience in the world has been denied the truth. The controlled media had to mute the great man's voice.

However, this book, *The Secret Behind Communism* will somewhat remedy that suppression, for it contains many important and relevant quotations from *Two Hundred Years Together,* including many of the revealing quotes that were the reason why the book was not published in English.

It wasn't the first time that Solzhenitsyn had raised the subject of the Jewish ethnic driving force behind Communism and its slaughters. In his famous *The Gulag Archipelago* books, in which he described his imprisonment by the Soviets, he pointed out that almost all the commanders of the Gulag camps were Jews, by famously including pictures (*shown on the left*) of six Jewish Chekist Gulag bosses of the 1930s.[2]

In *Two Hundred Years Together,* Solzhenitsyn wrote that he had taken their pictures from an official Soviet-era publication that boasted about the Gulags.

Despite Solzhenitsyn's efforts — and those of many others, including Frank Britton (some of his excellent work and research is included in this volume), the truth about the Jewish supremacist role in the creation, execution and maintenance of world Communism, and the "Russian" Revolution in particular, remains little-known. The reason for this is simple: The Jewish supremacist tribalists who influence major media in the West make sure that almost nothing is said about the fact that Jews, along with organized Jewish support worldwide, not only created Communism, but were the leaders who brought it into such grim reality. They were at the nexus of the greatest slaughter and mass human suffering in history.

This is the core of the secret behind Communism, exposed and overwhelmingly documented in this book.

The Paramount Jewish Role
in Communism: No Secret in Israeli Media

Ironically, Jewish historians are quite happy to discuss the leading Jewish role among themselves—although any Gentile who dares to raise the topic is immediately decried as an "anti-Semite." The Jewish role is written about only in the Jewish press.

A good example came with the article that appeared in the popular Israeli online Jewish Zionist news source, *YnetNews.com.*

net | **opinion** דעות

Sever Plocker

Stalin's Jews

We mustn't forget that some of greatest murderers of modern times were Jewish

Published: 12.21.06, 23:35 / Israel Opinion

Here's a particularly forlorn historical date: Almost 90 years ago, between the 19th and 20th of December 1917, in the midst of the Bolshevik revolution and civil war, Lenin signed a decree calling for the establishment of The All-Russian Extraordinary Commission for Combating Counter-Revolution and Sabotage, also known as Cheka.

Within a short period of time, Cheka became the largest and

Jewish historians and publications have no reluctance to point out in Jewish publications, in Israel and to Jewish readers around the world, the dominant role of Jews in the Bolshevik revolution in Russia. They even admit their key role in the greatest mass murders of all time. However, they find it important to cover it up in mainstream print and broadcasting media in Europe and America.

In December 2006 it shared an article with its Jewish readers called "Stalin's Jews," which tells facts about the Jewish role in mass murder that would certainly have been criticized as "anti-Semitic" if any gentile historian or publication had told them.

The article, written by well-known Jewish writer Sever Plocker, is subtitled:

> **"We mustn't forget that some of *(sic)* greatest murderers of modern times were Jewish"**

Plocker wrote:

"We cannot know with certainty the number of deaths Cheka was responsible for in its various manifestations, but the number is surely at least 20 million, including victims of the forced collectivization, the hunger, large purges, expulsions, banishments, executions, and mass death at Gulags.

"Genrikh Yagoda was the greatest Jewish murderer of the 20th Century, the GPU's deputy commander and the founder and commander of the NKVD. Yagoda diligently implemented Stalin's collectivization orders and is responsible for the deaths of at least 10 million people. His Jewish deputies established and managed the Gulag system."[3]

Genrikh Yagoda, murdered twice the number of people alleged against Adolf Hitler. Although Jewish scholars realize this fact, not 1 of 1000 gentiles even know his name.

To understand the incredible level of deception about the enormous Jewish crimes against humanity, just consider how the globalist Jewish-dominated media hides Yagoda's role in a genocide of at least 10 million human beings.

Jewish writers and a major Jewish Israeli website casually report to their Jewish readers that the Jewish Bolshevik, Yagoda, murdered twice the number of the alleged 5.1 million victims counted by the pre-eminent Holocaust historian, Raul Hilberg.

The Holocaust is "never forget."
The Bolshevik Holocaust is "never remember."

Yet, this Jewish genocidal murderer who ironically has an identical mustache to Hitler, and who murdered double the number of people than are alleged against Hitler, is completely unknown. Not one person in a thousand would be able to identify Yagoda's very distinctive name, much less associate it with mass murder.

Why does the media tell us that we should "never forget" the Jewish Holocaust, but in regard to the much bigger Bolshevik Holocaust the message is "never remember." This illustrates *The Secret Behind Communism* in a more profound way than this author ever could express.

Ethnic Hatred Expressed in Both Communism and Zionism

This book exposes the little-known fact that Zionism and Communism have the same ethnic and very similar ideological roots. Karl Marx was descended from a long line of Talmudic scholars, and he learned much of his Communist theory from Moses Hess. Hess later morphed into a rabid Jewish racial supremacist and Zionist while at the same time continuing to embrace the principles of Communism.

Tragically, the ethnic cleansings and murderous ways of the Jewish tribalists in Russia are being repeated in the Zionist ethnic cleansing of Palestine. Similar ethnic racism is at work in Palestine as it was in Russia, and in other European nations.

It can be seen in the ethnic genocide against the Ukrainians. The Jewish Bolsheviks purposefully murdered them to reduce their numbers, and then flooded their country with non-Ukrainians to destroy their national/ethnic unity (See: *Holodomor chapter*). Raphael Lemkin, father of the word *genocide,* wrote this in his article "Soviet Genocide in Ukraine."

Ukrainian Genocide by the Bolsheviks

The fourth step in the process [genocide] consisted in the fragmentation of the Ukrainian people at once by the addition to the Ukraine of foreign peoples...In this way, ethnic unity would be destroyed and nationalities mixed. Between 1920 and 1939, the population of Ukraine changed from 80% Ukrainian to only 63%...[4]

The Soviet Archives in Moscow has this revealing statement from a Bolshevik leader in Ukraine showing that genocide there was to break their ethnic unity in opposition to Bolshevik rule.

"Famine in Ukraine was brought on to decrease the number of Ukrainians, replace the dead with people from other parts of the USSR, and thereby to kill the slightest thought of any Ukrainian independence."[5]

This volume reveals how Israel today, and shockingly even Yad Vashem, honors one of the worst Bolshevik criminals of the Second World War, Ilya Ehrenburg, and shows how Zionists embrace the same ethnic hatreds as did their Bolshevik brethren.

The Israeli Holocaust Museum Honors Bolshevik Promoter of Genocide Who Hid Bolshevik Crimes from the World

Ehrenburg was a leading international propagandist for the Bolshevik state while it committed the worst mass murder in history. He was also the chief propagandist for the Red Army, who urged on the genocidal mass murder of Germans and other Eastern Europeans. *The Canadian Jewish News* states:

> Until his death in 1967, "his support for the Soviet state, and for Stalin, never wavered. His loyalty and service were acknowledged in 1952 when he received the Stalin Prize.[6]

He is most infamous for his viciously anti-German wartime propaganda. *The Canadian Jewish News* states:

> "As the leading Soviet journalist during World War II, Ehrenburg's writings against the German invaders were circulated among millions of Soviet soldiers." [7]

In one booklet called "Kill," Ehrenburg incites Soviet soldiers to treat Germans as sub-humans. Its final words include:

> "The Germans are not human beings. From now on the word German means to use the most terrible oath.... We shall kill. If you have not killed at least one German a day, you have wasted that day... If you cannot kill your German with a bullet, kill him with your bayonet. If there is calm on your part of the front, or if you are waiting for the fighting, kill a German in the meantime. If you leave a German alive, the German will hang a Russian and rape a Russian woman. If you kill one German, kill another--there is nothing more amusing for us than a heap of German corpses. Do not count days, do not count kilometers. Count only the number of Germans you kill. Kill the German--that is your grandmother's request. Kill the German--that is your child's prayer. Kill the German--that is your motherland's loud request. ... Kill."[8]

Ehrenburg's incendiary writings certainly contributed in no small measure to the orgy of murder and rape by Soviet soldiers against German and other Eastern European civilians.

The Canadian Jewish News further writes:

... The recent disclosure that Ehrenburg arranged to transfer his private archives to Jerusalem's Yad Vashem library and archive, while still alive, comes as a stunning revelation... Ehrenburg agreed... on condition that the transfer, and his will, remain secret for 20 years after his death.

So we discover that a dedicated Bolshevik Soviet leader whose propaganda hid the Bolshevik Holocaust, had secretly willed his private papers, not to the Soviet Union, but to the Zionist State, where he is honored today at Yad Vashem.

The honoring of a genocidal Bolshevik at Yad Vashem, the most important Jewish memorial to the Holocaust, speaks of an enormous hypocrisy that boggles the mind. Only in a deeply corrupted morality could the most important memorial in the world against genocide honor a man who supported genocide. More importantly, there is not a word of criticism in the press. It seems that one man's genocidal maniac is another's man's hero.

Zionist Israel today honors leaders who openly promote ethnic genocide in words just as horrific as Ehrenberg's. The former chief Sephardic rabbi of Israel, Rabbi Ovadia Yosef, calls for the extermination of the Palestinians. BBC quotes him:

"It is forbidden to be merciful to them. You must send missiles to them and annihilate them. They are evil and damnable," he was quoted as saying in a sermon delivered on Monday to mark the Jewish festival of Passover...

"The Lord shall return the Arabs' deeds on their own heads, waste their seed and exterminate them, devastate them and vanish them from this world," he said.

Rabbi Yosef is the spiritual head of the powerful Shas Party, one of the Israeli Prime Minister's closest allies. He has also said that "The only purpose of Gentiles on Earth is to serve Jews." Could one even imagine the world outrage if any political leader in America or Europe was in political partnership with someone who preaches that Jews must be exterminated? This alone reveals Zionist power in government and media across the world.

The Bolshevik Holocaust: Down the Memory Hole

Why there is vast knowledge and emotional attachment to a Holocaust perpetrated against Jews and so little attention on a larger Holocaust perpetrated *by* Jews, is clear. It is the result of Jewish influence in media and

government. We should have knowledge and thus passion for all victims of genocide, not just for a group favored by the press.

I begin with a short chapter from my book, *Jewish Supremacism*, for an introduction to the shocking historical data. After finishing *The Secret Behind Communism*, I urge you to read *Jewish Supremacism* and *My Awakening* for a deeper understanding of Jewish ethnic racism and extremism.

Then I explore a wealth of material that has gone down what George Orwell called the "memory hole" in his classic novel, *1984.*

I share with you some of Frank Britton's ground-breaking research on the topic, first published in 1952, and supplemented since that time, including my additions and updates to it. Then I delve into my own research and that of many other scholars on the topic. It is important for me to state that some of the text here is not my own, and I don't take credit for it all. However, I have edited and added to the text in places where needed. I am also indebted to some of the translations and the scholarship of Wolfgang Strauss who made key selections of translations into English from Solzhenitsyn's *Two Hundred Years Together.*

Some of the material is gleaned from articles and books by dozens of scholars on Bolshevism and its subsequent crimes. I obviously take no credit for their original research, but I have tracked down and compiled a great deal of this mountainous diverse data, made an analysis of it, and placed it here in a cohesive format along with my own editing and commentary.

The book seeks to answer crucial questions. Why has there been such a close relationship between Jewish tribalism and Communism all over the world? At first glance the two movements would seem to be incompatible.

How does one explain rich capitalist Zionist bankers such as Jacob Schiff, supporting Communist atheist movements?

How and why did Communist Jews who worshipped Trotsky transform into neo-conservatives who aren't very conservative?

Israel is an ethnic supremacist state. Israel promotes Jewish-only immigration, and segregated schools and housing of Jews and non-

Deir Yassin (above) and the ethnic cleansing of 700,000 Palestinians were born from the same misanthropic tribalism which drove the ethnic genocide of Russians, Ukrainians and other European peoples

Jews. Israel does not even allow a Jewish/Gentile marriage performed. It allows its Jewish citizens to own and to carry machine guns on the street.

Yet, those same Zionist Israel supporters overwhelmingly support the very opposite political agenda in every nation in which they dwell.

They predominantly support leftist and Marxist movements and ideologies in the Gentile nations in which they live, still today, decades after losing control of Communist Russia, but also embrace Zionism. Why?

Zionist influence over American and EU policy directly led to the Zionist ethnic cleansing of Palestinians, and the death and suffering of millions of innocents in by Zionist, tribalist-driven wars in the Mideast. What do these events and the Communist genocides have in common?

Racial hatred is shown as a clear motivation in the genocides of the Jewish Bolsheviks. Their motivation must be examined and

fully understood. Can one understand the crimes of Zionism without seeing their relationship to the crimes of Communism?

The Bolshevik Holocaust is an horrific story that all people who love life and freedom should learn the truth about if they are not to be doomed to repeat such horrors.

If the world had been aware of the Jewish tribalism behind Communism and the most massive violation of human rights in all of history, certainly the world would have averted crimes such as the horrific Iraq War, motivated by the Zionist agenda, and based entirely on lies. It was empowered by their symbiosis of media and government influence. Preventing the wars they have created in the Mideast would have saved millions of lives.

Many of the Zionist techniques of terrorism, ethnic cleansing, torture and murder in Palestine and across the region were learned long ago in their Bolshevik revolt against civilization.

Unmasking the ethnic tribalism and ethnic hatred behind The Red Terror is critical to preventing a globalist tyranny and future genocides. You may ask, *how so?*

The ethnic tribalist takeover and The Red Terror thankfully has been ended in Russia, after half-a-century of genocide against ethnic Russians and other captive European peoples. However, since then, that same racist tribalism has gained a remarkable degree of global supremacy today. Indeed, power-mad Zionists dominate the world's only Superpower, to the detriment of its own people and the world. So, exposing them and deposing them is crucial to every person on earth who loves freedom.

They are the ethnically driven source of Zionist power and its crimes, and they still, for the most part, control the leftist remnants of Communism. They also dominate the right through neo-conservativism. They are at the nexus of global media, government, and finance. Their pervading influence enables Israel to literally get away with murder.

Exposing their horrific crimes against humanity will help prevent their repetition. The perpetrators must not be allowed to repeat their crimes upon we the living and our children.

In the next few pages you will delve deep into *The Secret Behind Communism.*

--Dr. David Duke

Chapter 1
Communism with the Mask Off

The old yellow newsprint screamed: "COMMUNISM IS JEWISH!" Another issue of the newspaper called *Common Sense* trumpeted, "NAACP PART OF RED MASTER PLAN!" In one of the older issues a huge headline predicted, "RED DICTATORSHIP BY 1954!"

However, such a warning did not seem too credible when looked at in 1965 by a young man of fifteen. I found the *National Enquirer*-type headlines ludicrous, but it was hard to resist reading something that scandalous, even if just to laugh at it.

The Sharp Words of Mattie Smith

One of the regular volunteers at the Citizen's Council in New Orleans, Mattie Smith, an elderly lady in a flower-print dress and outlandish hat, saw me snickering at the lurid headlines and said quietly, "You know, it's true."

"Red Dictatorship by 1954?" I replied with a smile.

"No," she said, "Communism *is* Jewish. They are the ones behind it."

I thought I would humor the little old lady by politely arguing a bit with her. "Ma'am. How could that be?" I asked. "Communists are atheists; they don't believe in God. Jews believe in God, so how could they be Communists?"

"Do you know who Herbert Aptheker is?" she said, answering my question with one of her own.

"No," I replied, affecting nonchalance.

She was like a tightly coiled spring waiting for release. "He has the official role of chief theoretician of the Communist Party, USA, and he's listed in the *Who's Who in World Jewry*.[9] Leon Trotsky, the Communist who took over Russia with Lenin, was in *Who's Who in American Jewry*.[10] His real name is Lev Bronstein. Both are atheist Communists, and both are proudly listed as great Jews in these books published by the leading rabbinical organizations in the world."

Meekly, I offered, "Maybe they were listed because they were *once* Jews."

"You have so much to learn," she said with a sigh. "Under Israel's Law of Return, you can be an atheist Communist and still immigrate to Israel. There are plenty of them, too. You only qualify to immigrate if you are a Jew, and a Jew is described simply as being of Jewish descent. So, you see, you can be Jewish and still be an atheist and still be a Communist — and I tell, Communism *is* Jewish!"

"All Jews are Communists?" I retorted sarcastically.

"No, no, no," she emphatically replied, with much patience in the way she paced her words. "All Jews are not Communists, any more than all snakes are poisonous. But most leading Communists in America are Jews, as well as most of the convicted Russian spies in America, as well as the leaders of the New Left. And historically, most of the leading Commie revolutionaries in the first few decades of the Russian Revolution were Jewish as well!"

What Mrs. Smith said made me very uncomfortable. Although it was not yet time to leave, I claimed that I had to catch my bus back home. I left the office hurriedly. Mrs. Smith *had* to be wrong, but I just did not have the information I needed to refute her statements. I resolved to research the issue so that I could show her why she was wrong. Something else bothered me as well, for I felt a little guilty for even talking with someone who said such terrible things about Jews.

I was staunchly anti-Communist, and to suggest that Jews were behind the horrors of Communism was to me such a terrible allegation that my heart told me that it just could not be true. It was the first time I had been face to face with a person I presumed was an anti-Semite. I was soon running to catch my streetcar.

During the next couple of days I avoided even thinking about the issue, and I stayed away from the Citizens Council office. Finally I picked up and read the two copies of *Common Sense* I had taken home. One copy maintained that the NAACP was a Communist front organization dedicated to the eventual overthrow of our way of life. It purported that 12 Jews and one

African American had founded the NAACP, and that all of the founders were dedicated Marxists with decades of documented Communist affiliations.

The article asserted that the only major Black founder of the NAACP, W. E. B. Dubois, was an avowed member of the Communist Party who emigrated to Communist Ghana (where he eventually was buried). Furthermore, the scandalous publication purported that the NAACP was financed by Jewish money and always had a Jewish president. It said that a Jew, Kivie Kaplan, was the current NAACP president and that he was the real leader of the organization rather than its African American "front man," Roy Wilkins. Although the public perceived Wilkins as the NAACP leader, the paper asserted that he actually had the lower rank of national secretary.

The argument of *Common Sense* was that the Jews led and supported the integrationist NAACP because they were opposed to and demonized powerful African American nationalist leaders such as Marcus Garvey and later those who led the Nation of Islam. It said that they really had no interest in African Americans becoming self-reliant or self-supportive. It maintained that the Jewish leadership had an interest in racial pluralism, diversity and conflict only because it would offer certain advantages to the Jews as a group.

In addition *Common Sense* suggested that the real goal of organized Jewry was to take over the United States, and to do that they had to weaken, divide and dispossess the elite of the American European majority who made up ninety percent of the nation's population, and from which the American elite of academia, media, business and politics were drawn. Common Sense said that the plans were already in the works to see to it that Europeans became a minority in an America ruled by Jews.

How could that be I thought, that's crazy. America was soon to go to the moon, and NASA from top to bottom was European American. "We become a minority I thought. Crazy! Just Crazy!" Much later I discovered that Jewish extremists hated African American nationalist groups as much as they hated their European American enemies that they sought to supplant in America's elite. They sought to bend African American groups to the interests of Jewry rather than the true liberation of their own people. They demonized Black leaders like Minister Farrakhan who saw the paramount Jewish role in the historical slave trade and saw Jewish exploitation of the Black community.

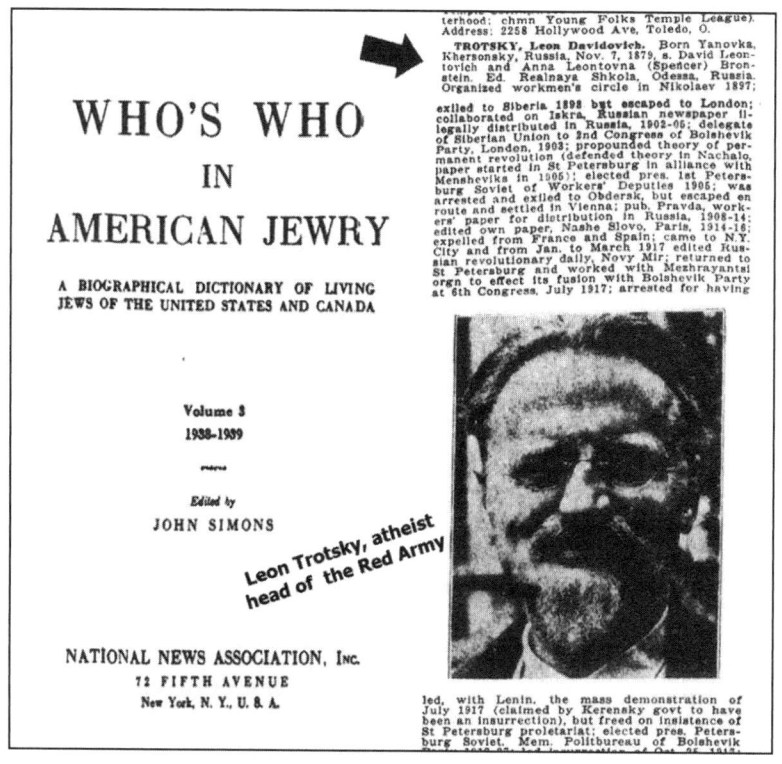

The other copy of *Common Sense* was no less startling. It had a long article asserting that international Communism was a Jewish creation and that the Russian Revolution had not really been Russian at all. Jews had supposedly financed and led Communism since its inception, and it alleged that they still thoroughly dominated the Communist movement in the United States and around the world.

This *National Enquirer* of the right quoted many names, dates and sources to support its incredible allegations. I was very skeptical of its assertions, but the information was too compelling to ignore. I had learned early on not to easily dismiss unpopular opinions.

Despite the article's strong documentation, the allegations seemed too bizarre to be true. How could it be that the largest and most powerful African American organization in America had been founded, financed, and run by Jews - and Marxist Jews at that — instead of African Americans?

How could something so incredibly amazing be kept so quiet that most people would not know about it? If the Russian Revolution was truly a revolution led by Jews rather than Marxist Russians, why was such an enormous historical fact ignored in our history books and in our popular media? Furthermore, I could not understand why wealthy and powerful capitalist Jews would foster race-mixing and Communism.

Father had often talked to me about the evils of Communism, and I had been thoroughly anti-Communist since reading books such as *The Conscience of a Conservative* by Barry Goldwater,[11] *None Dare Call It Treason* by John A. Stormer,[12] and *You Can Trust the Communists (To Be Communists)*[13] by Frederick Charles Schwarz. These books and others impressed upon me the penetration of Communist ideology throughout our society, media and government.

The Cuban Missile Crisis had occurred just three years before, and father's plans to build a fallout shelter were still fresh in my mind. He had even purchased food and other survival supplies for it.

During that period, the idea of nuclear war grew from an abstract idea to concrete anticipation. In the early 1960s, most communities tested the working order of air-raid sirens by sounding them daily at noon. Sometimes, when we lost track of time in school and the noon air-raid sirens went off, we wondered for a moment if the war was actually upon us.

During the Cuban crisis, most adults rationalized that thermonuclear war would not happen because it *must* not happen — because the very thought was too monstrous to contemplate. An 11-year-old is much more prone to believe that someone might pull the switch.

Years later, the world discovered that we had actually teetered much closer to nuclear war than most Americans had known at the time. The fact that I viewed Communists as putting my family in real danger of nuclear incineration contributed greatly to my visceral anti-Communist stance.

One of the *Common Sense* issues mentioned a full-page newspaper article written by Winston Churchill called "Zionism versus Bolshevism: A Struggle for the Soul of the Jewish People." The article had originally appeared in the *Illustrated Sunday*

Herald on February 8, 1920. Churchill had maintained that the world's Jews were being torn between an allegiance to Communism on the one hand and Zionism on the other.

> "There is no need to exaggerate the part played in the creation of Bolshevism and in the actual bringing about of the Russian Revolution by these international and for the most part atheistical Jews..."
>
> **Winston S. Churchill**

Churchill hoped the Jews would adopt Zionism as an alternative to what he called "diabolical" and "sinister" Bolshevism. In his well-written article, contemporary with the early years of the Russian Revolution, Churchill described Communism as a "sinister confederacy" of "International Jews" who "have gripped the Russian people by the hair of their heads and have become practically the undisputed masters of that enormous empire."14

The article shocked me enough that I had to check its authenticity. It turned out to be genuine. In fact, I found some Jewish references to it bewailing the fact that Churchill's article gave fodder to the anti-Semites of the world. The following is an excerpt from his amazing article.

In violent opposition to all this sphere of Jewish effort rise the schemes of the International Jews. The adherents of this sinister confederacy are mostly men reared up among the unhappy populations of countries where the Jews are persecuted on account of their race. Most, if not all, of them have forsaken the faith of their forefathers and divorced from their minds all spiritual hopes of the next world. This movement among the Jews is not new. From the days of Spartacus-Weishaupt to those of Karl Marx, and down to Trotsky (Russia), Bela Kun (Hungary), Rosa Luxembourg (Germany), and Emma Goldman (United States), this world-wide conspiracy for the overthrow of civilisation and for the reconstitution of society on the basis of arrested development, of envious malevolence, and impossible equality, has been steadily growing...and now at last this band of extraordinary personalities from the underworld of the great cities of Europe and America have gripped the Russian people by the hair of their heads and have become practically the undisputed masters of that enormous empire.

There is no need to exaggerate the part played in the creation of Bolshevism and in the actual bringing about of the Russian Revolution by these international and for the most part atheistical Jews...[15]

As important an historical figure as Churchill was, he was still only one voice. I rationalized that he could simply be wrong about the nature of the Russian Revolution. One of the *Common Sense* articles I read referred to a series of explosive documents (complete with file numbers) from the National Archives of the United States.

I wrote to my local Congressman, F. Edward Hebert, and asked if his office could obtain copies of the files for me. A couple of weeks later, on returning home from school, I found waiting for me a large manila envelope from the Congressman.

Certified by the seal of the United States of America, the documents were from the National Archives. They concerned intelligence reports from foreign governments and extensive reports from our chief intelligence officers in Russia during the time of the early days of the Communist revolution and the Russian Civil War.

The early 1920s were long before the establishment of the OSS and the CIA. The U.S. Army ran our international intelligence work at that time. One of our military intelligence officers in Russia during its revolutionary period was Captain Montgomery Schuyler.

He sent back regular reports to the chief of staff of U.S. Army Intelligence, who then relayed them to the Secretary of War and the President of the United States.

Reading through the lengthy reports gave me a glimpse into an historical period of which few Americans are aware. They reported horrible massacres of thousands of Russian aristocrats and intelligentsia, murdered simply because they could provide effective leadership in opposition to the Communists.

Many Americans are at least somewhat aware of Stalin's murder of millions. However, many millions also died in the early days of Bolshevism under Lenin and Trotsky, for it was these men who initiated the first mass killings and the Gulags.

The reports also stated, without equivocation, the Jewish nature of the revolution. In one of Schuyler's official, detailed reports, declassified in 1958, almost 50 years after he wrote and dispatched them, he states:[16]

> "It is probably unwise to say this loudly in the United States, but the Bolshevik movement is and has been since its beginning, guided and controlled by Russian Jews of the greasiest type..."
>
> Captain Schuyler, American army intelligence officer in Russia during the Russian Revolution. (In his official report)

In quoting the graphic language of this official report, my intention is not to offend; but Schuyler's report says what it says, whether we like it or not. In another report, written four months later, Captain Schuyler goes on to quote the evidence of Robert Wilton, who was then the chief Russian correspondent of the authoritative *London Times*. Wilton later went on to pen a number of best-selling books about the revolution, including the widely acclaimed *Russia's Agony* and *Last Days of the Romanovs*.[17] On June 9, 1919, Schuyler cites Wilton as follows:

> A table made up in 1918, by Robert Wilton, correspondent of the London Times in Russia, shows at that time there were 384 commissars including 2 Negroes, 13 Russians, 15 Chinamen, 22 Armenians and more than 300 Jews. Of the latter number 264 had come from the United States since the downfall of the Imperial Government.[18]

There was, of course, no reason to impugn the reporting of the *Times* or of Captain Schuyler. I couldn't believe my eyes as I scanned the papers dispersed across the plastic tablecloth on my dining room table. I wondered how it could possibly be true that the "Russian Revolution" had had only 13 ethnic Russians out of the 384 members of its top governing body. Churchill's description of "gripping the Russian people by the hair of their heads" came to life in the pages I received from our own National Archives.

Once I started checking out the leads I would glean from my reading, the National Archives kept providing me with the most incredible documents. Not only did our chief intelligence officer write to the President of the United States about the Jewish nature of Communism, so did our U.S. ambassador to Russia, David R. Francis. In a January 1918 cable to our government, he reported:

> The Bolshevik leaders here, most of whom are Jews and 90 percent of whom are returned exiles, care little for Russia or any other country but are internationalists and they are trying to start a world-wide social revolution. — David Francis, American Ambassador to Russia at the time of the Revolution.[19]

The National Archives also sent me copies from its files of communications from Scotland Yard and British Intelligence. The directorate of British Intelligence sent to America and other nations a lengthy report dated July 16, 1919, on Bolshevism abroad. It was called "A Monthly Review of the Progress of Revolutionary Movements Abroad." This lengthy report lists the

> **"There is now definite evidence that Bolshevism is an international movement controlled by Jews."**
> ---The Director of British Intelligence to the U.S. Secretary of State

Communist movements in the major nations of the world. The first sentence in the first paragraph on the first page of this British government report bluntly states that Jews control international Communism.[20]

Years later, as a student at Louisiana State University, I took a course entirely devoted to the Russian Revolution. Neither my professor in his lectures, nor my textbook (*The Soviet Achievement*)[21] made any mention of the historical Jewish-Russian conflict and the Jewish domination of the Communist Party.

The Jewish role in the Communist Revolution was, however, mentioned in many major Jewish publications such as the *Jewish Encyclopedia* and the *Universal Jewish Encyclopedia and Encyclopaedia Judaica*. It astounded me to find them actually boasting about the pivotal role of Jews in the Russian Revolution. They even pointed out the effort of the Communist Jews to disguise the Jewish role — a successful effort, for most Gentiles in America and Europe are still unaware of it.

> The Communist movement and ideology played an important part in Jewish life, particularly in the 1920s, 1930s and during and after World War II.... Individual Jews played an important role in the early stages of Bolshevism and the Soviet Regime.... The great attraction of Communism among Russian, and later also, Western Jewry, emerged only with the establishment of the Soviet Regime in Russia...
>
> Many Jews the world over therefore regarded the Soviet concept of the solution to the "Jewish question" as an intrinsically positive approach.... Communism became widespread in virtually all Jewish communities. In some countries Jews became the leading element in the legal and illegal Communist parties and in some cases were even instructed by the Communist International

to change their Jewish-sounding names and pose as non-Jews, in order not to confirm right wing propaganda that presented Communism as an alien, Jewish conspiracy.[22]

Trotsky's book, *Stalin,* written in exile, attempted to show that

Stalin had played only an insignificant role in the early days of the Communist takeover. Trotsky attempted to illustrate this point by reproducing a postcard widely circulated in the months following the revolution. The postcard depicted the six leaders of the revolution.

Shown are Lenin (who was at least one-quarter Jewish, spoke Yiddish in his home, and was married to a Jewess); Trotsky (real Jewish name: Lev Bronstein); Zinoviev (real Jewish name: Hirsch Apfelbaum); Lunacharsky (a Gentile); Kamenov (real Jewish name: Rosenfeld); and Sverdlov (Jewish).[23] Not only does the postcard show the Jewish domination of the revolution; it also illustrates the fact that the Jewish Communist leaders shown had changed their names, presumably to disguise the fact that they were Jews, just as reported in the *Encyclopaedia Judaica.*

Although the fact of Lenin's Jewish ancestry was kept quiet for many years, Jewish writers are now taking note of it. David Shub, author of *Lenin: A Biography,* stated in a letter to the Russian émigré paper *Novyi Zhurnal*[24] that Lenin's mother was Jewish at least on her father's side and probably so on her mother's side as well.[25] In addition, a French Jewish periodical, *Review de Fonds*

*Social Juif,*26 reported that a Soviet novelist, Marietta Shaguinian, was prevented by Soviet censorship from publishing evidence of Lenin's Jewish ancestry. A number of Jewish publications in recent years have disclosed Lenin's Jewish heritage, including the *Jewish Chronicle.*27

JEWISH CHRONICLE JULY 26 1991

Moscow magazine on Lenin's Jewish roots

By ZEEV BEN-SHLOMO
East Europe Correspondent

Vladimir Ilyich Lenin, the creator of the Soviet Union, often officially praised as the embodiment of the Russian national genius, had a Jewish grandfather, according to the Moscow mass circulation weekly, Ogonyok. There have been rumours to this

The Cheka, or secret police, had a Jew, Moses Uritzky, as its first chief. Most of the other subsequent leaders were also Jews, including Sverdlov and Genrikh Yagoda (which is Russian for "Yehuda," "the Jew") presided over the pogroms that killed millions. The Soviet propaganda minister during the war was a Jew, Ilya Ehrenburg, who notoriously distinguished himself by his exhortations of Soviet troops to rape and murder the women and children of Germany.28 Anatol Goldberg quoted Ehrenburg in his book, *Ilya Ehrenburg* as saying, "...the Germans are not human beings...nothing gives us so much joy as German corpses."29

Aron Solts   Naftaly Frenkel

Yakov Rappoport   Matvei Berman

lazar Kogan   Genrikh Yagoda

The Communist secret police, which underwent many name changes, including Cheka, OGPU, GPU, NKVD, NKGB, MGB, and KGB, was the most feared police agency in the history of the world. They imprisoned, tortured, or murdered more than 30 million Russians and Eastern Europeans.

Even the more conservative Soviet historians of the 1960s were placing the number of murdered at about 20 to 40 million — figures that do not include the millions more who were dispossessed, imprisoned, exiled, tortured, and displaced.

Nobel Prizewinner Aleksandr Solzhenitsyn in his opus, *The Gulag Archipelago*, using the research of a Soviet statistician who had access to secret government files, I. A. Kurganov, estimated that between 1918 and 1959, at least 66 million died at the hands of the Communist rulers of Russia.

Although that number may be far too high, in *The Gulag Archipelago II*, Solzhenitsyn affirms that Jews created and administered the organized Soviet concentration camp system in which tens of millions of Christians died. Pictured on page 79 of *The Gulag Archipelago II* are the leading administrators of the greatest killing machine in the history of the world.[30] They are Aron Solts, Yakov Rappoport, Lazar Kogan, Matvei Berman, Genrikh Yagoda, and Naftaly Frenkel. All six are Jews.

Interestingly, though, during this period of murder and mayhem, Jews were a protected class, so much so that the Communist Party took the unprecedented step of making expressions of anti-Semitism a counter-revolutionary offense, and thus punishable by death.[31]

The Jewish Voice in January, 1942, stated: "The Jewish people will never forget that the Soviet Union was the first country -- and as yet the only country in the world -- in which anti-Semitism is a crime."[32] The *Congress Bulletin* (Publication of the American Jewish Congress) stated: [33] [34] [35]

> **Anti-Semitism was classed as counter-revolution and the severe punishments meted out for acts of Anti-Semitism were the means by which the existing order protected its own safety.**

The Russian Penal Codes of 1922 and 1927 even went so far as to make anti-Semitism punishable by death. The book *Soviet Russia and the Jews* by Gregor Aronson and published by the American Jewish League Against Communism, quotes Stalin remarking on the policy in an interview in 1931 with the Jewish Telegraph Agency:

...Communists cannot be anything but outspoken enemies of Anti-Semitism. We fight anti-Semites by the strongest methods in the Soviet Union. Active Anti-Semites are punished by death under law.[36]

The Beginning of an Ethnic War

In school, I brought up these fascinating facts with some of my teachers. They in turn were as incredulous as I had been. One suggested that the Jewish involvement in the Communist Revolution might have been a result of the long-running historical persecution of Jews by the Tsars and, indeed, by much of the Russian intelligentsia. For instance, Tolstoy, Dostoyevsky, and many other prominent Russian writers had criticized Jewish machinations in their books and articles. Russians didn't like the fact that the Jews used the Russian language for doing business among Gentiles but spoke Yiddish among themselves. Jews were also accused of having an "us versus them" mentality rather than assimilating with the Christian majority.

There had been a running feud between the Russians and the Jews for centuries and from these conflicts arose "pogroms" to suppress the Jews. This war without borders can be illustrated by the Jewish reaction in the 1880s to the anti-Semitic Russian May Laws. The May Laws of 1882 attempted to restrict Jews from some professions and mandate resettlement of most Jews to their original area of the empire, the Pale of Settlement (a huge area, originally set up in 1772, encompassing an area about half the size of Western Europe, extending from the Crimea to the Baltic Sea, to which the Jews had been restricted)

In retaliation, Jewish international financiers did their best to destroy the Russian economy. *Encyclopaedia Britannica* describes what happened:

The Russian May Laws were the most conspicuous legislative monument achieved by modern Anti-Semitism.... Their immediate result was a ruinous commercial depression which was felt all over the empire and which profoundly affected the national credit. The Russian minister was at his wits end for money. Negotiations for a large loan were entered upon with the house of Rothschild and a preliminary contract was signed, when...the finance minister was informed that unless the persecutions of the Jews were stopped the great banking house would be compelled to withdraw from the operation....[37]

In response to the economic and other pressures put upon Russia, the Tsar issued an edict on September 3, 1882. In it he stated:

> For some time the government has given its attention to the Jews and to their relations to the rest of the inhabitants of the empire, with a view of ascertaining the sad condition of the Christian inhabitants brought about by the conduct of Jews in business matters....

> With few exceptions, they have as a body devoted their attention, not to enriching or benefiting the country, but to defrauding by their wiles its inhabitants, and particularly its poor inhabitants. This conduct of theirs has called forth protests on the part of the people,...(the government) thought it a matter of urgency and justice to adopt stringent measures in order to put an end to the oppression practiced by the Jews on the inhabitants, and to free the country from their malpractices, which were, as is known, the cause of the agitations.[38]

So, Jews had ample reason to attempt to overturn the Tsarist government of Russia, and there is direct evidence they did just that. The *Jewish Communal Register of New York City of 1917-1918*, edited and published by the Jewish community, profiles Jacob Schiff, who at that time was one of the wealthiest men in the world as head of the huge banking house of Kuhn, Loeb & Company. In the article it states how the firm of Kuhn, Loeb & Company "floated the large Japanese War Loans of 1904-1905, thus making possible the Japanese victory over Russia." It also goes on to say:

> Mr. Schiff has always used his wealth and his influence in the best interests of his people. He financed the enemies of autocratic Russia and used his financial influence to keep Russia away from the money market of the United States.[39]

Jacob Schiff actually gave somewhere between $17 million and $24 million to finance the Jewish-Communist revolutionaries in Russia, a sum that would be the equivalent of many hundreds of millions of dollars by today's dollar value. Rabbi Marvin S.

Andelman, in his book *To Eliminate the Opiate,* cites two sources documenting Schiff's financial support of the Communist Revolution and ultimate repayment by them.

Jacob Schiff is credited with giving twenty million dollars to the Bolshevik revolution. A year after his death the Bolsheviks deposited over six hundred million rubles to Schiff's banking firm Kuhn & Loeb.[40] [41] **(Loeb and Trotsky ne Bronstein, pictured below)**

It puzzled me that the violently anti-capitalist R Party would be supported by some of the most prominent capitalists in the world. But, I finally realized that the Russian Revolution was not ultimately about the triumph of an economic ideology, it was about the culmination of an age-old struggle between two powerful peoples — the Jews and the Russians — in an ethnic war that tragically ended in the totalitarian tyranny of the Communist dictatorship. Even worse, the score was ultimately settled in the terror of the blood-washed cellars of the Cheka and the frozen death of the Gulags.

The fact that supercapitalists such as Jacob Schiff could support a nakedly socialist regime such as Communism made me question whether there was something more to Communism than met the eye. What was it about Communism that made it so attractive to Jews, who were largely well-educated non-proletarians, when Communism was supposed to be, in Lenin's words, "a dictatorship of the proletariat"? Obviously, by and large, Jews were nothing like Marx's "workers of the world," for no group was more involved in capitalism or the manipulation and use of capital than the Jewish community.

I checked out the Communist personalities that Mattie Smith told me were in the Jewish *Who's Who in World Jewry*. Atheist Leon Trotsky as well as atheist Maxim Litvinov, the Soviet Minister of Foreign Affairs, are proudly listed in the directory of famous Jews compiled by the leading Jewish rabbinical groups of the world.

Winston Churchill, in his eloquent article "Zionism Versus Bolshevism: A Struggle for the Soul of the Jewish People," had argued that Communism and Zionism were distinct ideologies that were competing, as he put it, "for the soul of the Jewish

people." But something didn't seem quite kosher in this supposed titanic struggle, for it appeared that many Zionists also supported Communism and, at least in the early years, many Communists were sympathetic to Zionists. Millions of Jews, even supercapitalists such as Jacob Schiff, supported the Communist revolution in Russia. The struggle seemed to be like that of two brothers who might sometimes argue between themselves but who always stand together against their common enemies.

In 1975, I read a book called *Trotsky and the Jews*, written by Joseph Nedava and published by the Jewish Publication Society (Philadelphia, 1971). The book points out that before the Russian Revolution, Leon Trotsky (born Lev Bronstein) used to play chess with Baron Rothschild of the famous Rothschild banking family. What could the Rothschilds, the biggest banking house in Europe, possibly have in common with a leader who wanted to destroy capitalism and private property? Conversely, why would a dedicated Communist be a close friend of the most powerful "capitalist oppressor" in the world? Could it be that they saw Communism and Zionism as two very different avenues to a similar goal of power and revenge against the Tsars?

> **A Jewish journalist (M. Waldman) who knew Trotsky from the period of his stay in Vienna ("when he used to play chess with Baron Rothschild in Café Central and frequent Café Daily to read the press there").** 42

A number of questions arose: 1) Could Communism simply have been a tool they adapted to defeat and rule their Russian antagonists? 2) Did the Jews believe they were in conflict with only Russians or with other peoples as well? 3) Was Communism originally part of a strategic imperative that reached far beyond the confines of Soviet Russia? These were important questions. I thought that I might find their answers in the philosophical origins of Communism.

I resolved to investigate the ideological roots of Communism. I found *Das Kapital*43 and the *Communist Manifesto*44 in my public library. Karl Marx's books were obtuse, especially the parts describing the Hegelian dialectic, but they made some sense if one believed that mankind had a machine-like nature as Marx theorized. One of

Inside Judaica

Insights on questions of Jewish interest by Dr. Frederick Lachman, Executive Editor, Encyclopaedia Judaica

Q. Was Karl Marx A Jew?
A. Born in the Rhineland town of Trier (then West Prussia), Marx was the son of Jewish parents, Heinrich and Henrietta Marx. Heinrich Marx became a successful lawyer, and when an edict prohibited Jews from being advocates he converted to Protestantism in 1817. In 1824, when Karl was six years old, his father converted his eight children, the authoritative Encyclopedia Judaica reports. Heinrich, whose original name was Hirschel ha-Levi, was the son of a rabbi and the descendant of talmudic scholars for many generations. Hirschel's brother was chief rabbi of Trier. Heinrich Marx married Henrietta Pressburg, who originated in Hungary and whose father became a rabbi in Nijmegen, Holland.

my teachers made the often-repeated, poorly-thought-out comment that Communism was great in theory but faulty in practice. To my way of thinking, to be a great idea it must *work* in practice, and Communism obviously doesn't. There has never been a theory that has promised more human happiness yet delivered more poverty, mental and physical oppression, and more human misery and death.

Until I looked into the foundations of Communism, I had always thought Karl Marx was a German. In fact, I had read that Marx's father was a Christian. It turns out that his father, a successful lawyer, was a Jew who had converted to Christianity after an edict prohibited Jews from practicing law. Much later, in 1977, I read an article from the *Chicago Jewish Sentinel* boasting that Marx was the grandson of a rabbi and "the descendant of Talmudic scholars for many generations."[45] An excellent article in the *Barnes Review* points out the "Racism of Marx and Engels."[46]

Not only was Karl Marx from a long line of Talmudic scholars, he also hated Russians with a passion that could be described as pathological. I looked up Karl Marx in the Jewish encyclopedias, and I found to my amazement that the man who taught him many of the principles of Communism was Moses Hess. As incredible as it might seem, contemporary Zionist leaders venerate Moses Hess as the "forerunner" of modern Zionism. In *The Encyclopedia of Zionism in Israel*, under the entry for Moses Hess, is the following:

> **Pioneer of modern socialism, social philosopher, and forerunner of Zionism.... Hess was thus a forerunner of political and cultural Zionism and of socialist Zionism in particular. He became deeply involved in the rising socialist movement. Karl Marx and Frederick Engels acknowledged that they had learned much from him during the formative years of the movement.... —** *The Encyclopedia of Zionism in Israel.*[47]

After months of reading from many major, first hand sources, I realized that the elderly lady in the offices of the Citizens Council had been essentially right, at least about the origins of the Communist revolution. I felt as if I were sitting on the edge of a volcano. Every new piece of information seemed to both confirm and clarify the issue ever further.

In *The Last Days of the Romanovs*, Robert Wilton, on assignment for *The London Times* in Russia for 17 years, summed up the "Russian Revolution" in these words:

> **The whole record of the Bolshevism in Russia is indelibly impressed with the stamp of alien invasion. The murder of the**

Tsar, deliberately planned by the Jew Sverdlov and carried out by the Jews Goloshekin, Syromolotov, Safarov, Voikov, and Yurovsky, is the act, not of the Russian people, but of this hostile invader.[48]

In 1990, a major New York publisher, the Free Press, a division of Simon & Schuster, published a book by Israeli historian Louis Rapoport called *Stalin's War Against the Jews*. In it the author casually admits what we Gentiles are not supposed to know:

> Many Jews were euphoric over their high representation in the new government. Lenin's first Politburo was dominated by men of Jewish origins...
>
> Under Lenin, Jews became involved in all aspects of the Revolution, including its dirtiest work. Despite the Rs' vows to eradicate Anti-Semitism, it spread rapidly after the revolution — partly because of the prominence of so many Jews in the Soviet administration, as well as in the traumatic, inhuman Sovietization drives that followed. Historian Salo Baron has noted that an immensely disproportionate number of Jews joined the new Soviet secret police, the Cheka.... And many of those who fell afoul of the Cheka would be shot by Jewish investigators.
>
> The Collective leadership that emerged in Lenin's dying days was headed by the Jew Zinoviev, a loquacious, curly-haired...[49]

I began to realize that there was once widespread knowledge of the Jewish leadership of the "Russian Revolution," — an example can be found in the *National Geographic Magazine's* May 1907 edition. An article entitled "The Revolution in Russia" describes the Jewish leadership of the terroristic Communist Revolution:

> Revolutionary leaders nearly all belong to the Jewish race and the most effective revolutionary agency is the Jewish Bund,...The government has suffered more from that race than from all of its

other subjects combined. Whenever a desperate deed is committed it is always done by a Jew and there is scarcely one loyal member of that race in the entire Empire.[50]

The facts were indisputable. An enormous fact of history has been wiped away from the intellectual consciousness of the West as thoroughly as a file can be erased from the hard disk of a desktop computer. In his classic novel *1984*,[51] George Orwell wrote about historical truth "going down the Memory Hole." This had been the fate of the truth regarding the real perpetrators of the "Russian Revolution." I asked myself two questions: "Why was the historical truth about the Communist Revolution suppressed?" and "How, in a free world, could that suppression have been accomplished?" The first question had an obvious answer in the fact that the forces of international Jewry would not want it generally known that they were the primary authors of the most repressive and murderous evil in the history of mankind: Communism. Obviously, knowledge of that fact does not create good public relations for Jews.

The answer to the second question of "how" was more elusive. I realized that only very powerful forces could suppress important parts of the historical record and create a false impression of a "Russian Revolution" when there were *only 13 ethnic Russians* in the highest levels of the first Bolshevik government. Obviously the Jews historically did have a lot of power — as evidenced by Jacob Schiff, the Rothschilds, and others — but the power to change the perception of history — that seemed preposterous. Yet only a few months before, when Mattie Smith had told me at the Citizens Council that the Russian Revolution was Jewish, I had thought the idea was ridiculous. Now I knew differently, and I knew I was just beginning to discover a different reality in the world that was not mentioned by the *NY Times*.

One of the intrepid researchers that impressed me in those years was Frank Britton. The next few chapters will highlight his research with additional commentary.

Chapter 2
The Ethnic War On the Russian People

The following includes much of Frank Britton's historical research with my updating, editing and commentary added

UNDER the reign of Tsar Alexander I (Tsar 1801-1825) of Russia many of the restrictions against Jewish residence beyond the Pale of Settlement were relaxed, especially for the artisan and professional classes.

A determined effort was made to establish Jews in agriculture and the government encouraged at every opportunity the assimilation of Jews into Russian national life.

Nicholas I

Alexander's successor, Nicholas I (Tsar 1825-1855), was less inclined to favor Jewry, and in fact viewed their inroads into the Russian economy with alarm. He was much hated by the Jews.

Prior to his reign, Alexander I had allowed any male Jew the privilege of escaping compulsory military duty by paying a special draft-exemption tax. In 1827 Nicholas I abolished the custom, with the result that Jews were for

Tsar Alexander I

the first time taken into the Imperial armies.

In 1844, Nicholas I further antagonized Jewry by abolishing the institution of the Kahal, and in that same year he prohibited by law the traditional Jewish garb, specifying that all Jews should, except on ceremonial occasions, dress in conformity with Russian standards. These measures, and many others like them, were aimed at facilitating the assimilation of Jewry into Russian life.

The Tsarist government was much concerned by the Jews' failure to become Russianized, and viewed with extreme hostility the ancient Jewish custom of maintaining a separate culture, language, mode of dress, etc. — all of which contributed to keep the Jew an alien in the land of his residence.

It is to this determination to "Russianize" and assimilate Jewish extremists that we can ascribe the unusual efforts made by the Imperial government to provide free education to its Jews.

In 1804 all schools were thrown open to Jews and attendance for Jewish children was made compulsory. Compulsory education was not only a novelty in Russia, but in any country in the early 19th century.

In Russia education was generally reserved for a privileged few, and even as late as 1914 only 55% of her gentile population had been inside a school. The net result of the Imperial government's assimilation program was that Russian Jewry became the best educated segment in Russia. This eventually worked to the destruction of the Tsarist government.

Alexander II

The reign of Alexander II marked the apex of Jewish fortunes in Tsarist Russia. By 1880 they were becoming dominant in the

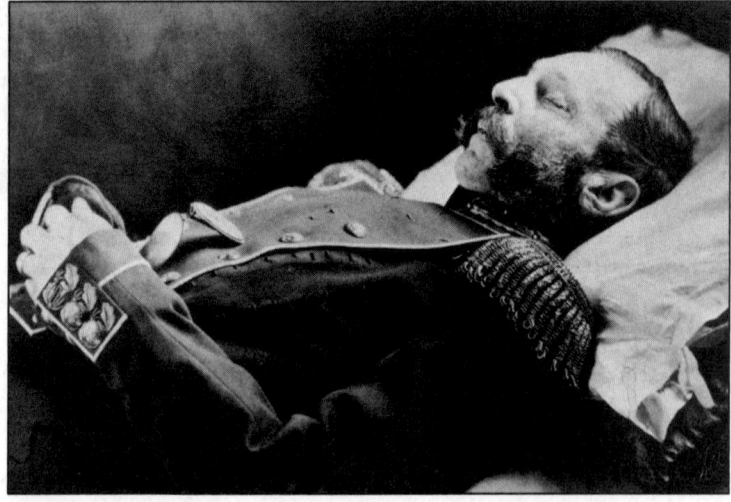

Tsar Alexander II lying in state after his assassination in a plot hatched in the home of the Jewess Hesia Helfman.

professions, in many trades and industries, and were beginning to filter into government in increasing numbers.

As early as 1861 Alexander II had permitted Jewish university graduates to settle and hold governmental positions in greater Russia, and by 1879 apothecaries, nurses, midwives, dentists, distillers, and skilled craftsmen were permitted to work and reside throughout the empire.

Nevertheless Russia's Jews were increasingly rebellious over the remaining restraints which still bound the greater part of Russian Jewry to the Pale of Settlement, and which, to some extent at least, restricted their commercial activities.

Herein lay the dilemma: the Imperial government could retain certain of the restrictions against the Jews, and by doing so incur their undying hostility, or it could remove all restraints and thus pave the way for Jewish domination over every phase of Russian life.

Certainly Alexander II viewed this problem with increasing concern as time went on. He lost a considerable amount of his enthusiasm for liberal causes after an attempt was made to assassinate him in 1866.

He dismissed his "liberal" advisors and from that time on displayed an inclination toward conservatism. This is not to say he became anti-Jewish, but he did show more firmness in dealing with them.

In 1879 there was another attempt on his life, and another in the following year when his winter palace was blown up. In 1881 a plot hatched in the home of the Jewess, Hesia Helfman, was successful. Alexander II was blown up and so ended an era.

The May Laws

The reaction to the assassination of Alexander II was instantaneous and far-reaching. There was a widespread belief in and out of the government, that if the Jews were dissatisfied with the rule of Alexander II—whom the crypto-Jew, D'Israeli, had described as "the most benevolent prince that ever ruled Russia"—then they would be satisfied with nothing less than outright domination of Russia.

Up to 1881 Russian policy had consistently been directed in an attempt to "Russianize" the Jew, preparatory to accepting him into full citizenship. In line with this policy, free and compulsory education for Jews had been introduced, repeated attempts had been made to encourage them to settle on farms, and special efforts had been made to encourage them to engage in the crafts.

Now Russian policy was reversed. Hereafter it became the policy of the Imperial government to prevent the further exploitation of the Russian people by the Jews. Thus began the death struggle between Tsar and Jew.

All through 1881 there was widespread anti-Jewish rioting all over the empire. Large numbers of Jews who had been permitted to settle beyond the Pale of Settlement were evicted.

In May of 1882 the May Laws (Provisional Rules of May 3, 1882) were imposed, thus implementing the new governmental policy of Alexander III (Tsar 1881-1894).

The May Laws shook the empire to its foundations. The following passage is taken from *Encyclopaedia Britannica*[52]:

> "The Russian May Laws were the most conspicuous legislative monument achieved by modern anti-Semitism ... Their immediate results was a ruinous commercial depression which was felt all over the empire and which profoundly affected the national credit.
>
> "The Russian minister was at his wit's end for money. Negotiations for a large loan were entered upon with the house of Rothschild and a preliminary contract was signed, when ... the finance minister was informed that unless the persecutions of the Jews were stopped the great banking house would be compelled to withdraw from the operation ... In this way anti-Semitism, which had already so profoundly influenced the domestic policies of Europe, set its mark on the international relations of the powers, for it was the urgent need of the Russian treasury quite as much as the termination of Prince Bismarck's secret treaty of mutual neutrality which brought about the Franco-Russian alliance."

Thus, within a period of 92 years (from the 3rd partition to 1882) the Jews, although constituting only 4.2% of the population, had been able to entrench themselves so well in the Russian economy that the nation was almost bankrupted in the attempt to dislodge them. And, as we have seen, the nation's international credit was also affected.

Tensions Between Jews and Tsarist Regime Rise

After 1881 events served increasingly to sharpen the enmity of Jewry toward Tsarism. The May Laws had not only restricted Jewish economic activity, but had attempted — unsuccessfully, as we shall see — to preserve Russia's cultural integrity.

Hereafter Jews were permitted to attend state-supported schools and universities, but only in ratio to their population. This was not unreasonable since Russia's schools were flooded with Jewish students while large numbers of her Gentile population were illiterate, but to the Jews this represented another bitter "persecution," and all the world was acquainted with the enormity of this new crime against Jewry.

Alexander III's Proclamation on Jewry

On May 23rd a delegation of Jews headed by Baron Gunzberg called on the new Tsar Alexander III (Tsar 1881-1894) to protest the May Laws and the alleged discrimination against Jewry.

As a result of the investigation which followed, Tsar Alexander III issued an edict the following Sept. 3rd, a part of which is given here:

Tsar Alexander III.

"For some time the government has given its attention to the Jews and to their relations to the rest of the inhabitants of the empire, with a view of ascertaining the sad condition of the Christian inhabitants brought about by the conduct of the Jews in business matters...

"During the last twenty years the Jews have gradually possessed themselves of not only every trade and business in all its branches, but also of a great part of the land by buying or farming it. With few exceptions, they have as a body devoted their

attention, not to enriching or benefiting the country, but to defrauding by their wiles its inhabitants, and particularly its poor inhabitants.

"This conduct of theirs has called forth protests on the part of the people, as manifested in acts of violence and robbery. The government, while on the one hand doing its best to put down the disturbances, and to deliver the Jews from oppression and slaughter, have also, on the other hand, thought it a matter of urgency and justice to adopt stringent measures in order to put an end to the oppression practiced by the Jews on the inhabitants, and to free the country from their malpractices, which were, as is known, the cause of the agitations."[53]

Ironically, although the world is conditioned to think that attempts to limit all kinds of Jewish influence are violations of human rights, the Tsars actually saw their efforts as a defense of the most basic human rights of their subjects. Of course, this perspective is certainly not allowed in a global media where the same forces are well-ensconced.

Who was right and who was wrong?

The time came when the Jewish Bolsheviks gained the upper hand and murdered the Tsar, his wife and children.

They went on to commit the greatest mass murder in human history. That sobering fact should historically answer the question who the ultimate violators of humanity actually were.

Chapter 3
Born of the same Roots:
Communism & Zionism

It was in this atmosphere that the twin movements of Marxism and Zionism began to take hold and dominate the mass of Russian Jewry. Ironically, both Zionism and Marxism were first promulgated by westernized German Jews.

Zionism, whose chief advocate was Theodore Herzl, took root in Russia in the 1880s in competition with Marxism, whose high priest was Karl Marx, grandson of a rabbi.

Eventually almost all Russian Jews came to identify himself with either one or the other of these movements.

The Jew Grigori Gershuni master-minded the terror against the Tsar's ministers. Meanwhile, Jews the world over spread hate propaganda against the Imperial government.

Jewish Terrorists in Russia

As an outgrowth of this political fermentation, there appeared at the beginning of the century one of the most remarkable terroristic organizations ever recorded in the annals of history.

This was the Jewish dominated Party of Socialists-Revolutionaries (PSR), which between 1901 and 1906 was responsible for the assassination of no less than six first ranking leaders of the Imperial government, including Minister of Education Bogolepov (1901); Minister of Interior Sipyagin (1902); Governor of Ufa, Bogdanovich (1903); Premier Viachelav von Plehve (1904); Grand Duke Sergei, uncle of the Tsar (1905); and General Dubrassov, who had suppressed the Moscow insurrection (1906).

Chief architect of these terroristic activities was the Kovno-born Jew, Grigory Gershuni, who headed the "terror section" of the Social Revolutionary Party and who was a cofounder of the party.

In charge of the "fighting section" was Yevno Azev, son of a Jewish tailor, and one of the principal founders of the party. Azev later plotted, but was unable to carry out, the assassination of Tsar Nicholas II. Azev was later exposed as also working as a police spy, and was forced to flee from the wrath of his erstwhile revolutionary comrades to exile in Germany.

Gershuni was arrested as a result of Azev's spy work, and was sentenced to life imprisonment. This marked the end of the terroristic activities of the party, but the effect of these political murders was far reaching. Never again was the royal family, or its ministers free from the fear of assassination.

Soon another prime minister would be shot down—this time in the very presence of the Tsar. This was the backdrop for the revolution of 1905.

Chapter 4
Bloody Sunday & the 1905 Revolution

THE revolution of 1905, like that of 1917, occurred in an atmosphere of war. On Jan. 2nd, 1905, the Japanese captured Port Arthur, and thereby won the decisive victory of the Russo-Japanese war.

Later in January there occurred a tragic incident which was the immediate cause of the 1905 revolution, and which was to affect the attitude of Russia's industrial population toward the Tsar for all time. This was the "Bloody Sunday" affair.

The Imperial government, in its attempts to gain the favor of the industrial population, and in its search for a way to combat Jewish revolutionary activity, had adopted the tactic of encouraging the formation of legal trade unions, to which professional agitators were denied membership. These trade unions received official recognition and were protected by law.

Father Gapon

One of the most outstanding trade union leaders — and certainly the most unusual — was Father Gapon, a priest in the Russian Orthodox Church. On the day Port Arthur fell a number of clashes occurred in St. Petersburg's giant Putilov works between members of Father Gapon's labor organization and company officials.

A few days later the Putilov workers went on strike. Father Gapon resolved to take the matter directly to the Tsar, Nicholas II (Tsar 1894-1917). On the following Sunday thousands of St. Petersburg's workmen and their families turned out to participate in this appeal to the "little father".

The procession was entirely orderly and peaceful and the petitioners carried patriotic banners expressing loyalty to the crown. At the palace gate the procession was met by a flaming volley of rifle fire. Hundreds of workmen and members of their families were slaughtered. This was "Bloody Sunday," certainly one of the blackest days in Tsarist history.

Was Tsar Nicholas II responsible for Bloody Sunday, as Marxist propagandists have claimed? He couldn't have been because he was out of the city at the time. Father Gapon had marched on an empty palace. But the harm had been done.

Bloody Sunday turned Russia's industrial population against the Tsar. Jewish agitators capitalized on this to promote the 1905 revolution. Chief leader of the 1905 revolt was Trotsky.

Revolution of 1905

Bloody Sunday marked the beginning of the 1905 revolution. For the first time the Jewish Marxists were joined by large numbers of the working class. Bloody Sunday delivered Russia's industrial population into the hands of the Jew-dominated revolutionary movement.

A strike broke out in Lodz in late January, and by June 22nd this developed into an armed insurrection in which 2,000 were killed.

Tsar Nicholas II acted at once to recover the situation. In early February he ordered an investigation (by the Shidlovsky Commission) into the causes of unrest among the St. Petersburg workers, and later in the year (August) he announced provisions for establishing a legislature which later came to be the Duma.

He also offered amnesty to political offenders, under which, incidentally, Lenin returned to Russia. But these attempts failed.

On October 20th the Jewish Menshevik-led All-Russian Railway union went on strike. On the 21st a general strike was called in St. Petersburg, and on the 25th there were general strikes in Moscow, Smolensk, Kursk, and other cities.

The St. Petersburg Soviet is Founded

On October 26th the revolutionary St. Petersburg Soviet was founded. This St. Petersburg Soviet assumed the functions of a national government. It issued decrees, proclaimed an eight hour day, freedom of the press, and otherwise exercised the prerogatives of a government.

From the very beginning the Soviet was dominated by the Menshevik faction of the Russian Social Democratic Labor Party, although the Social Revolutionary Party was also represented.

Its first president was the Menshevik, Zborovski, who was succeeded by Georgii Nosar. He in turn was succeeded by Lev Trotsky, who chiefly as a result of the prestige gained in 1905, became one of the guiding spirits of the October revolution in 1917.

Trotsky became president of the St. Petersburg Soviet on Dec. 9th, and a week later some 300 members of the Soviet, including Trotsky, were arrested. The revolution was almost, but not quite, over.

Parvus

On Dec. 20th the Jew, Alexander Lvovich Parvus (real name Israel Lazarevich Gelfand), assumed control of a new executive committee of the Soviet and organized a general strike in St. Petersburg which involved 90,000 workers. The next day 150,000 workers went on strike in Moscow, and there were insurrections in Chita, Kansk, and Rostov. But within a week the government had gained the upper hand and by the 30th of December the revolution was over.

Alexander Lvovich Parvus (real name Israel Lazarevich Gelfand).

Stolypin Reforms

As an outcome of the 1905 revolution, Tsar Nicholas II set about remedying the short-comings of his regime in a most commendable manner. At his decree, Russia was given representative government and a constitution.

An elective legislature — the Duma — was established, and free elections were held. By these measures and others which followed, Russia seemed well on the way to becoming a constitutional monarchy patterned after the western European model, and as a point of fact it was only the outbreak of World War I which prevented this from becoming a reality.

As would be expected, the Jewish revolutionary parties bitterly opposed these reforms, looking on them as merely a device by which the forces of revolution would be dissipated.

Actually these measures did succeed in pacifying the Russian masses, and the years between 1905 and 1914 were ones of comparative quiet and progress. No man deserves more credit for this state of affairs than Prime Minister Pyotr Arkadyevich Stolypin, who in the year following the 1905 revolt emerged as the most impressive figure in Imperial Russia.

From 1906 to 1911 it is no exaggeration to say that he dominated Russian politics. It was he who gave Russia the famed "Stolypin Constitution," which among other things undertook to guarantee the civil rights of the peasantry, which constituted 85% of Russia's population. His land reforms, for which he is most famous, not only gave the peasant the right to own land, but actually financed the purchase with government loans. Stolypin was determined to give the peasant a stake in capitalism, believing that "the natural counterweight of the communal principal is individual ownership."

Were the Stolypin land reforms effective? Bertram Wolfe, American Jewish Communist Party member and author, who is on all points anti-Tsarist and pro-revolutionary, had this to say[54]: "Between 1907 and 1914, under the Stolypin land reform laws, 2,000,000 peasant families seceded from the village mire and became individual proprietors. All through the war the movement continued, so that by Jan. 1, 1916, 6,200,000 peasant families, out of approximately 16,000,000 eligible, had made application for separation. Lenin saw the matter as a race with time between Stolypin's reforms and the next upheaval. Should an upheaval be postponed for a couple of decades, the new land measures would so transform the countryside that it would no longer be a revolutionary force. How near Lenin came to losing the race is proved by the fact that in 1917, when he called on the peasants to 'take the land,' they already owned more than three-fourths of it."

Premier Peter Arkadyevich Stolypin reformed Russia and would have brought peace had he not been assassinated by the Jew Mordekhai Bogrov.

Russian Jewry wanted revolution, not reform. As early as 1906, an attempt had been made to assassinate Prime Minister Stolypin when his country house was destroyed by a bomb. Finally in Sept. of 1911 the best Prime Minister Russia ever had was shot down in cold blood while attending a gala affair at the Kiev theatre. The assassin was a Jewish lawyer named Mordekhai Gershkovich Bogrov. Thus it was that Russia had since 1902 lost two Prime Ministers to Jewish assassins.

Many of Stolypin's reforms were carried out after his death. In 1912 an industrial insurance law was inaugurated which gave all industrial workmen sickness and accident compensation to the extent of two-thirds and three-fourths of their regular pay.

For the first time the newspapers of the revolutionary parties were given legal status. Public schools were expanded and the election laws were revised. In 1913 a general amnesty for all political prisoners was given. Not even the severest critic of Tsarism can deny that these measures represented a sincere attempt on the part of the Imperial government to bring about reform. Why in spite of all this, was the Tsar overthrown?

Chapter 5
The First World War Weakens the Tsar

ONE of the chief factors contributing to the destruction of the Imperial government was the onset of World War I. Before the war the Imperial military establishment had contained perhaps 1,500,000 professional troops, well trained and loyal to the crown, "but by 1917 the regular army was gone. Its losses for the first ten months of the war were reckoned as 3,800,000, or, to take the reckoning of the Quartermaster-General, Danilov, 300,000 a month, and the officers, who went into action standing, while commanding their men to crawl, were falling at twice the rate of the men."[55]

Altogether 18 million men were called to the colors, most of whom were conscripted from the peasantry. Although courageous in battle they proved politically unreliable and were easily incited by agitators. Large numbers of the industrial population were also drafted into the armies, and their places were taken by peasants, fresh out of the country.

As a result, Russia's principal cities came to be populated by a working class which was peasant in origin and habit of thinking, but which lacked the conservatism and stability which seems to go with tenure of the land. This new proletariat was in reality an uprooted and landless peasantry, poorly adjusted to city life, and easily stirred up by propagandists.

Now it should be remembered that the Russian revolution was carried out by a handful of revolutionaries operating mainly in the larger cities. While something like 85% of Russia's gentile population was rural, these country people took virtually no part in the revolt. Conversely only 2.4% of the Jewish population was actually situated on the farms; the great majority of the Jews were congregated in the cities.

Says the *Universal Jewish Encyclopedia*[56]: "... it must be noted that the Jews lived almost exclusively in the cities and towns; in Russia's urban population the Jews constituted 11%. Two additional factors are taken into consideration. The rural population took practically no part in political activity.

As a matter of fact, the Jews represented a substantial portion of Russia's educated class. Not only that, but the overwhelming majority of Russia's professional class were Jews.

So complete was the Jewish domination of the professions that only one out of eight of Russia's professional people were Gentile. In other words, the Jews, who constituted 4.2% of Russia's pre-war population comprised something like 87% of those who had critical positions of control in Russia's infrastructure.

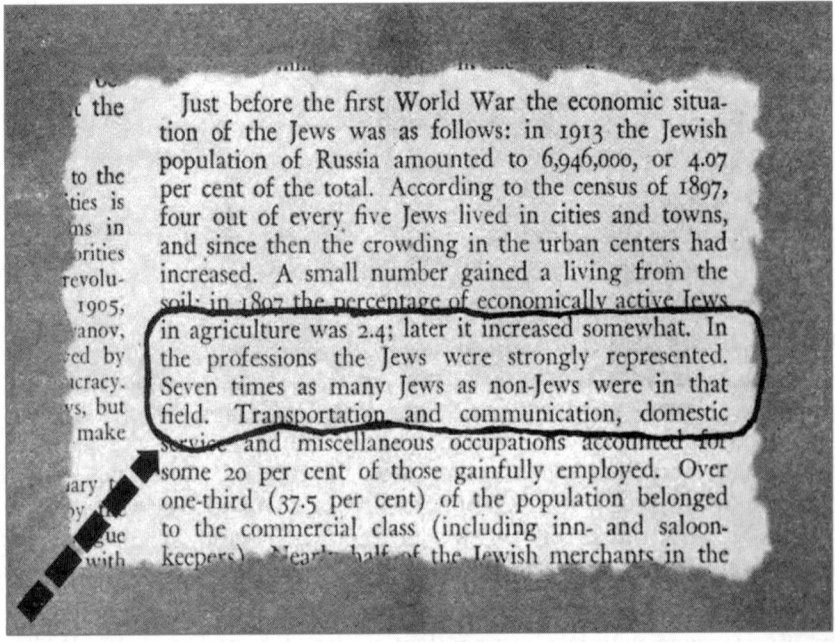

Just before the first World War the economic situation of the Jews was as follows: in 1913 the Jewish population of Russia amounted to 6,946,000, or 4.07 per cent of the total. According to the census of 1897, four out of every five Jews lived in cities and towns, and since then the crowding in the urban centers had increased. A small number gained a living from the soil: in 1897 the percentage of economically active Jews in agriculture was 2.4; later it increased somewhat. In the professions the Jews were strongly represented. Seven times as many Jews as non-Jews were in that field. Transportation and communication, domestic service and miscellaneous occupations accounted for some 20 per cent of those gainfully employed. Over one-third (37.5 per cent) of the population belonged to the commercial class (including inn- and saloon-keepers). Nearly half of the Jewish merchants in the

The above excerpt is taken from the *Universal Jewish Encyclopedia*.[57].

The Evacuations

Also significant was the fact that the theatre of war was situated in those areas most heavily populated by Jews. By 1914, it should be remembered, Russia's Jewish population was nearing the seven million mark. (The exact figure given in the *Universal Jewish Encyclopedia* is 6,946,000).

A substantial number of these resided in Russian-Poland, which was a war zone. The majority of those Jews, out of hatred for the Tsarist regime, were inclined to favor a German victory.

As a result, the Imperial high command was compelled to remove all Jews from the war area in the early part of 1915. In May of 1915, for example, the supreme command expelled all Jewish residents from the provinces of Courland and Grodno.

Altogether, nearly a half million Jews were forced to leave their homes in the military zone. These expellees were at first required to remain within the Pale of Settlement, but in August of 1915 they were permitted to settle in all cities in the empire.

Thus it was that as the war progressed a flood of Tsar-hating Jews began infiltrating the cities beyond the Pale.

Chapter 6
The March 1917 Revolution

The revolution occurred in March of 1917, in St. Petersburg, capital city of the Romanovs. From beginning to end the revolt involved an amazingly small number of people when we consider that the fate of 150 million Russians was at stake.

The revolt came, as we have tried to indicate, because of Jewish unrest, because of Jewry's dissatisfaction, and above all, because of Jewry's determination to destroy Tsarism.

By the Spring of 1917 Russia's unstable urban population had been thoroughly poisoned by this dissatisfaction. A food shortage in St. Petersburg fanned this dissatisfaction into the flame of revolution.

St. Petersburg in the third year of World War I was Russia's chief armaments production center, and by reason of this possessed the largest industrial population of any city in Russia. It also had the largest Jewish population of any city outside the Pale of Settlement.

By March, 1917, a breakdown in the Russian transportation system resulted in a severe food shortage in the city. At the same time, many of the city's factories began shutting down due to material shortages. Both of these factors were extremely important in the days immediately ahead.

The desperate food shortage affected virtually every family in the city. Furthermore, the enforced idleness of the working population—due to factory shutdowns—threw vast numbers of workmen onto the streets.

Day-by-Day Account

Given here is a day by day account of the events which resulted in the overthrow of the Tsar and the establishment of the Provisional Government:

March 5th: It was evident by this time—even to foreign visitors—that trouble was brewing. Bread lines were growing day by day, and factory workmen began to appear on the streets in large numbers. During the day the police began mounting machine guns in strategic places throughout the city.

March 6th: The government brought a large number of Cossack troops into the city in anticipation of trouble. Revolution was now freely predicted, and many of the shops in expectation of this began boarding up windows. The few remaining factories were closed by strikes and the police mounted more machine guns. The Tsar, who was visiting the troops at the front, still had not returned to the city. The Duma remained in session.

March 8th: Crowds of women began a series of street demonstrations in protest over the bread shortage. Agitators, many of whom were veterans of the 1905 revolution, began to take charge and organize diversionary demonstrations. Here and there the crowds sang the "Marseillaise" — regarded in Russia as a revolutionary song. A number of red flags appeared. At the corner of Nevsky Prospekt and the Catherine Canal mounted police, aided by Cossack cavalry, dispersed the crowds. There were no casualties. Significantly, however, the crowds had raised the red flag of revolution without being fired on.

March 9th: The Nevsky from Catherine Canal to Nicholai Station was jammed from early morning with crowds, which were larger and bolder than on the preceding day. Streetcars were no longer running. The Cossack cavalry, under orders to keep the Nevsky clear of demonstrators, repeatedly charged the mobs, and a few people were trampled. But it was observed that the cavalrymen used only the flats of their sabers, and at no time used fire arms. This encouraged the mob, which held the Cossacks in dread. Meanwhile, agitators were constantly at work.

March 10th: During the afternoon huge crowds collected around Nicholai Station. An American photographer, Donald Thompson, has described in vivid fashion the scene there[58]: "About two o'clock a man richly dressed in furs came up to the square in a sleigh and ordered his driver to go through the crowd, which by this time was in a very ugly mood, although it seemed to be inclined to make way for him. He was impatient and probably cold and started an argument. All Russians must have their argument. Well, he misjudged this crowd, and also misjudged the condition in Petrograd. I was within 150 feet of this scene. He was dragged out of his sleigh and beaten. He took refuge in a stalled street car where he was followed by the workingmen. One of them took a small iron bar and beat his head to a pulp. This seemed to give the mob a taste for blood. Immediately I was pushed along in front of the crowd which surged down the Nevsky and began smashing windows and creating general disorder. Many of the men carried red flags on sticks. The shops along the Nevsky, or most of them, are protected by heavy iron shutters. Those that were not had their windows smashed. I noticed about this time that ambulances were coming and going on the side streets. There were usually three or four people lying in each one."

Russian Jews demonstrate in favor of the Revolution, with banners in Hebrew proclaiming "Long live the Universal Workers Union" and "Long Life to the International Proletariat," March 1917.

The disorder now became general. The mobs turned their fury on the police, who barricaded themselves for a desperate last stand in the police stations. There they were slaughtered almost to the last man, and the prisons were emptied of their entire populations, including desperate criminals of every category.

March 11th: Widespread rioting continued on the 11th. Added to the terror of revolution were the degradations of the recently liberated criminal population. During the day the Duma sent the following urgent message to the Tsar, now entrained for St. Petersburg: "The situation is serious. There is anarchy in the capital. The government is paralyzed. The situation as regards transportation, and supplies, and fuel has reached a state of complete disorganization. Police dissatisfaction is growing. Disorderly shooting is taking place in the streets. Different sections of the troops are shooting at each other. It is necessary immediately to entrust a person who has the confidence of the country with the creation of a new government."

The Tsar's reaction was tragically out of keeping with the reality of the situation. It is doubtful that he even had an inkling of what was really transpiring. His reaction was to command the dissolution of the Duma. The overwhelming majority of the Duma's membership, — loyal to the Tsar — obeyed his command, with the result that the last vestige of governmental authority ceased to exist in the capital.

March 12th: The president of the dissolved Duma sent this last despairing message to the Tsar: "The situation is becoming worse. Immediate means must be taken, for tomorrow it will be too late. The last hour has struck and the fate of the fatherland and the dynasty is being decided."

Tsar Nicholas II may never have received the message: in any event he did not reply. And indeed, the hour was late.

At 1:00 A.M. on the morning of the 12th one of the regiments (the Volynski) revolted, killing its officers. By 11 A.M. six regiments had revolted. At 11:30 A.M. the garrison of the Peter and Paul fortress surrendered and joined the revolution.

The only section of the city which now remained under governmental control was the War Office, the Admiralty Building, and St. Isaac's Cathedral. The revolution was now an accomplished fact.

Tsar Nicholas II Abdicates

Four days later, on the 16th, Tsar Nicholas II, whose train never reached St. Petersburg, abdicated. The closing words of his written abdication announcement were: "May God have mercy on Russia".

The 12th of March marked the formation of two governing bodies which were to jointly rule Russia for the next 8 months. The first of these was the Provisional Committee of the Duma, consisting of 12 members headed by Prince Lvov.

This group served as the Provisional Government until overthrown in October by the Bolsheviks. At all times, however, it governed by the sufferance of the St. Petersburg Soviet, which was the second body organized on the 12th.

This St. Petersburg Soviet was in reality dominated by the Menshevik and Bolshevik factions of the Russian Social Democratic Labor Party, of whom the Mensheviks were by far the most powerful. A second party, the Social Revolutionary Party, was a minority party.

Eventually, as we shall see, the Bolshevik faction gained control over the St. Petersburg Soviet, and having done so, at once precipitated the October Revolution and established the regime which held power in Russia until the 1990s.

To better understand these events, it is necessary that we trace the history of these Mensheviks and Bolsheviks and their Russian Social Democratic Labor Party.

Chapter 7
The Origins of the Bolsheviks

WE must for the moment turn our attention to a group of revolutionary exiles who are important to this story because they and their disciples eventually became the rulers of Communist Russia. Head of this group, and the man who is generally recognized as Lenin's teacher, was George Plekhanov, a Gentile.

Plekhanov had fled Russia in the 1880s and settled in Switzerland. There with the aid of Vera Zasulich, Leo Deutsch (real name Lev), and Pavel Axelrod (real name Pinches Borutsch) — all Jews — he had formed the Marxist "Group for the Emancipation of Labor", and until 1901 was recognized as the leader of the group.

Lenin
Lenin (part Jewish) speaks - Trotsky and Lev Kamenev (both Jews) stand immediately to the right of the speaker's podium

Although Plekhanov was himself a Gentile, those around him were, with a few exceptions, Jewish. One of the technical exceptions was Lenin, who first became a disciple of Plekhanov, and later a competitor. Lenin was at least of partly Jewish ancestry, spoke Yiddish, was married to a Jew, and identified himself with the Jewish community. He even spoke frequently of the superiority of Jews over Gentiles.

Lenin (real name Vladimir Ilyich Ulyanov) was born on the banks of the Volga in the provincial city of Simbirsk in 1870. He was born to a station of comparative privilege, being the son of a government official whose title of "Actual State Counselor" carried with it the privilege of hereditary nobility. Lenin's father did not himself inherit the title, but acquired it as a reward of service as a school supervisor.

According to KGB files declassified in 2011, Lenin was part-Jewish, with his maternal grandfather being Jewish. This was too far back for Lenin to be classified as Jewish by either the orthodox Jewish community or society at large, but it may well have played a role in his fierce opposition to anti-Semitism. The first time his voice was recorded was a special message which outlawed anti-Semitism after the success of the Bolshevist seizure of power.

By every rule, "Lenin" should have become a respected member of Russian society. He was of middle class background, was university educated, and was admitted to the practice of law. That he did not do so can be ascribed in part to the fate of his older brother, Alexander, who in 1887 was executed for participating in an attempt on the life of Tsar Alexander II. This is said to have influenced Lenin to take up the career of a professional revolutionary. In any event the year of 1895 finds young Lenin—then 25—meeting in Switzerland with the leaders of the "Group for the Emancipation of Labor".

Shortly thereafter he returned to Russia in the company of young Julius Margo (Tsederbaum), a Jew who had already become prominent as an agitator in the Pale of Settlement, and who was one day to become the leader of the Menshevik faction. Their purpose was to raise funds for revolutionary activity. In St. Petersburg they became involved in a series of strikes which swept the city in 1895, and in the autumn of the same year Lenin, Martov, and a number of others were convicted and sent to prison for revolutionary activity.

In February of 1897 Lenin completed his prison term and began his period of exile in Siberia. He was permitted to travel to Siberia at his own expense and he took with him his Jewish wife, Krupskaya and her Yiddish speaking mother.

It should be explained that, contrary to popular belief, political exiles — unless convicted of a criminal act — were not imprisoned in Siberia; rather they were paroled there. In exile, the government provided a pension, sufficient usually to maintain an existence. To supplement this, the exile sometimes sought local employment (Trotsky worked as a bookkeeper) or they got funds from friends and family. Lenin received a government allowance of 7 rubles 40 kopeks monthly, "'enough to pay for room, board and laundry." [*Lenin* (abridgement by Donald P. Geddes)]

While in Siberian exile Lenin, Martov, and an accomplice Potresov, formulated the idea of an "All Russian Newspaper" which would serve to combine the thought and energies of the entire revolutionary movement.

The Marxists in 1900, as at all times in the future, were divided and subdivided into a great many factions. Lenin's idea was to weld these various factions into a single organization.

Iskra

Communism as an organized movement began with the publishing of *Iskra* ("The Spark") in December of 1900. Three years later, in 1903, the "Iskrists" joined with the Polish Social Democrats, the Jewish Bund, and others, to form the Russian Social-Democratic Labor Party (which later changed its name to the Communist Party).

Iskra, like every other Communist publication which followed, was mainly edited and controlled by Jews.

In February of 1900 Lenin was released from exile and applied for, and got, permission to go to Switzerland. In Geneva he joined the "Group for the Emancipation of Labor", and in December the Group began the publication of *Iskra*. The establishment of *Iskra* marked the beginning of Russian Marxism as an organized movement, and the beginning of Lenin's role as a party leader.

The editorial board consisted of the "oldsters", Plekhanov, Zasulich, Axelrod, and their disciples, Lenin, Potresov, and Martov. Lenin's Jewish wife, Krupskaya, was the board's secretary. Later, in 1902, young Trotsky (Bronstein) joined the editorial board, but without voting privileges.

Four of the above — Martov, Axelrod, Zasulich, and Trotsky — were Jews, while Plekhanov and Potresov were Gentiles.

It is interesting to note the editorial contributions of the first 45 issues of *Iskra*. The largest number of articles was written by Martov, who contributed 39. Next was Lenin, who wrote 32 articles, followed by Plekhanov with 24, Petresov with 8, Zasulich with 6, and Axelrod with 4. In addition, articles were written by Parvus, Trotsky, and Rosa Luxemburg all of whom were Jewish.

It is worth recording that the only other revolutionary paper in existence at this time was *Rabochee Delo* (Workers Cause), organ of the "Economist" faction, of which the Jew, Theodore Dan was the editor.

Iskra was actually printed in Munich, Germany. For a time the editorial board met in London, but in 1903 it was moved back to Geneva. From there copies of *Iskra* were smuggled into Russia by ship and courier. In this way Iskra built up an underground organization of professional revolutionaries, first known as "Iskrists", and later as Bolsheviks and Mensheviks.

In Switzerland, Axelrod eked out an existence by peddling yogurt, and Plekhanov is said to have addressed letters for an income. But the founders and leaders of Communism were not proletarians. Almost without exception they were highly educated Jewish intellectuals, few of whom had ever performed a useful day's labor.

Unification Congress of 1903

In 1903 a Unification Congress convened in Brussels, Belgium. Its purpose was to unite the various Marxist groups into the Russian Social Democratic Labor Party, which technically had been formed in 1898, but which had failed to bring unity.

Altogether, 60 voting delegates attended, four of whom were, or had been, workers. The rest were mostly Jewish intellectuals. Represented were the groups which had formed the party in 1898: The Jewish Bund, the Georgian Social Democrats, Rosa Luxemburg's Polish Social Democrats, and the Group for the Emancipation of Labor, now identified as "Iskrists".

The Maximalist's newspaper, *Rabochee Delo*, was also represented by 3 delegates. These groups, their leaders, and their disciples, made the revolution of 1917. Here, Communism as we know it, was born.

In early August the Belgian Police deported a number of delegates and the Unification Congress moved en masse to England, where it convened from August 11th to the 23rd. One very important outcome of the congress was the ideological split which divided the Iskrists into two camps: The Bolsheviks (majority faction), headed by Lenin, and the Mensheviks (minority faction), headed by Martov.

The final act of the congress was to elect Lenin, Plekhanov, and Martov to the editorial board of *Iskra*. This new board of three never actually functioned, due to the hostility between Martov and Lenin. After issue No. 53 Lenin resigned leaving it in the hands of Martov, Plekhanov, Axelrod, Zasulich and Petresov, the latter three being admitted to the board following Lenin's resignation.

Although Lenin's faction clung to the Bolshevik label, they did not at any time command a real majority in the party. Lenin had temporarily been able to dominate the Unification Congress when the Jewish Bund's delegation had walked out in a huff over party policy.

Because Lenin had been temporarily able to marshal a majority of the remaining delegates to his support, his faction had been identified as the Bolshevik, or majority faction, and always thereafter Lenin and his followers were known as Bolsheviks.

It is important to note that this Bolshevik-Menshevik split was among the Iskrists only. The two other major factions of the party—Rosa Luxemburg's Polish Social Democrats and the Jewish Bund—were neither Bolshevik nor Menshevik, although both factions usually teamed up with the Mensheviks on party policy. In 1917, however, both the Polish party and the Bund merged into the Bolshevik faction.

The Jewishness of the Mensheviks is obvious from this photograph of Avel Axelrod, Julius Martov and Alexander Martinov. *Norra Bantorget in Stockholm, Sweden,* May 1917.

Revolution of 1905

The 1905 revolution came unexpectedly. Jewish agitators, seizing upon the discontent engendered by Russia's defeat by the Japanese, and capitalizing on the "Bloody Sunday" incident— which we have already described—fanned the flames of insurrection into being what was to be a dress rehearsal of the 1917 revolution.

The revolt, coming so quickly on the heels of the Bloody Sunday incident, caught the party leadership by surprise. Lenin was in Geneva and he did not return to St. Petersburg until October — shortly before the Petersburg Soviet was organized.

Martov the Menshevik leader, returned at the same time. Rosa Luxemburg arrived in December, by which time the insurrection had ended. Axelrod got only as far as Finland, and Plekhanov never returned at all.

The 1905 revolution was principally led by second-string leaders, virtually all of whom were identified with the Mensheviks.

Trotsky, alone of the top leadership had sensed the significance of "Bloody Sunday," and at the first word of revolution he and a Jewish compatriot, Parvus, had struck out for St. Petersburg.

Using the pseudonym Yanovsky, he very quickly became a leading member of the Soviet, and by the end of October was generally recognized as the most influential member of the Executive Committee. In addition, he edited (with Parvus) the Menshevik organ, *Nachato*.

Later, under the pseudonym, "Peter Petrovich" he edited the *Russkyaya Gazeta*. On Dec. 9, as we have previously related, he was elected president of the St. Petersburg Soviet, and following his arrest Parvus assumed leadership of the revolt.

Although Lenin had been in St. Petersburg throughout the life of the St. Petersburg Soviet, neither he nor any member of his faction played a prominent part in its activities. When the 300 members of the Soviet were finally arrested, not a single prominent Bolshevik was among them. The revolution of 1905 was strictly a Menshevik affair.

The London Congress of 1907

In 1907 (May 13 — June 1) a fifth Congress of the Russian Social Democratic Labor Party was held, this time in London. This was by all accounts the most impressive one of all, and it was the last one held before the 1917 revolution. Represented at the Congress were:

* The Bolsheviks, led by Lenin — 91 delegates.

* The Mensheviks, led by Martov and Dan—89 delegates.

* The Polish Social Democrats, led by Rosa Luxemburg—44 delegates.

* The Jewish Bund, led by Rafael Abramovitch and M. I. Lieber—55 delegates.

* The Lettish Social Democrats, led by "Comrade Herman" (Danishevsky).

Altogether there were 312 delegates to the Congress, of whom 116 were, or had been, workers. Dominating the Congress were the great names of the party: there were the founders of the movement, Plekhanov, Axelrod, Deutch, and Zasulich—who after 1907 played roles of diminishing importance in party affairs—and their disciples, Lenin, Martov, Dan (Gurvich), and Trotsky.

There were Abramovich and Lieber (Goldman) of the Bund, and Rosa Luxemburg, the latter one day being destined to lead a revolution of her own in Germany.

Present also were Zinoviev, Kamenev, and Stalin, none of whom were important in 1907, but who are listed here because one day they would be the three most powerful men in Russia. Significantly all of those named were Jewish, excepting part-Jewish Lenin, Plekhanov, and Stalin.

Perhaps one of the most important matters taken up by the London Congress was the bitterly controversial question of "expropriations." It should be explained that Lenin's Bolshevik faction had to an increasing degree resorted to outlawry to replenish

Julius Martov, or L. Martov, the Jew whose real name Yuliy Osipovich Zederbaum, was born in Istanbul in 1873. He became the leader of the Mensheviks.

its finances: Robbery, kidnapping, and theft became regular party activities.

On one occasion a loyal Bolshevik married a rich widow to secure funds for the party treasury. These activities were referred to in party circles as "expropriations." The most famous expropriation was the Tiflis bank robbery, engineered by young Josef Stalin shortly after the London Congress.

The Mensheviks bitterly criticized these tactics, while Lenin stoutly defended them as a necessary means of raising capital. The "expropriation" question broke out again and again as a point of contention between the two factions. Actually a great deal of Lenin's strength came from this source. With money thus raised he was able to pay the traveling expenses of delegates to these various congresses, and this gave him a voting power which was probably out of proportion to his following.

Maxim Maximovich Litvinov, Born Meir Henoch Mojszewicz Wallach-Finkelstein, was a Russian revolutionary and prominent Soviet diplomat.

Lenin's opposition on the expropriation question came not only from Martov's Menshevik faction, but also from the Jewish Bund and Rosa Luxemburg's Polish Social Democrats. The Jewish Bund and Rosa Luxemburg's faction usually sided with the Mensheviks in these intra-party squabbles, and it was not until 1917, when they were actually incorporated into the Bolshevik faction, that Lenin was able to control the entire party.

The Tiflis bank robbery has now become a part of the legend which surrounds Stalin, and it is perhaps worthwhile to give it some attention. Although the robbery was engineered by Stalin, then a minor party worker, the actual holdup was carried out by an Armenian by the name of Petroyan, who is known in Russian history as "Kamo." Kamo's method was crude but effective: he tossed a dynamite bomb at a bank stagecoach which was transporting 250,000 rubles in currency.

In the resulting explosion some 40 people were killed and Kamo escaped with the loot, which consisted mainly of 500 ruble notes. The Bolsheviks encountered considerable difficulty in converting these 500 ruble notes into usable form. It was decided that agents in various countries would simultaneously cash as many as possible in a single day. The operation was not a complete success. The Jewess, Olga Ravich, who was one day to marry Zinoviev, was apprehended by police authorities, as was one Meyer Wallach, whose real name was Finklestein, and who is better known as Maxim Litvinov. Litvinov later became Commissar of Foreign Affairs (1930-39).

Three Communist Newspapers Launched: All Run by Jews

Grigory Yevseevich Zinoviev was born Ovsei-Gershon Aronovich Radomyslsky Apfelbaum, is best remembered as the longtime head of the Communist International and the architect of the several failed attempts to transform Germany into a Communist country during the early 1920s.

In the autumn of 1908 the Bolsheviks began publishing the *Proletariie,* with Lenin, Dubrovinsky, Zinoviev, and Kamenev (the latter two Jewish) as editors.

In the same year the Menshevik organ, *Golos Sotsial-Demokrata* began publication, edited by Plekhanov, Axelrod, Martov, Dan, and Martynov (Pikel), all of whom were Jewish with the exception of Plekhanov. In October of 1908, the *Vienna Pravda* was launched, with Trotsky as editor.

Lenin-Zinoviev-Kamenev Troika

In 1909 Lenin, Zinoviev and Kamenev formed a "troika." It was to endure until Lenin's death in 1924. Zinoviev and Kamenev were Lenin's inseparable companions. Later, when the Bolsheviks were in power, Trotsky would become co-equal with Lenin, and even something of a competitor, but Kamenev and Zinoviev were never Lenin's equals nor his competitors—they were his right and left hand. They would argue with him, and fight with him, and oppose him in party councils, but the "troika" was broken only when Lenin died.

January Plenum

In January of 1910, the 19 top leaders of the Party met in what historians refer to as the "January Plenum of the Central Committee." Its purpose was, as always, to promote party unity.

One outcome was that Lenin was compelled to burn the remainder of the 500 ruble notes from the Tiflis expropriation, which he had been unable to cash anyway. Another outcome of the January Plenum was the recognition of the newspaper, Sotsial Demokrata, as the general party newspaper. Its editors were the Bolsheviks, Lenin and Zinoviev, and the Mensheviks, Martov and Dan. Lenin was the only Gentile.

Trotsky's semi-independent *Vienna Pravda* was also declared to be an official party organ, and Kamenev was appointed to help edit it. Who could have foretold in the year 1910 that within seven short years this Yiddish crew would be the lords and masters of all Russia?

Germans Allow Lenin to Enter Russia

The 1917 revolution, like that of 1905, caught the top leaders of the party unprepared. Lenin and Martov were in Switzerland, and Trotsky was eking out an existence in New York's East Side.

Shortly after the March revolution, the German government arranged to ship Lenin, Martov, Radek, and 32 members of the party across Germany to Russia. The German strategy seemed to be based on the assumption—which later proved correct—that the Communists would work to sabotage the Russian war effort, now being prosecuted by the Provisional Government.

Perhaps the Lenin group had some such agreement with the Germans, no one knows. But one thing is certain: 48 hours after the Bolsheviks came to power, Trotsky began negotiations for an armistice. But that story comes later.

On April 3rd, just 23 days after the provisional government had been formed, Lenin and his party arrived in St. Petersburg. Within 7 months he and his faction would be the supreme dictators of all Russia.

Chapter 8
The Ground is Prepared

A description of the March Revolution which overthrew the Tsar has already been presented, and the process by which the establishment of the two governing bodies which came into existence on March 12th. They were named the Provisional Government and the St. Petersburg Soviet.

The St. Petersburg Soviet, although it controlled the mob, was reluctant to assume the responsibility of governing—at least in the beginning. The Soviet was originally organized by second-string leaders who were quite capable of stirring up trouble, but who had little capacity for leading a revolutionary government. Furthermore, it was not clear in the early days of the revolution as to what the final outcome would be.

St. Petersburg was, after all, only one city in the empire, and the attitude of the country as a whole, and of the soldiers at the front, was unknown. For this reason the Soviet preferred that the Provisional Government—which had some semblance of legitimacy—should temporarily rule.

The Petersburg Soviet, formed on March 12th was dominated by the Mensheviks under the leadership of the Jews Lieber, Dan and Martov. Later (in October) the Bolsheviks gained control when Trotsky became president and they immediately precipitated the October Revolution.

The Provisional Government

The Provisional Government was not a revolutionary body. Of its 12 members, only one, Kerensky, was a "Socialist." The others were typical upper-middle class members of the Duma, with possibly mild leanings to the left.

Head of the Provisional Government was Prince Lvov, whose reputation as a liberal may have qualified him for that position more than some of the others. This 12 man government had sprung into being simply because no other semblance of a government existed in St. Petersburg on March 12th—it did not in any way participate in the revolution.

The Jew Karl Radek, born Karol Sobelsohn, took part in the failed 1905 revolution in Poland, and then moved to Germany and finally to the Soviet Union. After the October Revolution, Radek became Vice-Commissar for Foreign Affairs.

In the months following the overthrow of the Tsar, however, its power grew considerably, so that by July when an abortive Bolshevik uprising occurred, the Provisional Government was able to quell the affair and arrest or force into hiding the Bolshevik leaders.

The Provisional Government undertook to continue the war against Germany. The great mass of people were, of course, patriotic Russians, and Germany was looked on as a dangerous threat to Russian sovereignty. The Provisional Government, during its entire tenure, was primarily occupied with the prosecution of the war.

The Provisional Government took two steps, however, which were to profoundly affect the revolution. The first, and most fateful, was the decision to permit the return of all exiled political prisoners from Siberia and abroad. By doing so it sealed the fate of Russia.

Here is the way one American writer, Edward Alsworth Ross, has described it[59] : "One of the first acts of the Provisional government, however, is to bring back to Russia the political victims of the autocracy. From Siberia about eighty thousand are brought out.

From Switzerland, France, Scandinavia, the United States, even from Argentina and other remote countries, come perhaps ten thousand who have been refugees from the tsar's vengeance. In all ninety thousand at least, virtually all of them of socialist sympathies, stream into European Russia in late April, May, June, and July. Honored by a grateful people for their voluntary sacrifices and sufferings they quickly rise to a commanding influence in the local soviets and carry them irresistibly toward the political left."

These ninety thousand exiles constituted the heart of the approaching Bolshevik revolution. They were almost to the last man professional revolutionaries, and with few exceptions they were Jewish.

Stalin, Sverdlov, and Zinoviev were among the exiles who returned from Siberia. Lenin, Martov, Radek, and Kamenev — as we have seen — returned from Switzerland. Trotsky returned, with hundreds of his Yiddish brethren, from New York's East Side.

The Coming Genocide of the Russian Gentile Elite

Let us take another quotation from the starry-eyed Edward Alworth Ross, whose prose is almost as poor as his judgment: "The bewildered leaderless Russian masses are thrilled and captivated by these ready, self-confident men who tell them just what they must do in order to garner for themselves the fruits of the revolution.

This is why refugees, obscure to us although not to Russians, who in exile had been obliged to work in our steel mills and tailor shops for a living, former residents of New York's "Eastside", who lived precariously from some Russian newspapers we Americans never heard of, will rise to be the heads of soviets and, later, cabinet ministers of a government ruling a tenth of the human race. In all modern history there is no romance like it."[60] When the Bolsheviks came to power, they systematically undertook to destroy every vestige of opposition by exterminating the upper classes of Russian society.

Soon these hordes of returning Jews would exercise the power of life and death over 150 million Russians. Soon every factory, every government bureau, every school district, and every army unit would function under the gimlet eye of a Jewish Commissar. Soon the blood of human beings would be oozing from under the doors of Communist execution chambers as tens of thousands of men and women were butchered like cattle in a slaughterhouse.

The Jew Fyodor Ilyich Dan (Real name Gurvitch) was one of the leading Mensheviks on the presidium of the Petrograd Soviet. He went to live in New York after the revolution where he died in 1947.

Soon five million landowners would be deliberately starved to death as part of a premeditated plan. Soon a move would be under way to exterminate the Gentile leader class of the entire nation by murdering every Gentile factory owner, and lawyer, and government leader, and army officer, and every other person who had been, or might be, a potential leader.

Soon the standing population of the slave labor camps would exceed 15 million. Soon every church and cathedral would be gutted and every priest and preacher would become a criminal in his own community.

Soon Russia would have a zombie-proletariat docile, willing to work, easily controlled, incapable of revolt ... Such was the "romance" of the Bolshevik revolution.

Constituent Assembly Elections

A second important act of the Provisional Government was to create the machinery for the election of a Constituent Assembly.

It was provided that delegates from all of Russia should be chosen in free elections, and these were to meet in a Constituent Assembly for the purpose of writing a constitution for Russia.

It was to be, as one writer puts it [61]: "a body encompassing the purposes of both the Continental Congress and the Constitutional Convention of the American Revolution."

When the Constituent Assembly did meet, in January of 1918, the Bolsheviks had already been in power a month.

"It met at the Tauride Palace in Petrograd and lasted less than 13 hours; from four in the afternoon of Jan. 18, to 40 minutes past four of Jan. 19, when it was dispersed by Bolshevik troops, chiefly soldiers of Lettish regiments."

One of the factors which precipitated the October Revolution was the forthcoming elections for the Constituent Assembly.

All-Russian Congress of Soviets

One other event occurred which was to affect the outcome of the revolution. This was the convening of the First All-Russian Congress of Soviets in St. Petersburg on June 3rd, 1917.

It should be explained that the word "soviet" means "council", or "committee". Following the March Revolution, literally hundreds of local revolutionary Soviets were organized all over Russia by the various Marxist parties.

It was decided that a congress of these soviets should meet for the purpose of unifying the forces of the revolution.

This first Congress of Soviets was dominated by the Mensheviks and Essars. (Essars = Social Revolutionary Party). The Bolsheviks had fewer than 40 delegates out of several hundred attending.

Before disbanding, the Congress of Soviets set October 20th (later changed to Nov. 7th) as the date for the convening of the next Congress. This date is extremely important because it marks the date of the Bolshevik Revolution.

When the Second Congress of Soviets did convene, on the evening of November 7th, the Bolsheviks had already gained control of the St. Petersburg Soviet and had overthrown the Provisional Government a few hours earlier.

The Bolsheviks were thus able to present the Second All-Russian Congress of Soviets with a "fait accompli". This Second Congress of Soviets became the official government of Communist Russia on that same evening of November 7th, 1917.

Lenin Returns

But now we must turn our attention back to Lenin and his party at the time of their arrival from abroad. When Lenin arrived in St. Petersburg in April of 1917, he found the St. Petersburg Soviet dominated by the Mensheviks, with the Essars (Social Revolutionaries) second in membership, and the Bolsheviks in the minority.

President of the Soviet was the Menshevik, Tcheidze, a "defensist" who strongly supported the war effort. Of the two vice-presidents, one was Skobelev, also a Menshevik, and the other was Kerensky, the only member of the 12 man Provisional Government who also belonged to the Soviet.

Although the Mensheviks controlled the St. Petersburg Soviet, they were badly divided among themselves. The main body of the Menshevik faction—the defensists—was headed by Theodore Dan (Gurvich) and M. I. Lieber (formerly of the Jewish Bund). The other group of Mensheviks,—the internationalists— was headed by Martov. Lenin bitterly criticized this state of affairs. He regarded the provisional government as an instrument of the "bourgeois" and he immediately and violently advocated its overthrow.

Throughout April, May, and June the Bolsheviks preached the destruction of the Provisional Government, and among the factory workers and the military garrisons around St. Petersburg this propaganda began to take effect. Under the slogan "all power to the Soviets", the Bolsheviks had succeeded by July in recruiting to their banners large numbers of the city's more radical elements.

The returning influx of exiles also enhanced the position of the Bolsheviks. These exiles were not all originally Bolsheviks, but they were almost without exception extremists, and they had waited a long time for revolution to come: they were hungry for power. And they were inclined to favor the Bolsheviks because they were the most radical advocates of direct action.

Trotsky, who had in 1905 begun as a Menshevik, and who had later been a "neutral", immediately joined the Bolsheviks on his return from New York. So it was with many others.

On July 17th this antigovernment agitation resulted in an unscheduled uprising by thousands of the city's inflamed worker-soldier population. In modern Russian history these are known as the "July Days".

Kerensky, who by now had become the dominant figure in the Provisional Government dealt with the insurrection with considerable firmness. The mob was fired on, and in the course of the next three days several hundred people were killed.

As a result of the "July Days" uprising, the top Bolshevik leadership was either arrested or forced to flee. Lenin and Zinoviev temporarily hid out in Sestroretsk, outside of St. Petersburg. Trotsky, Kamenev, and Lunacharsky (soon to become prominent) were arrested. Stalin, at that time an editor of *Pravda*, was not molested.

One result of the "July Days" was the collapse of the Provisional Government under the premiership of Prince Lvov. On July 20th, Kerensky (Adler) the Jewish Napoleon, became Prime Minister of a 'salvation of the revolution' government. Kerensky was quite an orator, and he applied himself to the task of whipping up enthusiasm for an offensive against the Germans. Although he met with moderate success at first, the offensive failed and Kerensky's influence declined steadily in the next three months.

Chapter 9
The Sixth Party Congress

IN August (8-16) the Russian Social-Democratic Labor Party held its Sixth Congress. This was the first one held since the London Congress of 1907, and it was the last one held before the Bolshevik Revolution, now only two months away. This Sixth Congress was completely a Bolshevik affair. The other factions merged with the Bolsheviks and ceased to exist; from this time on the Russian Social Democratic Labor Party WAS the Bolshevik Party. (Within a year the party officially changed its name to the Communist Party).

The most important act of the Sixth Congress was to elect the "October Central Committee", consisting of 26 members. This Central Committee was to rule the Bolshevik Party through the critical days of the October Revolution.

Who were the principal members of the "October Central Committee"? Let us take the words of Lev Trotsky as they appear in his book, *Stalin:*

> "In view of the Party's semi-legality the names of persons elected by secret ballot were not announced at the Congress, with the exception of the four who had received the largest number of votes. Lenin—133 out of a possible 134, Zinoviev—132, Kamenev—131, Trotsky—131".[62]

These four two months before the October Revolution, were the top leaders of the Bolshevik Party. Three were Jews and the fourth, Lenin, was part Jewish, spoke Yiddish and was married to a Jewess.

Trotsky Names Jews Who Ran Bolshevik Revolution

Trotsky's writings are extremely enlightening from a historical viewpoint. He hated Stalin and he wrote his book, Stalin, to prove that Stalin was a Johnny-come-lately, an upstart, and an usurper. He brings forth masses of evidence to show how unimportant Stalin was in Party councils during and immediately after the October Revolution.

In doing so, Trotsky again and again emphasizes who the really important leaders were. Let us take another typical comment from his book on Stalin as he describes the meetings of the October Central Committee shortly before the Bolshevik Revolution: "The 422 pages of the fourth volume, dealing with August and September, record all the happenings, occurrences, brawls, resolutions, speeches, articles in any way deserving of notice. Sverdlov, then practically unknown, was mentioned three times in that volume; Kamenev, 46 times; I, who spent August and the beginning of September in prison, 31 times; Lenin, who was in the underground, 16 times; Zinoviev, who shared Lenin's fate, 6 times. Stalin was not mentioned even once. Stalin's name is not even in the index of approximately 500 proper names."[63]

Thus, Trotsky again cites evidence to prove that Stalin was not an important figure in the Bolshevik Party in 1917. But in doing so he names the real leaders, who as before are the Jews, Kamenev, Zinoviev, Trotsky, and the up and coming Sverdlov. Lenin, often described as a Gentile,[actually as pointed out before, he was only part Gentile, he spoke Yiddish (The Jewish Language) and was according to Jewish authorities and preached that Jews are the superior race.

Because the top party leaders were either in prison or in hiding as a result of the abortive July Days uprising, the Sixth Party Congress was organized by the lesser lights of the party, of whom Sverdlov was the most active.

Lev Trotsky, ever anxious to discredit Stalin, gives us this description: "The Praesidium consisted of Sverdlov, Olminsky, Lomov, Yurenev, and Stalin. Even here, with the most prominent figures of Bolshevism absent, Stalin's name is listed in last place. The Congress resolved to send greetings to 'Lenin, Trotsky, Zinoviev, Lunacharsky, Kamenev, Kollontai, and all the others arrested and persecuted comrades'. These were elected to the honorary Praesidium."[64]

Here again, in the words of Trotsky, we have named the "most prominent figures of Bolshevism": Lenin, Trotsky, Zinoviev, Kamenev and Lunacharsky. And we know these were the most important leaders because they were the ones Kerensky had arrested or driven underground following the July Days revolt. Of these, only Lunacharsky was fully gentile; the others were Jewish or part Jewish: Lenin.

These facts show why the Jewishness of Communism is so immediately and indisputably apparent to anyone who has the slightest knowledge of Bolshevik history.

Trotsky, Lenin and Kamenev.

Chapter 10
Trotsky to Power: the Red Terror Begins

ON August 17th, Kamenev was released from prison, and exactly a month later Trotsky was also freed by the Kerensky regime. On Sept. 24th Trotsky was elected president of the St. Petersburg Soviet, displacing Cheidze, the Menshevik.

From this moment on the Bolsheviks were in control of the St. Petersburg Soviet. On October 29th the St. Petersburg Soviet voted to transfer all military power to a "Military Revolutionary Committee", headed by Trotsky. Revolution was now only days away.

Military Revolutionary Committee

The Military Revolutionary Committee, under the chairmanship of Trotsky, was organized for the express purpose of preparing the revolution. Time was running out and it was a matter of striking soon or not at all. The Constituent Assembly elections were only a few weeks off, and when it convened, Russia was to have a new government. There was another reason for striking soon.

The Second All-Russian Congress of Soviets was to meet on Nov. 7th. The Bolsheviks feared—and with reason—that the Kerensky government would arrest or disband the entire congress and thereby doom the revolt. For these reasons it was felt essential to overthrow the Provisional Government by or before the Second All-Russian Congress of Soviets convened on Nov. 7th.

On November 4th the Military Revolutionary Committee arranged huge mass meetings in preparation for the forthcoming revolt. On the following day the garrison of the Peter and Paul Fortress declared itself in alliance with the Bolsheviks.

On the 6th Kerensky made one last attempt to forestall revolution by ordering the arrest of the Military Revolutionary Committee, banning all Bolshevik publications, and ordering fresh troops to replace the St. Petersburg garrison. These measures were never carried out.

Headquarters of the Military Revolutionary Committee during the October Revolution was the Smolny Institute. From here, Trotsky commanded the forces which overthrew the Kerensky regime.

The Bolshevik Revolution

On the evening of November 6th, Lenin came out of hiding and joined the Military Revolutionary Committee at Smolny Institute which served as revolutionary headquarters. At two A.M. the following morning the revolution began.

By noon the city was largely in Bolshevik hands. At three P.M. Lenin delivered a fiery speech to the St. Petersburg Soviet — his first since July. At nine P.M. Bolshevik troops began their two day siege of the Winter Palace, last stronghold of the Provisional Government.

At eleven P. M. the Second All-Russian Congress of Soviets convened with the Bolsheviks in a clear majority. The Congress was now the official government of Russia. The Jew Kamenev, was elected its first President. Lenin became Premier. Trotsky was made Commissar of Foreign Affairs. Before dawn it had elected a Central Executive Committee under the chairmanship of Kamenev, who thus had the distinction of being the first President of the "Soviet Republic".

Within a few days (Nov. 21) the Jew, Sverdlov, succeeded Kamenev, and thus became the second Jewish president of the "Soviet Republic". A relatively minor figure in Bolshevik circles six months before the revolution, he very quickly became one of the five top men in the party. Before his early death two years later he had become the party's chief troubleshooter and had assumed absolute control over Russia's economic life.

The Constituent Assembly is Broken Up by the Bolsheviks

On November 25th, 8 days after the Bolshevik coup, free elections were held throughout Russia under machinery set up by the Provisional Government. The Bolsheviks, not yet completely organized, made no attempt to interfere with the elections, but when it became clear that they would command only a minority in the Constituent Assembly, they immediately laid plans to undermine its authority.

The Provisional Government had specified that the convocation of the Assembly should be in the hands of a special commission. The Bolsheviks arrested this commission, and substituted for it a "Commissary for the Constituent Assembly", headed by the Jew, Uritzky.

By this tactic the Bolsheviks were able to exert their authority over the Assembly. When the Assembly did finally convene, the Jew, Sverdlov, although not a delegate, took charge of the proceedings, and actually called the meeting to order. Ten hours later the Assembly was thrown into confusion when the Bolsheviks walked out.

Shortly thereafter Bolshevik troops brutally brought the Constituent Assembly to an end by ejecting the delegates and locking the doors to the building. This was the end of the Constituent Assembly. After having convened for only 13 hours, it disbanded, never to meet again. So ended Russia's hope for a constitution and a representative government.

In March, 1918, the Soviet Government moved its capital from St. Petersburg to Moscow. In the same month the Russian Social-Democratic Labor Party officially styled itself the Communist Party.

The Jew Moisei Solomonovich Uritsky, a member of the Bolshevik Central Committee. He played a leading part in the Bolsheviks' armed take-over in October and later was made head of the Petrograd Cheka (secret police). In this position, he coordinated the pursuit and prosecution of members of the nobility, military officers and ranking Russian Orthodox Church clerics--but left all rabbis alone. In fact, one of the first laws passed by the Bolsheviks after they seized power was to outlaw any anti-Jewish activity--which became punishable by death.

Trotsky as "War Commissar"

Meanwhile the enemies of the new regime were gathering strength. Before the year was over the Soviet Government was under attack on six war fronts. Some of these antiCommunist armies were organized by pro-Tsarist sympathizers; others were organized and financed by foreign governments.

These "White Russian" forces constituted a dangerous threat to the new regime, and in March Trotsky relinquished his post as

Commissar of Foreign Affairs to become Commissar of War, a position which gave him authority over the Soviet Government's entire military resources. It was he who organized and led the Red Army to victory. Not until 1921 were the last of the antiCommunist forces destroyed.

Head of the Red Army Leon Trotsky
"One of the greatest Jewish Generals in History."
—Jewish Encyclopedia, 1943 vol. 10, pg. 312.65

Chapter 11
Encyclopedia Judaica
on the "Russian Revolution"

THE *Encyclopaedia Judaica,* published in Jerusalem, Israel, is a widely-quoted reference book for all things Jewish. This work is open about the Jewish role in Communism, particularly early Communism. It even points out that it was so Jewish that Jewish leaders were instructed to change their names to hide the Jewish domination.

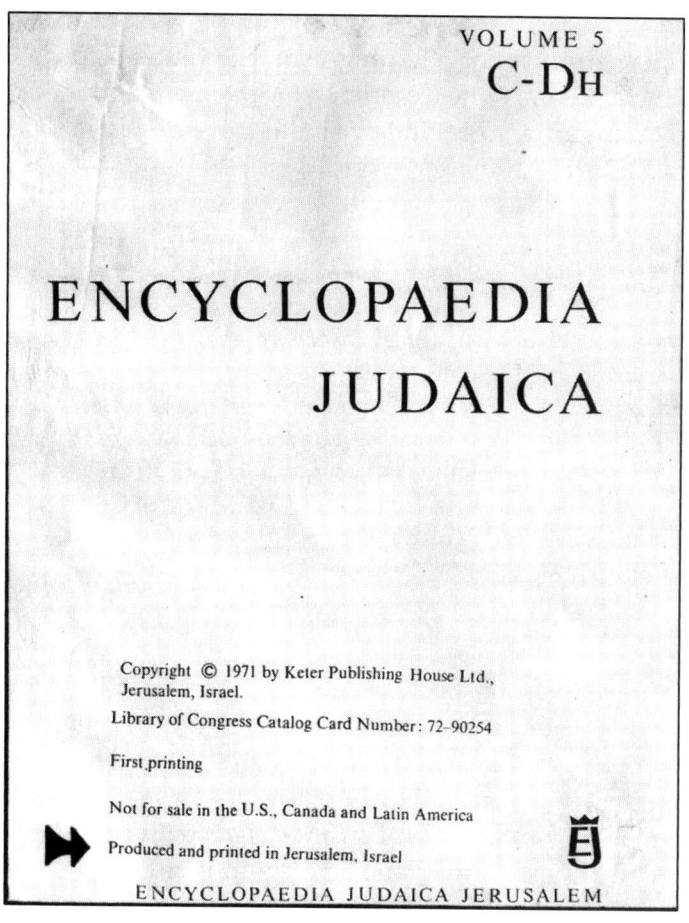

VOLUME 5
C-Dн

ENCYCLOPAEDIA

JUDAICA

Copyright © 1971 by Keter Publishing House Ltd., Jerusalem, Israel.

Library of Congress Catalog Card Number: 72-90254

First printing

Not for sale in the U.S., Canada and Latin America

Produced and printed in Jerusalem, Israel

ENCYCLOPAEDIA JUDAICA JERUSALEM

> COMMUNISM
>
> The Com-
> munist movement and ideology played an important part in
> Jewish life, particularly in the 1920s, 1930s, and during and
> after World War II.

Under the entry for "Communism" in volume 5, page 792, the following appears: "The Communist Movement and ideology played an important part in Jewish life, particularly in the 1920s, 1930s and during and after World War II."

> Communist trends became
> widespread in virtually all Jewish communities. In some
> countries Jews became the leading element in the legal and
> illegal Communist parties and in some cases were even
> instructed by the Communist International to change their
> Jewish-sounding names and pose as non-Jews, in order not
> to confirm right-wing propaganda that presented Commu-
> nism as an alien, Jewish conspiracy

On page 793, the *Encyclopaedia Judaica*[66] goes on to say that "Communist trends became widespread in virtually all Jewish communities. In some countries, Jews became the leading element in the legal and illegal Communist Parties."

On page 793, the *Encyclopaedia Judaica*[67] reveals that the Communist International (an organization which coordinated all Communist parties around the world) instructed Jews to change their names so as, the body said, "not [to] confirm right-wing propaganda that presented Communism as an alien, Jewish conspiracy."

Jewish Role in the Russian Communist Revolution

The *Encyclopaedia Judaica* describes in detail the important role that Jews played in creating the Soviet Union. On page 792 it says: "Individual Jews played an important role in the early stages of Bolshevism and the Soviet Regime."

> Individual Jews played an important role in the early stages of Bolshevism and the Soviet regime.

On page 794, it goes on to list the Jews prominent in the upper command of the Russian Communist Party. These included Maxim Litvinov (later to be the Soviet Union's foreign minister), Grigori Zinoviev, Lev Kamenev, Jacob Sverdlov, Lazar Kaganovich, and Karl Radek, among many others. [68]

> **Bolshevik Theory (1903–1917).**
> The Bolshevik faction (which in 1912–13 became the Bolshevik Party) contained a number of Jews who were active mainly in the field of organization and propaganda (rather than in theory and ideology, as was the case with the Jewish Mensheviks). They included such people as Maxim *Litvinov (Wallach), M. Liadov (Mandelshtam), Grigori *Shklovsky, A. Soltz, S. Gusev (Drabkin), Grigori *Zinoviev (Radomyslsky), Lev *Kamenev (Rosenfeld), Rozaliya *Zemliachka (Zalkind), Helena Rozmirovich, Yemeh *Yaroslavsky (Gubelman), Serafima Gopner, G. Sokolnikov, I. *Piatnitsky, Jacob *Sverdlov, M. Vladimirov, P. Zaluisky, A. Lozovsky, Y. Yaklovlev (Epstein), Lazar *Kaganovich, D. Shvartsman, and Simon *Dimanstein. Their number grew rapidly between the Russian revolutions of February and October 1917, when various groups and individuals joined the Bolsheviks; prominent among the new adherents were *Trotsky, M. Uritsky, M. Volodarsky, J. Steklov, Adolf Joffe, David Riazanov (Goldendach), Yuri *Larin, and Karl *Radek (Sobelsohn).

The organizer of the revolution was Trotsky, who prepared a special committee to plan and prepare the coup which brought the Communists to power. According to the *Encyclopaedia Judaica,* this committee, called the Military Revolutionary Committee, had five members, of whom three were Jews.

The politburo, the supreme governing body of Russia immediately after the Communist Revolution, had four Jews among its seven members, according to page 797 of the *Encyclopaedia Judaica.*

Lenin was ardently pro-Jewish, and branded anti-Semitism as

> **Soviet Practice (1917-1939).**
>
> During the Revolution Jews played a prominent part in the party organs. The Politburo elected on Oct. 21, 1917, had four Jews among its seven members. The Military Revolutionary Committee, appointed to prepare the coup, was headed by Trotsky and had two Jews among its five members.

"counterrevolutionary" (*ibid.* page 798). A statement against anti-Semitism was made by Lenin in March 1919 and was "one of the rare occasions when his voice was put on a phonograph record to be used in a mass campaign against the counterrevolutionary incitement against the Jews," according to page 798 of the

> Anti-Semitism was branded as being counterrevolutionary in nature, and persons participating in pogroms or instigating them were outlawed (by a special decree issued by the Council of Commissars in July 1918, signed and personally amended by Lenin to sharpen its tone). A statement against anti-Semitism made by Lenin in March 1919 was one of the rare occasions on which his voice was put on a phonograph record, to be used in a mass campaign against the counterrevolutionary incitement against the Jews. The regime made every effort to denounce the pogroms and punish the persons taking part in them, even when they were Red Army personnel. When the civil war came to an end, a law was passed against "incitement to hatred and hostility of a national or religious nature," which, in effect, also applied to anti-Semitism, including the use of the pejorative epithet *Zhid.*

Encyclopaedia Judaica.[69] Furthermore, one of the first acts passed by the new Soviet Communist government was to outlaw anti-Semitism (ibid. page 798).

Chapter 12
Winston Churchill
the Truth about Bolshevism

THE preponderance of Jews in the inner sanctum of the Communist Revolution in Russia was well-known at the time, and it is only since the end of the Second World War that this fact has been suppressed. A good example of the contemporary awareness of the Jewish nature of early Russian Communism can be found in the writing of the young Winston Churchill, later to become prime minister of Great Britain.

On February 8, 1920, Churchill wrote a full page article for the *Illustrated Sunday Herald* which detailed Jewish involvement in Communism. The article, titled *Bolshevism versus Zionism, the struggle for the Soul of the Jewish People,* said that Jews were split between Communism and Zionism. Churchill favored the Jewish nationalists, and appealed to what he called "loyal Jews" to ensure that the Communist Jews did not succeed.[70]

Churchill went further and blamed the Jews for "every subversive movement during the nineteenth century," writing:

> "This movement among the Jews [the Russian Revolution] is not new. From the days of Spartacus Weishaupt to those of Karl Marx, and down to Trotsky (Russia), Bela Kuhn (Hungary), Rosa Luxembourg (Germany), and Emma Goldman (United States), this world-wide conspiracy for the overthrow of civilisation and for the reconstitution of society on the basis of arrested development, of envious malevolence, and impossible equality, has been steadily growing.

> "It played, as a modern writer, Mrs. [Nesta] Webster, has so ably shown, a definitely recognisable part in the tragedy of the French Revolution. It has been the mainspring of every subversive movement during the Nineteenth Century; and now at last this band of extraordinary personalities from the underworld of the great cities of Europe and America have gripped the Russian people by the hair of their heads and have become practically the undisputed masters of that enormous empire.

"Terrorist Jews.

"There is no need to exaggerate the part played in the creation of Bolshevism and in the actual bringing about of the Russian Revolution by these international and for the most part atheistical Jews. It is certainly a very great one; it probably outweighs all others. With the notable exception of Lenin, the majority of the leading figures are Jews. Moreover, the principal inspiration and driving power comes from the Jewish leaders. Thus Tchitcherin, a pure Russian, is eclipsed by his nominal subordinate Litvinoff, and the influence of Russians like Bukharin or Lunacharski cannot be compared with the power of Trotsky, or of Zinovieff,

ILLUSTRATED SUNDAY HERALD, FEBRUARY 8, 1920.   Page 5.

ZIONISM versus BOLSHEVISM.
A STRUGGLE FOR THE SOUL OF THE JEWISH PEOPLE.
By the Rt. Hon. WINSTON S. CHURCHILL.

Mr. Churchill inspecting his old regiment, the 4th Hussars, at Aldershot last week.

Good and Bad Jews.

"National" Jews.

Terrorist Jews.

International Jews.

"Protector of the Jews."

A Home for the Jews.

Duty of Loyal Jews.

the Dictator of the Red Citadel (Petrograd), or of Krassin or Radek—all Jews.

"In the Soviet institutions the predominance of Jews is even more astonishing. And the prominent, if not indeed the principal, part in the system of terrorism applied by the Extraordinary Commissions for Combating Counter-Revolution has been taken by Jews, and in some notable cases by Jewesses. The same evil prominence was obtained by Jews in the brief period of terror during which Bela Kun ruled in Hungary. The same phenomenon has been presented in Germany (especially in Bavaria), so far as this madness has been allowed to prey upon the temporary prostration of the German people. Although in all these countries there are many non-Jews every whit as bad as the worst of the Jewish revolutionaries, the part played by the latter in proportion to their numbers in the population is astonishing"[71]

Churchill also pointedly accused Leon Trotsky of wanting to establish a "world-wide Communistic state under Jewish domination."

Chapter 13
American Intelligence
on the "Russian Revolution"

THE American Army Intelligence Service had its agents in Russia at the time of the Communist revolution, and the Jewish nature of that revolution is accurately reflected in those reports.

An American Senate subcommittee investigation into the Russian Revolution heard evidence, put on congressional record, that "In December 1919, under the presidency of a man named Apfelbaum (Zinovieff) . . . out of the 388 members of the Bolshevik central government, only 16 happened to be real Russians, and all the rest (with the exception of a Negro from the US) were Jews" (S. Doc. No. 62, 1919).

However, none of these authorities quoted above dared to use the language of a US Military Intelligence officer, Captain Montgomery Schuyler, who sent two reports to Washington in March and June 1919. These reports described in graphic detail

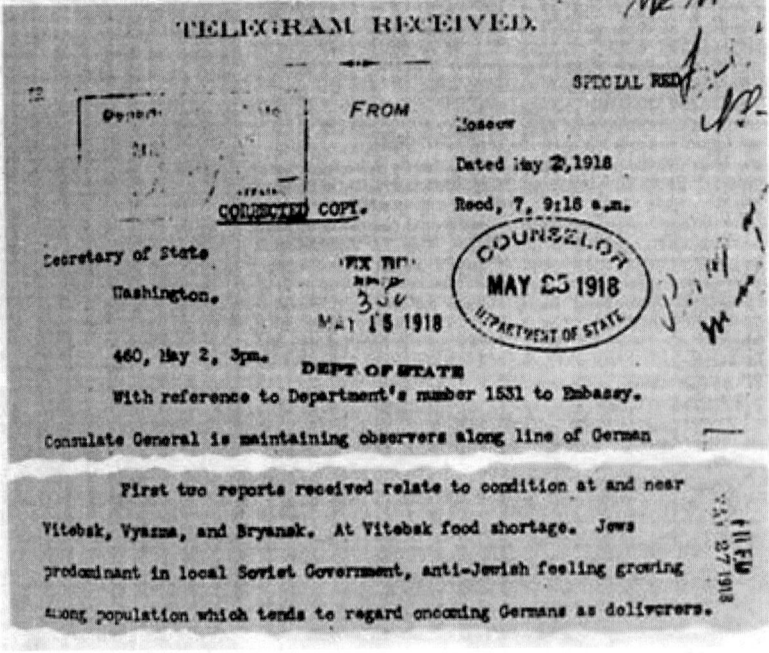

the Jewish role in the Russian Revolution, and were only declassified in September 1957. The originals are still in the US National Archives in Washington and are open for public inspection.

The first report, sent from Omsk on March 1, 1919, contains the following paragraph: "it is probably unwise to say this loudly in the United States but the Bolshevik movement is and has been since its beginning, guided and controlled by Russian Jews of the greasiest type."[72]

The second report, dated June 9, 1919, sent from Vladivostok, said that of the "384 commissars there were 2 Negroes, 13 Russians, 15 Chinamen, 22 Armenians and more than 300 Jews. Of the latter number 264 had come to Russia from the United States since the downfall of the Imperial Government."[73]

The Jewish domination of the commissar elite of the early Soviet Union ensured that any forms of anti-Semitism were regarded as "counterrevolutionary," and anti-Jewish agitation was entered into the Soviet law books as a capital penalty crime.

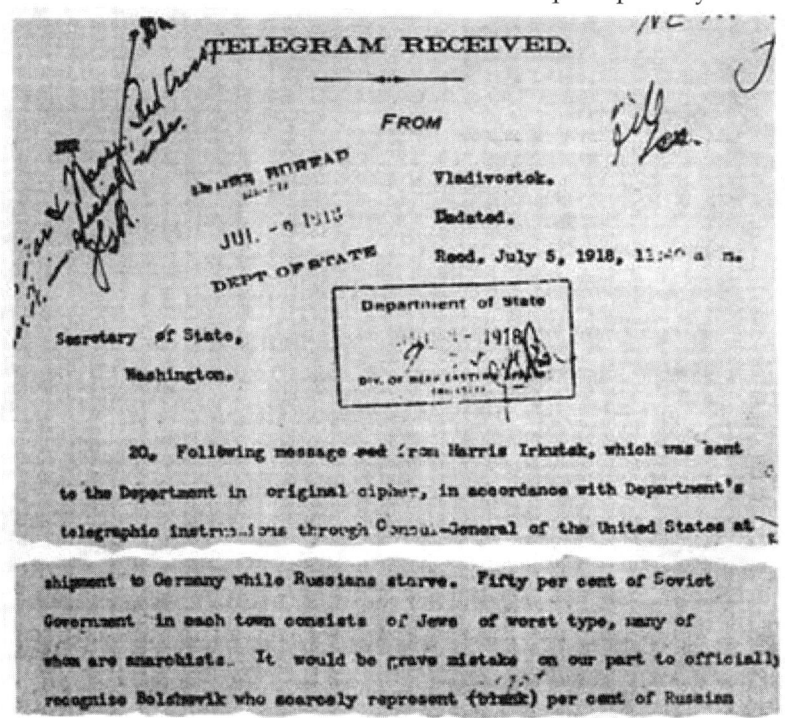

In reply please
refer to No. _____   383.9 Mil. Int. Report.

PERSONAL AND CONFIDENTIAL   Schuyler

DECLASSIFIED
DoD Dir. 5200.9 Sept. 27, 1958
WNR by [illegible], Date 8-12-63   WAR DEPARTMENT
AMERICAN EXPEDITIONARY FORCES, SIBERIA.
OFFICE OF THE CHIEF OF STAFF
INTELLIGENCE SECTION

March 1, 1919.

My dear Colonel Barrows:
    I have just received your letter of January 29th, forwarded by
Baron Boyen of General Romanovsky's staff, who has just arrived in
Omsk. I was of course much interested in your news, as I had been
[text cut off]

WAR DEPARTMENT
AMERICAN EXPEDITIONARY FORCES, SIBERIA.
OFFICE OF THE CHIEF OF STAFF
INTELLIGENCE SECTION

-2-

    Ever since then however, he has shown himself in so far as he
could safely do so, more and more liberal, and I have no hesitation in
saying that I firmly believe that his own opinions and frame of mind
are far more liberal than the outside world gives him credit for. He
is unfortunate in this that he has had to depend upon the mailed fist
to maintain his position and to keep his government from being overridden
by the Bolshevik elements which are numerous in every city in Siberia.
    It is probably unwise to say this loudly in the United States but
the Bolshevik movement is and has been since its beginning, guided and
controlled by Russian Jews of the greasiest type, who have been in the
United States and there absorbed every one of the worst phases of our
civilization without having the least understanding of what we really
[text cut off] not mean the use of the word liberty which has
[text cut off]

HEADQUARTERS, AMERICAN EXPEDITIONARY FORCES, SIBERIA

Vladivostok, Siberia,
June 9th, 1919.

From: Captain Montgomery Schuyler.

To: The Chief of Staff

Subject: General Report - Omsk.

    1. In compliance with orders of the Commanding General
(Secret) October 25th, 1918, I left Vladivostok on November
20th, 1918 and proceeded to Omsk which I reached on Decem-
[text cut off] I left that city also in compliance with
the new regime would be expected to bring some sort of
modern government into the country. These hopes were frus-
trated by the gradual gains in power of the more irrespon-
sible and socialistic elements of the population guided by
the Jews and other anti-Russian races. A table made in
April 1918 by Robert Wilton, the correspondent of the London
Times in Russia, shows that at that time there were 384
"commissars" including 2 negroes, 13 Russians, 15 Chinamen,
22 Armenians and more than 300 Jews. Of the latter number
264 had come to Russia from the United States since the
downfall of the Imperial Government. It is only since the

^

-2-

Chapter 14
The London Times Unmasks Bolshevism

THE most exhaustive description of the Jewish composition of the Bolsheviks was made by Robert Wilton, a foreign correspondent for *The Times* of London, the world's most respected newspaper.

Robert Wilton, distinguished correspondent of the London Times published the most complete list of Jews in the Bolshevik Government.

In 1920 he published a book in French, *Les Derniers Jours des Romanofs* (The Last Days of the Romanovs), where he showed the ethnic composition of the Bolshevik government in Moscow.

The Central Committee was composed the following way: Trotsky (Jew); Zinoviev (Jew); Larine (Jew); Juritsky (Jew);

Volodarsky (Jew); Kamenev (Jew); Smidovitj (Jew); Jankel (Jew); Steklov (Jew); Lenin (Russian, allegedly part-Jewish); Krylenko (Jew); Lunacharsky (Russian).

The Council of People's Commissars had a similar composition: President: Lenin (Russian); Foreign Affairs: Tjitjerin (Russian); Nationalities: Stalin (Georgian); Agriculture: Protian (Armenian); Public Education: Lunacharsky (Russian); Financial Advisor: Larine (Jew); Food: Schlichter (Jew); Army and Navy: Trotsky (Jew); State Control: Lander (Jew); Public Land: Kauffman (Jew); Work: Schmidt (Jew); Social Aid: Lelina (Jew); Religion: Spitzberg (Jew); Interior Affairs: Zinoviev (Jew); Hygiene: Anvelt (Jew); Finance: Goukovsky (Jew); Press: Volodarsky (Jew); Elections: Uritsky (Jew); Justice: Steinberg (Jew); Refugees: Fenigstein (Jew); Refugees (ass.): Savitj (Jew); Refugees (ass.): Zaslovsky (Jew).

The Central Executive Committee looked the same: Sverdlov (chairman): Jew; Avanessov (secretary): Armenian; Lenin: Russian, allegedly partly-Jewish; Bruno: Lithuanian; Bukharin: Russian; Starck: German; Wolach: Czech; Encukidze: Georgian; Krylenko: Russian; Kaoul: Lithuanian; Lunacharsky: Russian; Peterson: Lithuanian; Peters: Lithuanian; Stoutchka: Lithuanian; Terian: Armenian; Souriupa: Ukrainian; Tjavtchevadze: Georgian; Achkinazi: Imeretian; Telechkine: Russian; Babtjinsky: Jew; Weinberg: Jew; Gailiss: Jew; Sachs: Jew; Ganzburg: Jew; Danichevsky: Jew; Scheinmann: Jew; Landauer: Jew; Erdling: Jew; Linder: Jew; Dimanstein: Jew; Krassikofsach: Jew; Ermann: Jew; Joffe: Jew; Karkline: Jew; Knigissen: Jew; Kamenev: Jew; Zinoviev: Jew; Kaprik: Jew; Latsis: Jew; Lander: Jew; Roudzoutas: Jew; Rosine: Jew; Smidovitch: Jew; Steklov: Jew; Sosnovsky: Jew; Skrytnik: Jew; Trotsky: Jew; Teodorovitj: Jew; Uritsky: Jew; Feldmann: Jew; Froumkine: Jew; Scheikmann: Jew; Rosental: Jew; Karakhane: Jew; Rose: Jew; Radek: Jew; Schlichter: Jew; Schikolini: Jew; Chkliansky: Jew; Pravdine: Jew.

And finally, the Extraordinary Commission: Dzerjinsky (chairman): Pole; Peters (vice chairman): Lithuanian; Karlson: Lithuanian; Latzis: Lithuanian; Janson: Lithuanian; Daybol:

Lithuanian; Antonof: Russian; Alexandrevitj: Russian; Saissounce: Armenian; Deylkenen: Lithuanian; Vogel: German; Zakiss: Lithuanian; Chklovsky: Jew; Kheifiss: Jew; Zeistine: Jew; Rasmirovitch: Jew; Kronberg: Jew; Khaikina: Jew; Schaumann: Jew; Leontovitch: Jew; Jacob Goldine: Jew; Glaperstein: Jew; Kniggisen: Jew; Schillenkuss: Jew; Rivkine: Jew; Delafabre: Jew; Tsitkine: Jew; Roskirovitch: Jew; Sverdlov: Jew; Biesensky: Jew; Blioumkine: Jew; Routenberg: Jew; Model: Jew; Pines: Jew; Sachs: Jew; Liebert: Jew.

Above is a reproduction of a banner displayed by the Bolsheviks on the first anniversary of the Communist Revolution. After having butchered the royal family and a substantial part of the nation's ruling class, the Bolsheviks set out to "educate" the Russian people to the joys of proletarian life. The above poster, incidentally, again reveals the Jewishness of the Communist leadership: of the twelve shown, five are Jews and one (Lenin) is married to a Jewess. To the right of Lenin: Pokrovsky, Kamenev, Sverdlov, Lunacharsky, Kollontai, Krylenko, Zinoviev, Bukharin, Trotsky, Rykov, Radek.

Chapter 15
The Executioners of the Red Terror

SHORTLY after the March Revolution of 1917, the Tsar had applied for permission for himself and his family to leave the country. Nicholas II was closely related to the royal families of England and Denmark, and he felt exile there was preferable to remaining a prisoner in his own land.

The Provisional Government had been inclined to grant his request, but the St. Petersburg Soviet had blocked the move and the royal family had been transferred to Ekaterinburg, in south Russia.

The Jew Yakov Mikhailovich Yurovsky, head of the Cheka secret police in Ekaterinburg at the time when the Tsar and his family (below) were kept prisoners at the Ipatiev House in that town. After conferring directly in Moscow with the president of the Russian Soviet Republic (the Russian part of the USSR), a Jew by the name of Yakov Sverdlov, Yurovsky and a Cheka team murdered the entire Imperial family and their retainers by shooting them in a cellar of the Ipatiev House. The bodies were removed to the countryside, where they had initially been thrown into an abandoned mine shaft. The following morning, when rumors spread in Ekaterinburg regarding the disposal site, Yurovsky removed the bodies and buried them in a pit on Koptyaki Road, a since-abandoned cart track 12 miles north of the city. Yurovsky was rewarded for his murderous work: in 1921 he was promoted and became Chief of the Gold Department of the Soviet State Treasury. He died of natural causes in 1938.

Jewish Cheka Agents Murder the Tsar

There, in 1918, they were housed in the home of a local merchant named Ipatiev. On July 17th anti-Bolshevik troops advanced on Ekaterinburg and the local commissar, a Jew by the name of Yorovsky, ordered the family — and their household servants — executed.

Yorovsky personally dispatched Nicholas with a pistol shot in the head. The rest of the family was executed by a firing squad. Their bodies were then soaked in oil and burned.

Above: The Jew Yakov Mikhaylovich Sverdlov, first president of the Russian Soviet Republic. He died in 1919 of influenza,

and is buried in the Kremlin Wall Necropolis, in Moscow, along with other high-ranking Bolsheviks. In 1924, the town of Ekaterinburg, where the Jew Yurovsky (who was personal friend with Sverdlov) had murdered the Tsar, was renamed Sverdlovsk in honor of the murder and Sverdlov. It retained this name until 1991, when it was changed back to Ekaterinburg (also called Yekaterinburg). A statue of Sverdlov in the town, as can be seen below. Sverdlov's son Andrei had a long career as an officer for the Soviet security organs (NKVD, OGPU). His niece Ida married the NKVD chief, the Jew Genrikh Yagoda.

Ekaterinburg was renamed "Sverdlovsk", in honor of the Jew, Yakov Sverdlov, president of the "Soviet Republic" at the time of the Tsar's execution. It was only renamed Ekaterinburg in 1991, following the fall of the Soviet Union.

The infamous Jewish Bolshevik murderer, Yakov Sverdlov

On August 30, 1918, the Jew, Uritzky — then head of the "Cheka" — was assassinated. On the same day, Lenin was seriously wounded in an assassination attempt. The assassins (Fanny Kaplan and Leonid Kannegisser) were both Jewish, and both members of the Jewish-led Social Revolutionary Party who had turned on the Bolsheviks for smashing up the Constituent Assembly.

The Bolsheviks used these acts as an excuse for instituting the Red Terror, which began the following day, and which in a sense has continued to the present. Space simply does not permit us to give an adequate description of what followed. The entire membership of the Communist Party, which in 1918 numbered perhaps no more than 100,000, was turned into an instrument of murder. Its aims were two-fold; to inspire dread and horror among the Russian masses, and to exterminate the middle and upper classes i.e., the "bourgeoisie".

Men and women were executed or imprisoned not because of any offense, but simply because they belonged to the "enemy class". And this definition eventually included every merchant, professional person and landowner. Not only were these "class enemies" exterminated, but members of their families fell victim as well. The Bolsheviks cleverly adopted the practice of making hostages of the families of those who resisted the new order.

David Shub in his slavishly pro-Marxist book, *Lenin,* gives the following description of the Red Terror in St. Petersburg[74]: "Little time was wasted sifting evidence and classifying people rounded up in these night raids. Woe to him who did not disarm all suspicion at once. The prisoners were generally hustled to the old police station not far from the Winter Palace. Here, with or without perfunctory interrogation, they were stood up against the courtyard wall and shot. The staccato sounds of death were muffled by the roar of truck motors kept going for the purpose." This was the Red Terror in action.

The tragedy of all this cannot be measured by numbers alone; these people were the best that Russia had. They were the leader class. They were the priests, and lawyers, and merchants, and army officers, and university professors. They were the cream of Russian civilization.

The total effect was much the same as it would be in any country. With its small middle and upper class exterminated, Russia's peasant and worker population accepted Jewish Bolshevism without protest.

The Russian masses, deprived of their spokesmen and leaders were simply incapable of counter-revolution. That was what the Red Terror set out to accomplish.

Chapter 16
Exporting the Revolution

A basic tenet of Marxist ideology was, and is, the promotion of world revolution. The Bolshevik leadership undertook in 1919 to further this aim by establishing the Third International, which convened in March of 1919. Its presiding officer was Lenin, and its first president was the Jew, Zinoviev, who remained its head until 1926.

The prime objective of the Third International was to establish Communist parties in the various countries of the world, and to lend them aid and assistance in overthrowing their respective governments. Prospects of success were bright in the spring of 1919.

The Jewess Rosa Luxemburg's Revolution in Germany

The first country to experience a Communist revolution outside of Russia was Germany. The German government, which had abetted the Bolshevik coup in 1917 by facilitating Lenin's return to Russia via the sealed railway car, was in 1918 faced with a revolution of its own.

Rosa Luxemburg

In many respects the German Revolution paralleled the one in Russia. As World War I reached the climactic year of 1918, and as German manpower losses mounted, the Jew-dominated German Social Democratic Party spread the seeds of defeatism among the German population much as the Bolsheviks had done in Russia.

On November 3rd a mutiny broke out in the navy at Kiel, followed by rioting by the Social Democrats. On November 9th the Kaiser renounced his throne and the Social Democrats proclaimed a Socialist Republic. Two days later, on Nov. 11th, they agreed to an Armistice with the Allies.

There now occurred an event which was to embitter the German people against the Jews for all time, and which eventually contributed to the rise of Adolf Hitler. This was the demobilization of the German armies.

It should be explained that Germany did not surrender by the terms of the November 11th Armistice; the agreement was that all German armies were to withdraw to the pre-war boundaries of Germany as a preliminary to a negotiated peace.

But as the German armies retreated to German soil, the Revolutionary government, fearful lest the Revolution be upset, ordered them demobilized. On November 11th Germany still possessed the mightiest military machine on earth; thirty days later it had nothing. Instead of being able to negotiate peace on the terms of Wilson's Fourteen Points, a helpless and prostrate Germany got the Versailles Treaty.

No sooner had the German armies been demobilized than the more extreme elements of the Social Democratic Party, led by Rosa Luxemburg, laid plans to seize control of the revolution as the Bolsheviks had done in Russia.

The Munich Bolshevik Revolution

John Toland in his book *Hitler* (p. 76), stated

"In Munich another insurrection broke out on November 7, (1918). It was led by Kurt Eisner, a small elderly Jew wearing a black floppy hat which, large as it was, couldn't contain a shock of wild hair. Epically untidy, he was a living cartoon of the bomb-throwing Red."[75]

He declared Bavaria "A free state" the day after the one year anniversary of the Bolshevik revolution in Russia and made himself Minister-President of Bavaria. Two other Jews, Lujo Brentano and Villa Jaffe, served for a little while as People's Commissar for Trade and finance minister, respectively.

He was shot only three months later by "a right wing nationalist" of Jewish ancestry, then another Jew, Ernst Toller, proclaimed Bavaria a Soviet Republic on April 6, 1919, with several Jews in leading positions.

It was a total farce. His deputy for Foreign Affairs, (a psychiatric patient at that) for instance, declared war on Switzerland. Six days later, on April 12, 1919, the Communist party seized power with yet another Jew as the leader, Eugen Leviné. Now the farce became a bloody farce with several hostages taken from the elite, at the instigation of Lenin.

Eight men were accused as right-wing spies and executed. On May 3, 1919 the Communist adventure ended. Loyal elements of the army and Freikorps entered Bavaria in a force of about 40,000 men, defeated the Communists and executed Leviné along with 700 others. In the street fights another 1000 supporters of the revolutionary government had been killed[76]

Aided by funds provided by the Soviet ambassador, the Jew Joffe, Rosa Luxemburg's "Spartacus Bund" in January of 1919 attempted to overthrow the revolutionary government.

The revolt, following bloody street fighting, was quelled and its leaders, Rosa Luxemburg and her fellow Jew Karl Liebknecht, were imprisoned and later executed by German army officers.

Following the execution of Rosa Luxemburg, the Third International dispatched the Jew, Karl Radek, to lead the party.

Later the Jewess, Ruth Fischer, assumed control of the German Communist party, and remained at its head till 1924.

Bela Kun's Reign of Terror in Hungary

Following World War I, Hungary also had a Communist Revolution. In this case the instigator was the Jew, Bela Kun (Cohen), who imposed a Communist regime on the country in the spring of 1919.

Bela Kun had participated in the Bolshevik Revolution in Russia, and following the Armistice, he and a group of Jewish

revolutionaries, using forged passports, moved into Hungary and established the Communist newspaper, *Voros Ursay* (Red News).

Well supplied with finances by the Soviet government, and aided by the pro-Communist resident Jewish population, Kun quickly became the dictator of all Hungary. Bela Kun proceeded to follow the pattern of the Bolshevik revolution. Says *Encyclopaedia Britannica*: "Kun's programme was to 'arm at once, and forcibly transfer every industry and all landed property without conservation into the hands of the proletariat.' At first he collaborated with the Social Democrats[77] but soon shouldered them aside, nationalized all banks, all concerns with over 200 employees, all landed property over 1000 ac., every building other than workmen's dwellings.

All jewelry, all private property above the minimum (e.g. two suits, 4 shirts, 2 pair of boots and 4 socks) was seized; servants abolished, bathrooms made public on Saturday nights; priests jailed with the insane, criminals and shopkeepers, employing paid assistants were declared unfit for society and their businesses taken from them.

The result of this program was, as in Russia, economic and social chaos. The nationalization of every private bathroom in a country cannot be accomplished without profoundly affecting the social and moral tone of its society.

Neither can the land, buildings, and industries of a nation be nationalized without creating havoc. As in Russia, such a program could only be enforced by resorting to the Red Terror.

During the Hungarian Soviet Republic in 1919, the Heroes Square of Budapest was completely covered by red textile and at the basement of the obelisk a new statue was erected: Marx with a worker and a peasant. The statues of Hungarian national heroes were toppled. Hungarian national symbols were banned, and many Hungarian historic monuments were destroyed.

During Bela Kun's three month reign of terror, tens of thousands of people — priests, army officers, merchants, landowners, professional people — were butchered. The communizing of the country's industrial and agricultural resources produced a famine in the cities, and this, combined with the peasantry's antipathy for the Jews, resulted in Kun's eventual overthrow.

In an amazingly frank report, the *New International Year Book of 1919*[78] has summarized the situation:

"One of the chief weaknesses in the new regime was antipathy to the Jews. In the country districts the feeling was widespread that the revolution had been a movement on the part of the Jews to seize the power for themselves, and the remark was frequently heard that if the Jews of Budapest died of starvation, so much the better for the rest of the country. The government of Bela Kun was composed almost exclusively of Jews who held also the administrative offices. The Communists had united at first with the socialists who were not of the extremely radical party, but resembled somewhat the Labor parties or trade unionists groups in other countries. Bela Kun did not, however select his personnel from among them, but turned to the Jews and constituted virtually a Jewish bureaucracy."

After three months of blood, murder, and pillage, Bela Kun was deposed and interned in a lunatic asylum. Later he was released and returned to Russia, where he assumed control of the Red Terror organization the Cheka, in South Russia.

One repercussion was the association of Hungary's Jews with the suffering inflicted by the Communists; since Kun and most of his colleagues were clearly Jewish[79] many Hungarians recognized a Jewish element in the Bolshevist conspiracy afoot in central Europe.

As Louis Birinyi observed: "The personnel of the "government" were selected from the ranks of the agitators, about ninety-five per cent of 'whose names tell us that they were of Jewish origin.' The country then was divided into districts, and at the head of each district a commissar was placed. It was not uncommon for the Bolsheviks to appoint janitors of Jewish churches to the office of commissars who held in the hollow of their hands the life or death of the people in their districts. Terror squads were organized, and the "red terror" was in full swing."[80]

Chapter 17
Trotsky in Decline

LENIN died of a brain hemorrhage in January of 1924. By this time the Communists had become firmly entrenched. The civil wars were over and every vestige of organized resistance to Jewish-Bolshevism had been destroyed. On Lenin's death the party leadership fell to fighting among itself.

Lenin had, as early as May of 1922 suffered a paralytic stroke which affected his speech and motor reflexes. In December he suffered a second stroke, and his place was taken by a triumvirate composed of Zinoviev, Kamenev, and Joseph Stalin. Shortly afterwards Lenin suffered another stroke, and in 1924 he died.

Trotsky and Lenin

In the early days of the new regime Trotsky had enjoyed near equality with Lenin in prestige and power. Outside of Russia, Lenin-Trotsky were regarded as a duality, and in current literature of that period their names were often hyphenated.

The outside world had therefore fully expected Trotsky to assume Lenin's mantle as party leader. But after 1922 Trotsky's prestige in the Politburo had declined rapidly, as we shall see.

In the year the triumvirate began to function, the Politburo was composed of Lenin, Zinoviev, Kamenev, Trotsky, Bukharin, Tomsky, and Stalin. The Lenin-Zinoviev-Kamenev "troika" had, of course, been dominant so long as Lenin was active, but now Zinoviev and Kamenev, as the surviving members of the "troika," regarded themselves as Lenin's rightful successors, and they looked on Trotsky as a competitor.

Into this picture Stalin insinuated himself. He allied himself with Kamenev and Zinoviev, and the three were able to turn the Politburo against Trotsky. Stalin thus became the junior member of the triumvirate.

Trotsky describes the situation this way [*Stalin,* ibid page 48, 337] "Used as a counterweight against me, he was bolstered and encouraged by Zinoviev and Kamenev, and to a lesser extent by Rykov, Bukharin and Tomsky. No one thought at the time that Stalin would someday loom away above their heads. In the first triumvirate Zinoviev treated Stalin in a circumspectly patronizing manner; Kamenev with a touch of irony."[81]

Zinoviev was considered to be the senior triumvir, and he gave the opening address at the 12th Party Congress, a function

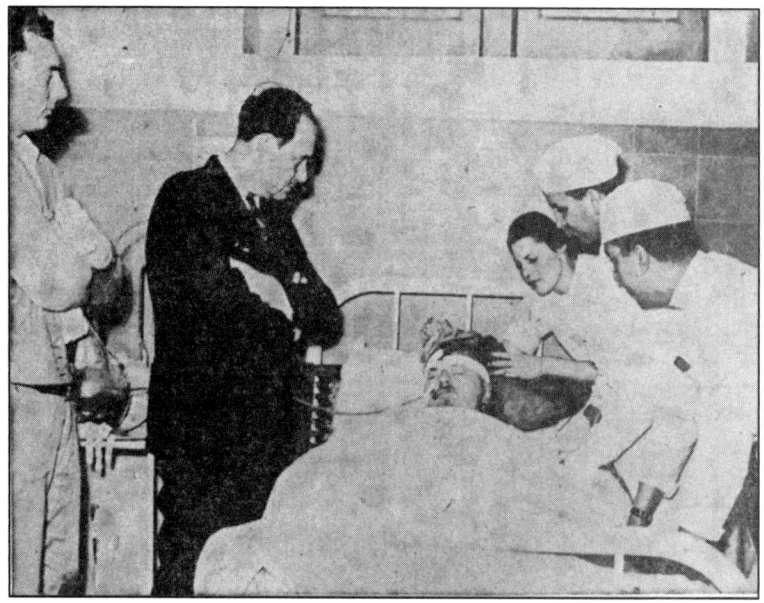

After falling out with Stalin, Trotsky was expelled and forced into exile in Mexico. There, in 1940, he was assassinated by an NKVD agent with an ice-pick blow to the head. Above, Trotsky on his deathbed in hospital, Mexico City.

heretofore reserved to Lenin. Zinoviev was not well received in this capacity, and before the Congress had adjourned, Stalin's control over the party machine gave him a dominant position in the triumvirate. This was the situation shortly after Lenin's death.

Stalin to Power

Stalin now moved to consolidate his position. In April of 1925 he engineered Trotsky's removal as War Commissar. In the same month he broke with Zinoviev and Kamenev and allied himself with politburo members Bukharin, Rykov, and Tomsky, Trotsky, Zinoviev, and Kamenev now united their forces in opposition to Stalin.

But now it was too late. In February of 1926 Zinoviev was expelled from the Politburo, then from the presidency of the St. Petersburg (Leningrad) Soviet, and finally as president of the Third International. Less than a month later (October 23) Trotsky and Kamenev were also expelled from the Politburo.

This marked the end of any effective resistance to Stalin. The next year Zinoviev, Kamenev, and Trotsky were removed from the party's Central Committee, and shortly afterwards all three were expelled from the party. In 1929 Trotsky was exiled abroad. In June of 1930 Stalin became the supreme dictator of Russia.

His closest associate throughout this time was the Jew Lazar Moiseyevich Kaganovich, who in 1917 was leader of the Bolshevik party in Belarus. During the October Revolution, Kaganovich was the leader of the revolt in Homel.

Chapter 18
Lazar Kaganovich:
Mass Murder & the Holodomor

In May 1922, when Stalin became the General Secretary of the Communist Party, he transferred the Jew Kaganovich to his apparatus to command the Organizational Department or Orgburo of the Secretariat.

The Jew Lazar Kaganovich, is possibly the greatest single mass murderer in all history. Responsible for the deaths of at least 20 million people plus the Ukrainian starvation Holocaust, he personally signed execution orders for at least 36,000 people.

Kaganovich was a devoted servant of Stalin, and in 1933 he became Chairman of the Commission for the Vetting of the Party Membership. This allowed him to ensure that anyone opposed to Stalin was expelled from the party, leading to a purge which historians have incorrectly presumed to be anti-Jewish, simply because so many Jews were Communists, and some prominent ones such as Trotsky had fallen out with Stalin. In reality, the Soviet purges of the 1930s were directed by this Jew.

Kaganovich's department was responsible for all assignments within the apparatus of the Communist Party, and thus had one of the most important positions in the Soviet state.

In 1924, Kaganovich became a member of the party's Central Committee and from 1925 to 1928, he was also the First Secretary of the Communist Party of the Ukrainian SSR.

In 1930, Kaganovich became a member of the Soviet Politburo and the First Secretary of the Moscow Obkom of the Communist Party (1930–1935) and Moscow Gorkom of the Communist Party (1931–1934).

He supervised the implementation of many of Stalin's economic policies, including the collectivization of agriculture and rapid industrialization. During the 1930s, he oversaw the destruction of many of Moscow's oldest monuments, including the Cathedral of Christ the Savior.

When Kaganovich gleefully destroyed the Church of the Savior he let loose his deep Jewish hatred for Russia, Christianity and all of its values. He pronounced:

"There is Mother Russia stripped of her skirt."

Kaganovich was given the task of implementation of the collectivization policy that caused a catastrophic 1932–33 famine

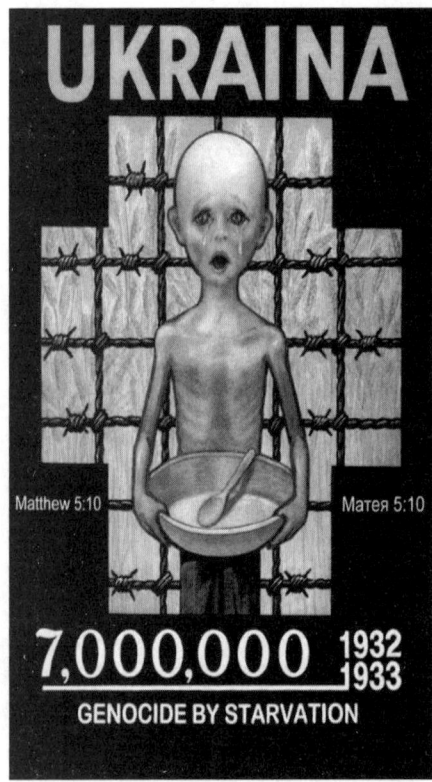

known as the Holodomor in the Ukraine. During this man-made famine, anywhere between 3.8 and 8 million Ukrainians died of starvation in a peacetime catastrophe unprecedented in European history. Kaganovich personally oversaw grain confiscations during the same period.

Similar policies also inflicted enormous suffering on the Soviet Central Asian republic of Kazakhstan, the Kuban region, Crimea, the lower Volga region, and other parts of the Soviet Union.

On January 13, 2010, the Kiev Appellate Court found Kaganovich posthumously guilty of genocide against Ukrainians during the catastrophic Holodomor famine.

The Department of Wet Affairs

In 1930 Kaganovich organized a special department of the Soviet secret police, with himself as the head. It was referred to as the department of "wet affairs," with "wet" meaning "bloody."

This was the section which handled clandestine mass executions, of the sort carried out later at Vinnitsa and at Katyn, and at a thousand other places throughout the Soviet Union over the next two decades.

The massacre of thousands of Polish officers at Katyn — uncovered by the Germans during World War II — was blamed on the Nazis orginally, although the truth of Kaganovich's role was later uncovered following the fall of the Soviet Union.

When the German Army invaded the Soviet Union in 1941, it was Kaganovich who was the savior of the Jews: he arranged for the evacuation of all Jews from the frontier areas and their resettlement far to the east, where they would be safe from the Germans. His policy was to let the Ukrainians and the Russians bear the brunt of the German invasion, but protect the Jews from hardship and danger at any cost.

Khrushchev Accuses Kaganovich

When the Gentile Communist Nikita Khrushchev accused Kaganovich in 1957 at a Soviet Party Congress of having

murdered 20 million Russians during his career, Kaganovich didn't even deny it. He only accused Khrushchev of being a murderer too. "Your hands are blood-stained too," Kaganovich told him.[82]

Khrushchev pointed out that the difference was that he, Khrushchev, had merely followed Kaganovich's orders, while it had been Kaganovich who had formulated the policies of mass murder and had given the orders for carrying out those policies.

Kaganovich was therefore one of the worst mass murderers in history. The Jewish association with the mass murder in the Ukraine was one of the primary reasons that the Nazis were greeted as liberators in World War II by the Ukrainians, and why so many of them joined up with the German forces to fight the Soviets.

After Stalin's death and fall from grace. Kaganovich was expelled from the Communist Party, but lived quietly in Moscow until his own death from natural causes in 1991.

The Real Ethnic Hatred Behind the Holodomor

Here is a quote from a Communist leader speaking in the Kharkiv region in 1934:

> **"Famine in Ukraine was brought on to decrease the number of Ukrainians, replace the dead with people from other parts of the USSR, and thereby to kill the slightest thought of any Ukrainian independence."**[83]

This is typical of the Jewish tribalist modus operandi. The supreme tribalists want to stop any nationalist, or patriotic movement based on heritage and relatedness. Destroy every other people's sense of heritage and solidarity while they themselves practice the most intense ethnocentrism on Earth.

Raphael Lemkin, the father of the term *genocide* made the ethnic genocidal motivation of the Jewish Bolsheviks in Ukraine very clear:

> In a 1953 lecture in New York City, Lemkin described the "destruction of the Ukrainian nation" as the "classic example of Soviet genocide," ...to eliminate (Ukrainian) nationalism...the Ukrainian peasantry was sacrificed...a famine was necessary for the Soviet and so they got one to order...if the Soviet program succeeds completely, if the intelligentsia, the priest, and the peasant can be eliminated [then] Ukraine will be as dead as if every Ukrainian were killed, for it will have lost that part of it which has kept and developed its culture, its beliefs, its common ideas, which have guided it and given it a soul, which, in short, made it a nation...This is not simply a case of mass murder. It is a case of genocide, of the destruction, not of individuals only, but of a culture and a nation."[84]

Lemkin also showed how the reduction of the Ukrainian population and the introduction of non-Ukrainian people would undermine Ukrainian aspirations for freedom.

> The fourth step in the process consisted in the fragmentation of the Ukrainian people at once by the addition to the Ukraine of foreign peoples and by the dispersion of the Ukrainians throughout Eastern Europe. In this way, ethnic unity would be destroyed and nationalities mixed. Between 1920 and 1939, the population of Ukraine changed from 80% Ukrainian to only 63%. In the face of famine and deportation, the Ukrainian population had declined absolutely from 23.2 million to 19.6 million, while the non-Ukrainian population had increased by 5.6 million. When we consider that Ukraine once had the highest rate of population increase in Europe, around 800,000 per year, it is easy to see that the Russian policy has been accomplished.[85]

One can see the same process that was taking place at the same time in Palestine with mass migrations of Jews into an area that had only a tiny percentage of Jews for two thousand years. And it is easy to see the Jewish tribalist role in similar policies to prevent any national sentiment and cohesion to resist Jewish tribalist power in European nations.

Meanwhile, as will be seen, in Moscow Jewish officials busily set up a special Jewish State within the USSR.

Chapter 19
The "Soviet Zion"
and Plans for a Jewish Homeland

THE special status accorded to Jews under Stalin was underlined with the 1934 announcement that a Jewish Autonomous Oblast situated in the Russian Far East, in Birobidzhan, was being set aside for Jews as a homeland, their own little Israel in the USSR, but like Israel most Jews around the world, they wanted a Jewish State, but did not go live there.

The Jewish autonomous region was the result of Stalin's nationality policy, which allowed for the Jews of the Soviet Union to receive a territory in which to pursue Yiddish cultural heritage within a socialist framework. According to the 1939 population census, 17,695 Jews lived in the region (16% of the total population). The Jewish population peaked in 1948 at around 30,000, about one-quarter of the region's population.

A giant menorah still dominates the main square in Birobidzhan. L'Chayim, Comrade Stalin! ("To Life, Comrade Stalin") a documentary on Stalin's creation of the Jewish Autonomous Region and its settlement, was released by The Cinema Guild in 2003.

On March 28, 1928, the Presidium of the General Executive Committee of the USSR passed the decree "On the attaching for Komzetof free territory near the Amur River in the Far East for settlement of the working Jews."

The decree meant "a possibility of establishment of a

Jewish administrative territorial unit on the territory of the called region".

On August 20, 1930 the General Executive Committee of RSFSR accepted the decree "On formation of the Birobidzhan national region in the structure of the Far Eastern Territory".

The State Planning Committee considered the Birobidzhan national region as a separate economic unit. In 1932 the first scheduled figures of the region development were considered and authorized.

The Organization for Jewish Colonization in the Soviet Union, a Jewish Communist organization in North America, successfully encouraged the immigration of some U.S. residents, such as the family of George Koval (later recruited as a Soviet spy in America).

The Jewish Autonomous Oblast

On May 7, 1934, the Presidium of the General Executive Committee accepted the decree on its transformation into the Jewish Autonomous Region within the Russian Federation. In 1938, with formation of the Khabarovsk Territory, the Jewish Autonomous Region (JAR) was included in its structure.

The Jewish oblast plan was a Soviet attempt to reconcile the Jewish Communists and the Zionists. It dealt with two thorny issues: Judaism, which ran counter to official state policy of atheism; and Zionism — the advocacy of a Jewish national state in Palestine — which contradicted Soviet views of nationalism.

Stalin's theory on the National Question regarded a group as a nation only if it had a territory, and since there was no Jewish territory, per se, the Jews were not a nation and did not have national rights.

Jewish Communists argued that the way to solve this ideological dilemma was by creating a Jewish territory, hence the ideological motivation for the Jewish Autonomous Oblast. Politically, it was also considered desirable to create a Soviet Jewish homeland as an ideological alternative to Zionism and the theory put forward by Socialist Zionists such as Bert

Borochov that the Jewish Question could be resolved by creating a Jewish territory in Palestine.

Thus Birobidzhan was important for propaganda purposes as an argument against Zionism which was a rival ideology to Marxism among left-wing Jews.

The Jewish Anti-Fascist Committee

The Jewish Anti-Fascist Committee (JAC) was founded in 1942 on Stalin's order. It was headed by the Jew Solomon Mikhoels, the director of the Moscow State Jewish Theater. The JAC spread Communist propaganda throughout Eastern Europe and elsewhere, assuring Jewish audiences that the Soviet Union was pro-Jewish.

Itzik Feffer and Solomon Mikhoels from the JAC at a meeting with Albert Einstein during their trip to the United States in 1943.

Ilya Ehrenburg

Ilya Grigoryevich Ehrenburg was one of the most prominent Jewish members of JAC, and he was among the most prolific and notable authors of the Soviet Union. He was one of the co-authors of the "Black Book," which was a Soviet propaganda piece on alleged German atrocities. Ehrenburg's lies reached new heights with the "Black Book" which claimed that the Nazis killed Jews with "vacuum chambers," "steam chambers" and "mass electrocution" in swimming pool-sized chambers with movable floors.

Ehrenburg was the chief propagandists for the Red Army. He brutally urged on the genocidal mass murder of all Germans.

Ehrenburg is perhaps most infamous for his viciously anti-German wartime propaganda. In the words of the Canadian Jewish News: "As the leading Soviet journalist during World War II, Ehrenburg's writings against the German invaders were circulated among millions of Soviet soldiers." His articles appeared regularly in Pravda, Izvestia, the Soviet military daily Krasnaya Zvezda ("Red Star"), and in numerous leaflets distributed to troops at the front.

In one leaflet headlined "Kill," Ehrenburg incited Soviet soldiers to treat Germans as sub-human. The final paragraph concludes:

JAC member, Ilya Ehrenburg, spoke in New York in 1946.

"The Germans are not human beings. From now on the word German means to use the most terrible oath. From now on the word German strikes us to the quick. We shall not speak any more. We shall not get excited. We shall kill. If you have not killed at least one German a day, you have wasted that day ... If you cannot kill your German with a bullet, kill him with your bayonet. If there is calm on your part of the front, or if you are waiting for the fighting, kill a German in the meantime. If you leave a German alive, the German will hang a Russian and rape a Russian woman. If you kill one German, kill another -- there is nothing more amusing for us than a heap of German corpses. Do not count days, do not count kilometers. Count only the number of Germans killed by you. Kill the German -- that is your grandmother's request. Kill the German -- that is your child's prayer. Kill the German -- that is your motherland's loud request. Do not miss. Do not let through. Kill."[86]

Ehrenburg's incendiary writings certainly contributed in no small measure to the orgy of murder and rape by Soviet soldiers against German civilians.

Until his death in 1967, "his support for the Soviet state, and for Stalin, never wavered," the *Canadian Jewish News* notes.

His loyalty and service were acknowledged in 1952 when he received the Stalin Prize. In keeping with official Soviet policy, he publicly criticized Israel and Zionism.

The Canadian Jewish News further writes:

" ... The recent disclosure that Ehrenburg arranged to transfer his private archives to Jerusalem's Yad Vashem library and archive, while still alive, comes as a stunning revelation. The reason this information has come to light only now is that Ehrenburg agreed to transfer his archive on condition that the transfer, and his will, remain secret for 20 years after his death. On Dec. 11 [1987], with the 20-year period expired, Israel's daily Maariv related Ehrenburg's story..."

A supposed dedicated Bolshevik Soviet leader, it turned out that he secretly willed his private papers, not to the Soviet Union but to the Zionist State, where he is honored at Yad Vashem.

JAC Visits America

In 1943, Mikhoels and the Jew Itzik Feffer became the first official representatives of Soviet Jewry to visit the West, where they went on a seven-month tour in the U.S., Mexico, Canada and Britain to meet with influential Jews.

In the U.S., they were welcomed by the pro-Communist Jews Albert Einstein and B.Z. Goldberg, and the American Jewish Joint Distribution Committee. (B.Z. Goldberg was the son-in-law of Sholom Aleichem, who wrote *Fiddler on the Roof*, a much-publicized propaganda piece for theaters, glorifying Jewish life in Russia without mentioning any Communist connections.)

They also participated in the largest pro-Soviet rally ever held in the United States, on July 8, 1943 in New York. Another participant was Rabbi Stephen Wise, chairman of the World Jewish Congress.

They met with Chaim Weizmann, head of the Zionist Organization, and first president of Israel; Charlie Chaplin, who had made the anti-German propaganda movie *The Great Dictator*; the Jew *Marc Chagall*, who was a much-praised Jewish artist and a leader of the "modern art" movement; the Black *Paul Robeson*, an actor and pro-Communist activist in the Black "civil rights" movement; and the Jew Lion Feuchtwanger, a writer from Germany who wrote well-publicized anti-German books and praised the Soviet Union.

A Soviet group formed in 1942, the Jewish Anti-Fascist Committee (JAC) was hugely successful in its war propaganda, as its stories of German atrocities against civilians and in concentration camps were presented as fact in Western media. Many members of the JAC were also strong supporters of Israel, something that Stalin briefly supported. Eventually however many of the members, including Mikhoel, were purged and killed by Stalin's secret police.

The JAC also propagated the idea of a Jewish homeland in the Soviet Union, and the organization received a letter from Stalin which read as follows: "The creation of a Jewish Soviet republic will once and forever, in a Bolshevik manner, within the spirit of Leninist-Stalinist national policy, settle the problem of the state legal position of the Jewish people and further development of their multi-century culture. This is a problem that no one has been capable of settling in the course of many centuries. It can be solved only in our great socialist country."

According to the Jew Grigory Kheifets, who was the Soviet vice-consul in San Francisco from 1941 to 1944 and also San Francisco KGB station chief, the letter went on to propose a plan to make the Crimean Socialist Republic a homeland for Jewish people from all over the world.

Coordination and execution of this plan to lure investors was entrusted to Kheifets and became known as the "California in the Crimea" option.

Ultimately all these plans for a "Soviet Zion" came to nothing as the world Zionist movement opted to seize Palestine as a Jewish homeland, even if it meant driving out the Arabs already living there.

Chapter 20
The Greatest Mass Murderers
in all of Human History

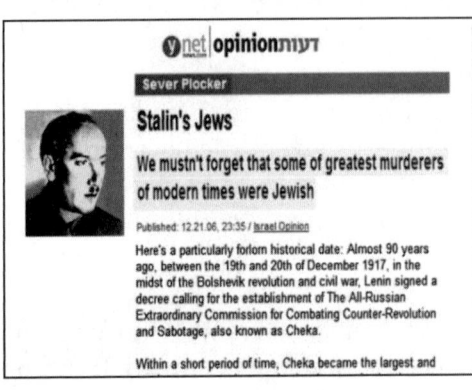

IN 2006, a remarkable article — and admission — appeared in the Israeli news source *Ynet News*. Titled "Stalin's Jews" and written by Jewish columnist Sever Plocker. His article confirmed the terrible crimes which Jewish Communists had committed under Stalin.[87]

The article for its Israeli, Jewish audience starts out by saying:

> **"We must not forget that some of greatest murderers of modern times were Jewish,"**

He then goes on to make a number of startling confessions:

> **"Here's a particularly forlorn historical date: Almost 90 years ago, between the 19th and 20th of December 1917, in the midst of the Bolshevik revolution and civil war, Lenin signed a decree calling for the establishment of The All-Russian Extraordinary Commission for Combating Counter-Revolution and Sabotage, also known as Cheka.**

> **"Within a short period of time, Cheka became the largest and cruelest state security organization. Its organizational structure was changed every few years, as were its names: From Cheka to GPU, later to NKVD, and later to KGB.**

> **"We cannot know with certainty the number of deaths Cheka was responsible for in its various manifestations, but the number is surely at least 20 million, including victims of the forced collectivization, the hunger, large purges, expulsions, banishments, executions, and mass death at Gulags.**

> **"Whole population strata were eliminated: Independent farmers, ethnic minorities, members of the bourgeoisie, senior officers, intellectuals, artists, labor movement activists,**

"opposition members" who were defined completely randomly, and countless members of the Communist party itself.

"In his new, highly praised book *The War of the World,* Historian Niall Ferguson writes that no revolution in the history of mankind devoured its children with the same unrestrained appetite as did the Soviet revolution. In his book on the Stalinist purges, Tel Aviv University's Dr. Igal Halfin writes that Stalinist violence was unique in that it was directed internally.

"Lenin, Stalin, and their successors could not have carried out their deeds without wide-scale cooperation of disciplined 'terror officials,' cruel interrogators, snitches, executioners, guards, judges, perverts, and many bleeding hearts who were members of the progressive Western Left and were deceived by the Soviet regime of horror and even provided it with a kosher certificate.

"And us, the Jews? An Israeli student finishes high school without ever hearing the name Genrikh Yagoda, the greatest Jewish murderer of the 20th Century, the GPU's deputy commander and the founder and commander of the NKVD.

"Yagoda diligently implemented Stalin's collectivization orders and is responsible for the deaths of at least 10 million people.

"His Jewish deputies established and managed the Gulag system.

The Jew Genrikh Yagoda, director of the NKVD, the Soviet Union's Stalin-era security and intelligence agency.

After Stalin no longer viewed him favorably, Yagoda was demoted and executed, and was replaced as chief hangman in 1936 by Yezhov, the "bloodthirsty dwarf."

"Yezhov was not Jewish but was blessed with an active Jewish wife. In his book Stalin: Court of the Red Star, Jewish historian Debag Montefiore writes that during the darkest period of terror, when the Communist killing machine worked in full force, Stalin was surrounded by beautiful, young Jewish women.

"Stalin's close associates and loyalists included member of the Central Committee and Politburo Lazar Kaganovich. Montefiore characterizes him as the "first Stalinist" and adds that those starving to death in Ukraine, an unparalleled tragedy in the history of human kind, did not move Kaganovich.

"Many Jews sold their soul to the devil of the Communist revolution and have blood on their hands for eternity. We'll mention just one more: Leonid Reichman, head of the NKVD's special department and the organization's chief interrogator, who was a particularly cruel sadist."

Yagoda (center) inspecting the construction of the Moscow-Volga canal, built by slave labor from the Gulags.

"In 1934, according to published statistics, 38.5 percent of those holding the most senior posts in the Soviet security apparatuses were of Jewish origin. Even if we deny it, we cannot escape the Jewishness of 'our hangmen,' who served the Red Terror with loyalty and dedication from its establishment. After all, others will always remind us of their origin."[88]

The Gulags: Jewish-Run Concentration Camps

As mentioned above, the infamous Soviet Gulags were under the direct control of the Jew Yagoda. He was not the only such Jew involved in the running of these camps, in which millions died. In fact Solzhenitsyn and many Jewish writers noted this.

The most famous revelation about the Jewish nature of the Gulags was that of famous dissident Alexander Solzhenitsyn. Speaking from personal experience as a Gulag prisoner, Solzhenitsyn gave a candid account of Jews in charge of the Soviet prison camps in his book, *Two Hundred Years Together.*

According to his observations, Jews made up a clear preponderance in the Gulag administration and in the early Bolshevik government, saying that of the 22 ministers in the first Soviet government, three were Russian, one Georgian, one Armenian and 17 were Jews. In addition, he points out, from personal experience once again, that "two thirds of the Kiev Cheka" (secret police) were Jews.

In 1937, another book appeared in Germany called *Jewish-Run Concentration Camps in the Soviet Union,*[89] which revealed that

Communist Jews were the commandants of 11 out of the 12 main Gulags.

Another prominent Jewish writer, Yuri Slezkine in his Judeocentric book, The Jewish Century, agrees with Leonard Schapiro's comment that "anyone who had the misfortune to fall into the hands of the Cheka stood a very good chance of finding himself confronted with and possibly shot by a Jewish investigator" (p. 177).[90]

During the 1930s the secret police, then known as the NKVD, "was one of the most Jewish of all Soviet institutions" (p. 254).[91]

Chapter 21
Iron Curtain Dictators

IN the Communist satellite nations, as in Russia, Jews occupied almost every key position of power. Perhaps no better proof of this can be found than in John Gunther's book, *Behind the Iron Curtain*.[92] Gunther revealed that in post-war Poland, Hungary, Romania, and Czechoslovakia, Jews played leading roles in all the one-party Communist states. Given here is a brief description of these "Iron Curtain Dictators."

The Jew Rákosi, on the far left, during the 1949 "Second World Festival of Youth and Students" Communist **front meeting.**

Hungary

The three "Muscovites" mentioned by Gunther are the Jews, Matyas Rakosi, Erno Gero, and Zoltan Vas—numbers one, two and three in the post-war Hungarian government, set up by the Soviet military commander of Hungary who disregarded the result of an election in November 1945 (in which the Communist Party only polled 17% of the vote) and installed a one-party Communist state.

Rakosi was born Mátyás Rosenfeld in present-day Serbia and was the *de facto* ruler of Communist Hungary between 1945 and 1956—first in his capacity as General Secretary of the Hungarian

Erno Singer/Gero

Communist Party (1945–1948) and later as General Secretary of the Hungarian Working People's Party (1948–1956). After Stalin's death, Rakosi was recalled to the Soviet Union and placed in internal exile until his death in 1971.

Erno Gero (born Erno Singer) was briefly in 1956 the most powerful man in Hungary as first secretary of its ruling Communist party. An early Hungarian Communist, Gero fled Hungary for the Soviet Union after Béla Kun's brief Communist government was overthrown in August 1919. During his two decades living in the USSR, Gero was an active KGB agent. Through that association, Gero was involved in Comintern — the international organization of Communists — in France, and also fought in the Spanish Civil War.

Gero became a member of Hungary's High National Council (provisional government) in 1945, and was appointed to a senior government post after the Soviet military commander disregarded the result of an election in November 1945 (in which

the Communist Party only polled 17% of the vote), and installed a one-party Communist state. Gero was Rákosi's right-hand man, but was removed from power following Stalin's death. After a period of exile in the Soviet Union, he was allowed to return to Hungary where he lived until his death in 1980.

Zoltan Vas

Zoltan Vas (*on left*) was a longtime Communist who was appointed government commissioner for Budapest public supplies in February 1945, and also served as mayor of Budapest the same year. "Elected" to the one-party state parliament in November 1945, Vas served as secretary of the Economic Supreme Council until 1949, when he was appointed president of the National Planning Office. He was on the Central Committee of the Hungarian Communist Party in 1956, and an alternate member and then full member of the Political Committee from 1948 to 1953. From February 1954, he headed the Materials and Produce Management Secretariat set up within the government secretariat. Like the other Stalinists, he was forced from power after the Soviet dictator's death. He died in 1983.

Poland

The post-war government of Poland was dominated by Jewish Communists as well. The most important of which were named Minc, Skryeszewski, Modzelewski, and Berman. The first

The Jew Hilary Minc

three were of cabinet rank, while Jacob Berman's official position was that of Under-Secretary of State — a minor office. Actually, Berman, who was a Soviet citizen, was the undisputed boss of Poland.

Hilary Minc, an economist and a Communist veteran who had spent the years 1939-1944 in Russia and was well known by Stalin, was second in rank only to Jacob Berman. He was the economic dictator and the author of the Three Year Plan. Minc was vice-premier and member of the Politburo from 1944 to 1956, when he resigned and admitted his "errors and misjudgments."

According to the book by Polish national hero and journalist Stefan Korbonski called *The Jews and the Poles in World War II*, in the decade up to 1955, Poland acquired Jewish overlords not only in government and the Communist party but in the secret police, in the administration of justice, and in the machinery of political indoctrination.

"To realize his plan of seizing total control of Poland, Stalin formed two teams: one to satisfy appearances and the Western Allies, the other to actually rule Poland. The first was headed by the Polish Communist Wanda Wasilewska and the other by Jacob Berman, whom Stalin knew well," Korbonski wrote.

The Jew Jacob (Jakub) Berman. He was in charge of the notorious State Security Services Urzad Bezpieczenstwa – the largest secret police in Polish history and one of its most repressive institutions. Berman was the brother of Adolf Berman, a Zionist activist who emigrated to Israel in 1950.

"The choice of Berman was connected with his Jewish origin, which exonerated him from suspicions of Polish patriotism and advocacy of Poland's independence. Stalin regarded the Jews as cosmopolitans whose loyalties would be to Zionism rather than the country of their residence.

"Jacob Berman, who was a Soviet citizen, was camouflaged in the secondary position of undersecretary of state at the Foreign Office and later at the Office of the Cabinet, from which he exerted control over all branches of the government. He had a direct telephone line to the Kremlin and to Stalin himself. That telephone was used on one occasion, after office hours, by William Tonesk, a Polish American who described the event in his interview published in the *New York Polish Daily* of June 9, 1987.[93]

The principal instrument of Berman's power was his total control of the Ministry of State Security, which began under Stalin's instructions to liquidate all centers of possible opposition, often by simply murdering persons suspected of advocating Poland's independence, especially former members of the Home Army, which fought the Germans during the occupation."

The team assembled by Berman at the beginning of his rule consisted of the following, all of them Jewish:

1. **General Roman Romkowski** (Natan Grünsapau-Kikiel), was vice-minister of State Security, He was a member of the then-illegal Communist Youth Organization and was trained in the Komintern "Lenin School." As vice-minister of State Security, Berman's confidant supervised the departments of investigation, training, and invigilation. He also managed the secret treasury of the Politburo, controlled by Jacob Berman, Hilary Minc, and Boleslaw Bierut, a Russified Pole promoted by Stalin. Bierut had served many years as an international agent of the Comintern.

2. **General Julius Hibner**, born David Schwartz, was a Communist who had served in the civil war in Spain in the years 1936-1938.

He was aide to the minister of State Security, charged with the Border Defense Corps and the Internal Security Corps. In 1951-1956 he was commander of the internal military forces and in 1956-1960 vice-minister of the interior.

3. **Luna Brystygier** was director of the fifth department of the Ministry of State Security.

4. **Colonel Anatol Fejgin** was director of the tenth department of the Ministry of State Security, his job was the tracing and liquidation of all Western influences and the collection of damaging material about Party members, with the exception of Bierut.

5. **The security police colonel Joseph Swiatlo** was in his youth a member of the Union of Young Communists. Two massive steel closets in his office contained material which incriminated every important personality from Berman down and was kept for purposes of blackmail.

6. **Colonel Joseph Rozanski** (Goldberg), a former clerk in a Warsaw law office and a veteran Communist, was the director of the investigation department of the Ministry of State Security. Charged with abuse of power and extensive use of torture, Rozanski was first sentenced in December 1955 to five years of imprisonment and then to fifteen. He was held in luxuriously appointed quarters and released ten years ahead of time. Upon his release, he settled in Israel.

7. **Colonel Czaplich** (fictitious name) who headed the third department of the Ministry of State Security, was charged with the prosecution of the Home Army, the organization of resistance against the Nazis during the war. He was nicknamed "Akower" (a Jewish version of the initials "A.K") of the Home Army. He displayed somewhat less cruelty than the other Bezpieka bosses.

8. **Zygmunt Okret** was the director of the archives department of the Ministry, in charge of records and personal files.

The above were far from being the only Jewish officials of the Ministry. Victor Klosiewicz, a Communist and member of the Council of State, stated in his interview conducted by Teresa Toranska: "Accounts had to be settled in 1955 and it was unfortunate that all the department directors in the Ministry of State Security were Jews."

The reason was Stalin's decision not to use Poles, whom he did not trust, but a more cosmopolitan element. The situation was aptly described by Abel Kainer in his essay "The Jews and Communism," in the political quarterly *Krytyka*:

> "The archetype of the Jew during the first ten years of the Polish People's Republic was generally perceived as an agent of the secret political police. It is true that under Bierut and Gomulka (prior to 1948) the key positions in the Ministry of State Security were held by Jews or persons of Jewish background. It is a fact which cannot be overlooked, little known in the west and seldom mentioned by the Jews in Poland. Both prefer to talk about Stalin's anti-Semitism (the "doctors" plot, etc.). The machine of Communist terror functioned in Poland in a matter similar to that used in other Communist ruled countries in Europe and elsewhere. What requires explanation is why it is operated by Jews. The reason was that the political police, the base of Communist rule, required personnel of unquestionable loyalty to Communism. These were people who had joined the Party before the war and in Poland they were predominantly Jewish."

Roman Zambrowski, born Rubin Nussbaum, who held several dominant political positions. In 1947 he was deputy speaker of the Seym (parliament) and its actual master over the ineffectual speaker Wiadyslaw Kowalski.

Another senior Jew was Tadeusz Zabludowski, the ruthless director of the Office of the Press, Publications and Entertainments, which was in fact the office of censorship. He was responsible for banning books and exerted total control over every publication, including books and theater performances as well as films and radio programs. He was assisted by Julia Minc, the wife of Hilary Minc, who headed the Polish News Agency, which was awarded the monopoly in the distribution of news and the management of the press.

Roman Werfl, a Communist since his youth and a journalist, was successively the editor of such periodicals as *Nowe Widnokregi, Glos Ludu,* and *Nowe Drogi.* He was the director of the "I Csiazka I Wiedza" publishing house, which enjoyed a monopoly of book publishing.

Leon Kasman was the editor of the official Party organ; he had been a Communist already before the war.

One of the dominant figures in the field of publishing and propaganda was Jerzy Borejsza, brother of the secret police colonel Joseph Rozanski, who set the policy of the press and its goals. He was assisted by "general" Victor Grosz and was promoted during the war in the Soviet Union from enlisted man to general for political services. He was the head of the political education department of the Polish army and was charged with the Communist indoctrination of the troops.

An important role was also played by Eugeniusz Szyr, a veteran of the Spanish civil war and a member of the "Union of Polish Patriots" formed in Moscow. He held the office of vice-premier.

Key positions in the Communist Party were held by Arthur Starewicz, secretary of the central committee of the Party, also a member of the Union of Polish Patriots, generally known as "The Muscovites."

A different role was assigned to Adam Schaff, a prewar Communist and a scholar and professor. He dedicated himself to the spreading of Marxist philosophy and published numerous works on the subject.

Zygmunt Modzelewski

The key positions in the Ministry of Foreign Affairs were held by Jews, often with assumed Polish names. Wincenty Rzymowski, a Pole, served as front man, with the title of minister, but the actual control was in the hands of vice-minister Zygmunt Modzelewski. The office of the ostensible minister of foreign affairs was later held by such insignificant figures as Stanislaw Skrzeszewski, who was a school teacher in Krakow before the war, as well as others, including Stefan Werblowski, greeted at the airport on his return from abroad by a delegation of Jewish officials, Marian Naszkowski and others. The control of the ministry was in the hands of Mieczyslaw Ogrodzinslcj, who adopted a Polish name as did his colleagues.

An important diplomatic role was played by Julius Katz-Suchy, Poland's delegate to the United Nations, and Manfred Lachs, who served as chairman of the legal committee of the UN Assembly and was later appointed a member of the International Tribunal in The Hague. There were many ambassadors and consuls, among them Henryk Strasburger and Waclaw Szymanowski; Consul Tadeusz Kassern, who became disenchanted with the system and committed suicide; Eugene Milnilciel, ambassador in London; Ludwik Rajchman, head of a Polish economic mission to the United States, and many others. In addition to the key personalities mentioned here, a very heavy proportion of the senior and middle-level officials were also Jewish.

The Ministry of Justice was under the control of Leon Szajn, the vice-minister and pre-war president of the leftist Association of Legal Aides and wartime member of the Union of Polish

Patriots sponsored by Stalin in Moscow. After the war he was assigned to the Democratic Party, kept by the Communists to ensure appearances of pluralism for the benefit of the West. He soon became the secretary general of that party, as well as vice-minister of justice.

His principal assistants were Stefan Rozmaryn and the prosecutor Jacob Sawickj, Jews who together with Colonel Stefan Kurowski, represented Poland's legal contingent at the Nuremberg trials of the Nazi leaders. Kurowski ended his career as the chief justice of the Supreme Court, which counted several Jewish judges, among them Mieczyslaw Szerer.

Among other members of the ruling Jewish-Communist elite were: Stefan Zolkiewski, minister of education in the years 1956-1959, who made Communist indoctrination the first priority; Ludwik Grosfeld, former minister of finance of the government in exile, who after his return to Poland joined the Communist National Council.

Emil Sommerstein, a prewar member of parliament, was appointed minister for war reparations; the eminent poet Julian Tuwim, who returned to Poland from the West in 1946 to become an enthusiastic champion of Communist rule; Wladvslaw Matwin, one of the founding members of the Moscow Union of Polish Patriots, who held several important positions, among them that of editor of the chief Communist press organ, the *Trybuna Ludua* (Tribune of the People).

Anthony Aister was vice-minister of the Interior; Stefan Arski, well-known journalist and senior official of the Communist Party; Isaac Kleinerman, head of the office of the presidium of the National Council; Jacob Prawin, Party activist; and Ozias Szechter, a veteran Communist.

As a result, a popular anti-Communist uprising in Poland in October 1956 took on a strong anti-Semitic undertone.

Although the Polish government suppressed the uprising, it flared up again in 1968. As a result, non-Jewish Communists forced a large number of leading Jewish Communists to resign, as described in the *Kracow Tygodnik Powszechnw* of March 20, 1988:

"Between the second half of 1967 and that of 1968, 341 officers of Jewish origin were dismissed from the army. They were also ousted from the Communist party ...

"In Warsaw, 483 persons were removed from senior official positions. 365 of them from the ministries and central agencies. 49 from academic posts and 24 from the press and cultural institutions. ...

"Six ministers and vice-ministers were removed from office, 35 directors and department heads ... about 70 professors and lecturers ... by mid-1969 over 20,000 Jews emigrated from Poland."[94]

Poland's Jewish bureaucracy was perhaps the largest of any Iron Curtain country outside of Russia proper.

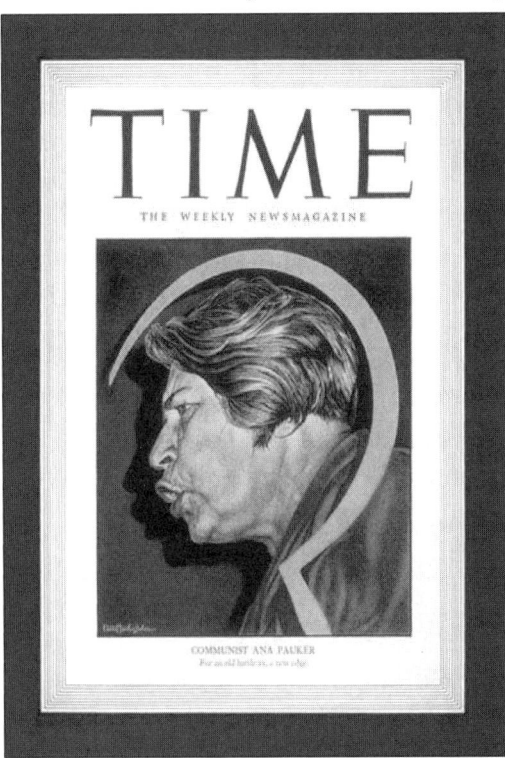

COMMUNIST ANA PAUKER
For an old battle-ax, a new edge.

Hanah Rabinsohn, better known as Ana Pauker.

Romania

Anna Pauker (born Hannah Rabinsohn) was a Romanian Communist leader and served as the country's foreign minister in the late 1940s and early 1950s. She was the unofficial leader of the Romanian Communist Party after World War II.

She was born in Bucharest of orthodox Jewish parents. Her father (who was a Kosher butcher) and a brother resided in Israel. When the Red Army entered Romania in 1944, Pauker became a member of the postwar government and in November 1947, was appointed Foreign Minister. But it was her position in the Communist Party leadership that was paramount: As a member of the 4-person Secretariat of the Central Committee and formally Number Two in the leadership, Pauker was widely believed to have been the actual leader of the Romanian Communists in all but name during the immediate postwar period.

In 1948, *Time* magazine featured her portrait on its cover and described her as "the most powerful woman alive".

Infamous as the "Iron Lady" of Romanian Communist politics, she was unreservedly Stalinist and served as Moscow's primary agent in Romania. Like so many Stalinists, once her idol had fallen from grace, she was sidelined and died in 1960.

Yugoslavia

The only non-Jewish dictator behind the Iron Curtain was Marshal Tito of Yugoslavia, which fact probably explains his later revolt against orthodox Communist rule from the Kremlin.

Markus Wolf, photographed in 1989.

But Tito was tutored by the Jew, Mosa Pijade. Says John Gunther of Pijade: "He is Tito's mentor ... Whatever ideological structure Tito may have, he got from this shrewd old man."

Czechoslovakia

The secretary-general of the Communist party in Czechoslovakia, whom John Gunther identified as a Jew dictator, was Rudolph Slansky. Holding the post of the party's General Secretary after World War II, he was one of the leading creators and organizers of Communist rule in Czechoslovakia. After the leader of Yugoslavia, Josip Tito, broke away from the domination of the Soviet leader, Joseph Stalin instigated a wave of "purges" of the respective Communist Party leaderships, to prevent more defections from among the Soviet Union's Central European "satellite" countries.

In November 1951 Slánský and 13 other Communist Party functionaries (of who 11 were Jews) were arrested on charges of fomenting "Trotskyite-Titoist-Zionist activities in the service of American imperialism." Slánský was found guilty and hanged in Pankrác Prison in 1952.

East Germany

That part of Germany under Soviet rule at the end of the Second World War was reconstituted into a one-party state called the "German Democratic Republic" under Communist rule.

Once again, Jews played a leading role in creating that state's infrastructure, but the most prominent Jew of all was Markus Wolf, who was head of the General Intelligence Administration (Hauptverwaltung Aufklärung), the foreign intelligence division of East Germany's Ministry for State Security (MfS, commonly known as the Stasi). He was the MfS's number two for 34 years, which spanned most of the Cold War. The Stasi set up a spy apparatus, both domestically and foreign, to rival that of the KGB, and were known to be as brutal, if not more so.

Shortly before German reunification Wolf fled Germany and sought political asylum in Russia. It was denied, and when he returned to Germany he was arrested by the police. In 1993 he was convicted of treason and sentenced to six years imprisonment. This was later quashed by the German supreme court, because Wolf was acting from the territory of the then-independent GDR.

In 1997 he was convicted of unlawful detention, coercion, and bodily harm (perpetrated against victims of the Stasi), and was given a suspended sentence of two years imprisonment. Wolf died in 2006.

Chapter 22
Russians Rise Up & Zionism Surges

THE struggle between Zionist Jews (who endorsed the basic economic and social principles of Communism, as can be seen to this day in Israel's kibbutzes, where everything is communally owned by the kibbutz members) and Communist Jews who (correctly) regarded Zionism as another form of nationalism, grew ever more intense after Stalin's death.

Many leading Jews had already fallen afoul of the Communist hierarchy, especially in the Great Purges of the 1930s. Zionists eventually came into open conflict with the Soviet authorities, particularly after the creation of the state of Israel, which was also (correctly) viewed by hardline Gentile Communists as an illegal state formed on land stolen from the Palestinians through illegal Jewish immigration.

World War II and the Rise of Russian Nationalism

The outbreak of the Second World War — and the invasion of the Soviet Union by Germany in 1941 irreparably altered the make-up of Soviet society. Jewish involvement in the horrors of Communism was an important factor in Hitler's desire to destroy the USSR and in the anti-Jewish actions of the German National Socialist government. Jews and Jewish organizations were also important forces in inducing the Western democracies to side with Stalin rather than Hitler in World War II.

By late 1941, many observers around the world fully expected the Soviet Union to collapse in the face of the massive German military victories on the Eastern Front. The USSR's ruling elite, fighting for its very existence, called upon the one reserve it had always, ideologically speaking, disdained: Russian nationalism.

In exhorting the Russian people to fight the German invaders, Soviet propaganda switched from being purely an ideological struggle between National Socialism and Communism, into one pitting Russian nationalism and independence against German aggression and imperialism.

This shift—in effect a call to Russian nationalism, instead of "worker internationalism," can be said to mark the turning point in Jewish influence in the Soviet Union.

Jewish Control Wanes in the Soviet Union

Despite their decline as a result of the growth of Russian nationalism, Jews still maintained an important role in the Communist elite of the USSR right to the very end of that state, as outlined in the book *The Jewish Century* by Yuri Slezkine (Princeton, NJ: Princeton University Press, 2004).[95]

According to Slezkine—a Jewish author—Jewish elite status in the USSR persisted despite the Great Terror of the late 1930s, which disproportionately affected the political elite. On the whole Jews were underrepresented as victims of the Great Terror. And although the Jewish percentage of the political elite did decline after the purges of the late 1930s and the promotion of former peasants and working class Russians, this did not affect Jewish predominance as a professional, cultural, and managerial elite.

Jewish elite status remained even after the purge was expanded to all sectors of the Soviet elite, due at least partly to "the widespread sense [among Russians] that the great victory [in World War II] entitled them to a greater role in decision making."[96]

Slezkine shows the very high percentages of Jews in various institutions in the late 1940s, including the universities, the media, the foreign service, and the secret police. For example, the deans among philosophers, historians, and legal scholars were ethnic Jews, and, as already noted, Jews constituted 80% of the Soviet Academy of Science Institute of Literature. As for the Jewish role as "vanguard of the working class," Jews still made up 23% of the staff at the Trade Union Council's publication *Trud* even after a purge that cut their numbers in half.

The campaign against the Jews began only after the apogee of mass murder and deportations in the USSR, and was much less lethal than those mounted against a long list of other ethnic groups, whose typical fate was deportation under the most brutal of circumstances (Cossacks, Chechens, Crimean Tatars, Volga

Germans, Moldavians, Kalmyks, Karachai, Balkars, Ingush, Greeks, Bulgars, Crimean Armenians, Meskhetian Turks, Kurds, and Khemshins).

The campaign against the Jews was also much less consistent and effective than the Soviet campaigns against the children of the former elite—the factory owners, the Cossack officers, and the middle classes and intelligentsia—had been[97.]

Unlike the purges of the 1930s that sometimes targeted Jews as member of the elite (albeit at far less than their percentage of the elite), the anti-Jewish actions of the late 1940s and early 1950s were targeted at Jews because of their ethnicity. Similar purges were performed throughout Soviet-controlled Eastern Europe[98]

> **"All three regimes [Poland, Romania, Hungary] resembled the Soviet Union of the 1920s insofar as they combined the ruling core of the old Communist underground, which was heavily Jewish, with a large pool of upwardly mobile Jewish professionals, who were, on average, the most trustworthy among the educated and the most educated among the trustworthy."[99]**

Speaking of the situation in Poland, Khrushchev supported the anti-Jewish purge with his remark that "you have already too many Abramoviches."

Whereas in the 1920s and 1930s children of the pillars of the old order were discriminated against, now Jews were not only being purged because of their vast overrepresentation among the elite, but were being discriminated against in university admissions. Jews, the formerly loyal members of the elite and willing executioners of the bloodiest regime in history, now "found themselves among the aliens."[100]

Jews retained their elite status and occupational profile until the collapse of the Soviet Union in 1991, but "the special relationship between the Jews and the Soviet state had come to an end—or rather, the unique symbiosis in pursuit of world revolution had given way to a unique antagonism over two competing and incommensurate nationalisms."[101]

Rise of Russian Nationalism Creates "Anti-Semitism"

As Slezkine explains, the response of the Russians was "massive affirmative action"[102] aimed at giving greater representation to underrepresented ethnic groups. Jews were targets of suspicion because of their ethnic status, barred from some elite institutions, and limited in their opportunities for advancement.

The Russians were taking back their country, and it wasn't long before Jews became leaders of the dissident movement and began to seek to emigrate in droves to the United States, Western Europe, and Israel. Despite still possessing elite social status and suffering far fewer disabilities than many groups (e.g., the overwhelming majority of the Soviet population was not allowed to live in cities and some Christian sects were banned), Jews perceived the situation as "anti-Semitic."

Jewish dissidents whose parents had run the Gulags, the deportations, and the state-sponsored famines, now led the "urgent call for social justice."[103]

Zionists Come to Dominate Russian Jewry

Applications to leave the USSR increased dramatically after Israel's Six-Day War of 1967, which, as in the United States and Eastern Europe, resulted in an upsurge of Jewish identification and ethnic pride. The floodgates were eventually opened by Gorbachev in the late 1980s, and by 1994, 1.2 million Soviet Jews had emigrated — 43% of the total.

By 2002, there were only 230,000 Jews left in the Russian Federation, 0.16% of the population. These remaining Jews nevertheless exhibit the typical Ashkenazi pattern of high achievement and overrepresentation among the elite, including six of the seven oligarchs who emerged in control of the Soviet economy and media in the period of de-nationalization.[104]

Perhaps unsurprisingly, this dénouement did not result in any sense of collective guilt among Soviet Jews[105] or among their American apologists. Indeed, American Jewish media figures who were blacklisted because of Communist affiliations in the 1940s are now heroes, honored by the film industry, praised in newspapers, their work exhibited in museums.

At the same time, the cause of Soviet Jews and their ability to emigrate became a critical rallying point for American Jewish activist organizations and a defining feature of neoconservatism as a Jewish intellectual and political movement. For example, Richard Perle, a key neoconservative, was Senator Henry Jackson's most important security advisor from 1969 to 1979 and organized Congressional support for the Jackson-Vanik Amendment linking U.S.-Soviet trade to the ability of Jews to emigrate from the Soviet Union. The bill was passed over strenuous opposition from the Nixon administration. Jewish activist organizations and many Jewish historians portray the Soviet Jewish experience as a sojourn in the land of the "Red Pharaohs."[106]

The victory over National Socialism set the stage for the tremendous increase in Jewish power in the post-World War II Western world, in the end more than compensating for the decline of Jews in the Soviet Union.

As Slezkine shows, the children of Jewish immigrants assumed an elite position in the United States, just as they had in the Soviet Union and throughout Eastern Europe and Germany prior to World War II. This power facilitated the establishment of Israel, the transformation of the United States and other Western nations in the direction of multiracial, multicultural societies via large-scale immigration, and the consequent decline in European demographic and cultural pre-eminence.

Anti-Zionism versus Anti-Semitism

In this way, the Soviet Union gradually became tainted as "anti-Jewish" when in fact at worst it became anti-Zionist.

The Western media, firmly under the control of Jewish Supremacists, helped propagate this idea and even coined the phrase "refuseniks" for those Zionist Jews who attempted to leave the Soviet Union for Israel in the 1970s.

Ironically, many of those who fought with the Zionists were Communist Jews. For example, after Stalin's death the Jewish Organization B'nai B'rith in the United States wrote in its magazine, the *B'nai B'rith Messenger:* "To show that Russia treats its Jews well, Soviet Premier Nikita Khrushchev this week remarked at a reception at the Polish Embassy that not only he himself and Soviet President Klementi Voroshilov, but also half the members of the Presidium have Jewish wives. Mr.

Khrushchev made this remark to Israeli Ambassador Joseph Avidar, who was amongst the guests."

According to a report in *The Canadian Jewish News,* November 13, 1964, the president of the Soviet Union at that time, Leonid Brezhnev, was married to a Jewess, and his children were raised as Jews. Confirmed Jews in his government were: Leonid Kantorovitj, head of the economy; Dimitri Dymshits, head of the industry; and Lev Shapiro, regional secretary of Birobidjan.

The Rise of the Jewish Oligarchs

As time went on, fewer and fewer Jews occupied the top positions in Soviet society, but retained their positions in the lower echelons. This became obvious when the Soviet Union collapsed in the early 1990s. Jews who had faithfully served the Soviet state emerged, with mysteriously acquired wealth, to buy up large sectors of Russia's denationalized infrastructure.

In this way, most of the oil, gas and natural reserves of Russia

Boris Berezovsky.

were snapped up by now "reformed" ex-Communist Jews, and the list of Jewish oligarchs became legendary and well-known both inside and outside of Russia. In a short time, these oligarchs accumulated almost half the wealth in Russia. The most prominent oligarchs were Boris Berezovsky, Mikhail Friedman, Mikhail Khodorkovsky, Vladimir Potanin, Vladimir Gusinsky and Alexander Smolensky — and they were all Jews.

Berezovsky also controlled the state television station and several newspapers, while Gusinsky's media empire controlled NTV, Russia's only national independent TV station, as well as major radio and print outlets.

Other famous Jewish oligarchs included Roman Abramovich; Oleg Deripaska; Viktor Vekselberg; Leonid Nevzlin; Eugene Shvidler; Vladimir Dubov; German Khan and Alexander Abramov.

According to the *Jerusalem Post*[107], there is an "army of Jewish billionaires" in Russia, — the Jewish Supremacist oligarchs who made their fortunes in that country after the collapse of Communism.

Mikhail Khodorkovsky photographed behind bars while on trial in Moscow. In 2004, Khodorkovsky was one of the richest people in the world, ranked 16th on Forbes list of billionaires. He was arrested in 2003 and charged with fraud, found guilty and sentenced to nine years in prison in May 2005. While still serving his sentence, Khodorkovsky was charged and found guilty of embezzlement and money laundering in December 2010, extending his prison sentence to 2017.

Many of these Jewish oligarchs were prosecuted or had charges brought against them. Some managed to escape and flee to Israel (such as Boris Berezovsky who then went to Britain) Others, such as Mikhail Khodorkovsky, were unable to flee in time and sentenced to prison for their swindling and insider trading by which they had accumulated their wealth.

The significant point to be learned from the Jewish oligarchs is that they were all able to rise to significant positions of influence in the later years of the Soviet Union, giving lie to the claim that the Soviets were anti-Jewish.

The most that can be said, as mentioned above, was that the Soviet state officially became anti-Zionist, viewing Israeli nationalism as a threat to international socialism. Individual Communist Jews who displayed no overt loyalty to Zionism or Israel, still held significant positions of power in the Soviet Union right to its end.

In 1984 Aleksandr Solzhenitsyn was interviewed by Nikolay Kazantsev, a monarchist Russo-Argentine journalist, for *Nasha Strana,* a Russian language newspaper based in Buenos Aires. In the interview he said:

"We (Russia) are walking a narrow isthmus between Communists and the World Jewry. Neither is acceptable for us... And I mean this not in the racial sense, but in the sense of the Jewry as a certain world view. Jewry [today] is embodied in capitalist globalism. Neither side is acceptable to us..." He also described the United States as a "province of Israel."[108]

Chapter 23
Jews Come to America

JEWISH historians divide Jewish immigration into the U. S. into three phases: the Sephardic or Spanish Period, the German Period and the Russian-Polish Period.

Jews Expelled from Southern U.S. States in 1862 Because of Fraud and Exploitation during Federal Occupation

In 1862, at the height of the American Civil War, Union Army general (and later president of America) Ulysses Grant expelled all Jews from the Southern U.S. states (the Confederacy) which were under his military control.

The reason for this move was that unscrupulous Jews from the North had moved in on the prostrate southern states and were engaging in all manner of black market, smuggling and swindling activities. The only way Grant thought he could stop this exploitation was to ban Jews from entering those territories.

On December 17, 1862, Grant wrote to the Assistant Adjutant General of the US Army:

> "I have long since believed that in spite of all the vigilance that can be infused into post commanders, the specie regulations of the Treasury Department have been violated, and that mostly by the Jews and other unprincipled traders. So well satisfied have I been of this that I instructed the commanding officer at Columbus to refuse all permits to Jews to come South, and I have frequently had them expelled from the department. But they come in with their carpet-sacks in spite of all that can be done to prevent it. The Jews seem to be a privileged class that can travel anywhere.
>
> "They will land at any wood yard on the river and make their way through the country. If not permitted to buy cotton themselves, they will act as agents for someone else, who will be at a military post with a Treasury permit to receive cotton and pay for it in Treasury notes which the Jew will buy at an agreed rate, paying gold."

HEAD QUARTERS, 13th ARMY CORPS,
DEPARTMENT OF THE TENNESSEE,
Oxford, Miss., Dec. 17th, 1862.

GENERAL ORDERS,
    No. 12.

1. The Jews, as a class, violating every regulation of trade established by the Treasury Department, and also Department orders, are hereby expelled from the Department.

2. Within twenty-four hours from the receipt of this order by Post Commanders, they will see that all of this class of people are furnished with passes and required to leave, and any one returning after such notification, will be arrested and held in confinement until an opportunity occurs of sending them out as prisoners unless furnished with permits from these Head Quarters.

3. No permits will be given these people to visit Head Quarters for the purpose of making personal application for trade permits.

BY ORDER OF MAJ. GEN. U. S. GRANT.

JNO. A. RAWLINS,
Assistant Adjutant General.

(OFFICIAL :)

Assistant Adjutant General.

HEAD QUARTERS, 13th ARMY CORPS,
DEPARTMENT OF THE TENNESSEE,
Holly Springs, Miss., Jan. 6, 1863.

GENERAL ORDERS,
    No. 2.

In pursuance of directions from the General-in-Chief of the Army, General Orders No. 12, from these Headquarters, dated Oxford, Miss., December 17th, 1862, is hereby revoked.

BY ORDER OF MAJ. GEN. U. S. GRANT.

JNO. A. RAWLINS,
Assistant Adjutant General.

[OFFICIAL :]

Assistant Adjutant General.

General Ulysses S. Grant's General Order No. 12, a repetition of General Order No. 11, which contained the revocation issued by President Abraham Lincoln.

On December 17, 1862, General Ulysses S. Grant issued General Orders No. 11. This order banished all Jews from Tennessee's western military. General Orders No. 11 declared:

"1. The Jews, as a class, violating every regulation of trade established by the Treasury Department, are hereby expelled from the Department.

2. Within 24 hours from the receipt of this order by Post Commanders, they will see that all of this class of people are furnished with passes required to leave, and anyone returning after such notification, will be arrested and held in confinement until an opportunity occurs of sending them out as prisoners, unless furnished with permits from these headquarters.

3. No permits will be given these people to visit headquarters for the purpose of making personal application for trade permits.

By order of Major Gen. Grant."

The expulsion order caused an uproar amongst the Jews, who petitioned President Abraham Lincoln to rescind the order. This duly happened and they were allowed back in to continue with the practices to which Grant had so strongly objected.

Ironically, Grant's expulsion order was based on the same kinds of conduct that led to the vast migration of Jews to America, exploitive activities of the tribe in European nations that also led to previous expulsions.

Sephardic Period

Since colonial America was still a pioneer country, there were almost no Jews here before the American Revolution. In 1776 there were certainly no more than a few score of Sephardic Jews in the entire country.

Modern Jewish historians have tried to prove the existence of two Jewish privates in Washington's armies, but the question is of no consequence either way. By 1830 — 50 years after the Declaration of Independence, and 220 years after the founding of Jamestown — there were an estimated 10,000 Jews in the U.S., comprising perhaps 1/5th of 1 percent of the total population.

German Period

During this period a fairly steady trickle of German Jews came to the U.S. mainly from Germany, so that by 1880 they numbered about 250,000, out of a total population of 50 million — about 1/2 of 1 percent.

Russian-Polish Period

Following the assassination of Tsar Alexander II in 1881, vast numbers of Russian Jews inundated America; between 1881 and 1917, the Jewish population increased by 1200% — to more than three millions!

World War I and the Russian Revolution added to this influx. Many Jews left Poland when as a result of the Versailles Treaty, it was made independent of Soviet Russia; others fled Russia during the counterrevolution and civil war which raged in 1918-1919-1920.

The White Russian Armies, regarding Bolshevism as a Jewish movement, showed little mercy to those Jewish communities falling into their hands. Many Jews, fleeing these anti-Communist armies, eventually made their way to the U.S.

This flood of immigration continued until 1924, when the Johnson-Lodge bill temporarily brought it to a halt. However, when the Roosevelt administration came to power in 1932, the barriers were once again lowered, so that in the calendar year of 1939, 52.3% of all immigrants admitted to the U.S. were Jewish.

After 1945, this influx has continued under so-called "Displaced Persons" (DP) legislation, with the result that approximately half of the world's Jewish population has now congregated here.

In 2010, official Jewish sources estimated America's Jewish population to be 5,275,00 - only 100,000 greater than the same estimate in 1949 (when it was claimed that there were 5,185,000 Jews in America). This figure is clearly incorrect and a realistic estimate will be at least two to three million more than that, anywhere between seven and nine million.

New York: Second Largest Jewish City in the World

The newly arrived Jews settled in the metropolitan centers, New York alone absorbing approximately half of the total Jewish immigration. But the "ghettoization" of the East-European Jews in the United States was the result not of objective forces only: it was as much the result of the immigrant's desire to retain all they could of their old way of life" — Page 218, *The Jewish People, Past and Present,* Central Yiddish Culture Organization (CYCO) New York.[109]

New York City has been the staging ground for the Jewish invasion of the U.S. Here the Jewish immigrant found a ghetto-like environment similar to the one he left in east-Europe. There he learned the language and customs of the country and gathered the know-how and capital to buy up business on the Main Street of Los Angeles, or Dallas, or Chicago.

Many lower class Jews, unable to learn the language or raise the capital, or being otherwise unequipped to go into business or the professions, settled in New York to become workers and craftsmen. Thus, after the war, we find Ben Gold's Communistic fur workers union, and David Dubinsky's "socialistic" garment workers union, which consisted almost entirely of Jews. This situation changed somewhat in the latter part of the twentieth century as manufacturing moved increasingly to the Far East. Nonetheless, as would be expected, New York City has been the seed-bed for Communism in the United States.

Chapter 24
The U.S. Communist Party

THE American Communist Party has never been very large. In 1940, it had an estimated 80,000 members; by the late 1950s this had dwindled to less than 10,000.

On first appearances this would seem to rule it out as a significant force in American politics. But appearances can be

The Ghetto, New York City

A postcard from the early 20th Century in New York showing the Jewish ghetto in the city.

deceptive. Unlike the mass-recruited Communist parties of France and Italy, the American Communist party is small, carefully chosen, well disciplined, and fanatical.

Few — perhaps no one — of its membership has been recruited from the sweaty-shirt strata.

Its members are college professors and union leaders, physicists and government workers, reporters, playwrights and business executives, actors and newspaper reporters. Some of its members are wealthy; almost all are well educated.

The first Communist Party of America (CPA) was founded in September 1919, after splits between the already existing Socialist Party movements — all of which were heavily Jewish-dominated.

Benjamin "Ben" Gitlow, the son of Russian Jews, was one of the leading founder members. Gitlow was charged in 1919 with attempting to incite the violent overthrow of the United States, and served two years in Sing Sing prison.

According to page 804 of the *Encyclopaedia Judaica,*

> "the list of Jews who played a prominent role in the leadership and factional infighting of the American Communist Party is a long one . . . Many American Jewish authors and intellectuals, some of whom later recanted, were active in editing Communist publications and spreading party propaganda . . . among them Michael Gold, Howard Fast, and Bertram Wolfe.

Jewish Communists in Labor Movement

For the first half of the 20th century, the Communist Party played a very prominent role in the U.S. labor movement from the 1920s through the 1940s, having a major hand in founding most of the country's first industrial unions while also becoming known for fighting for integration in workplaces and communities.

Jewish historian Ellen Schrecker, in her article "Soviet Espionage in America: An Oft-Told tale"[110] said that the CPUSA was a "Stalinist sect tied to a vicious regime and the most dynamic organization within the American Left during the 1930s and '40s."

Jewish women, mostly Eastern European immigrants in New York City, helped to lead the Communist cause and were a vital component of its rank and file. Notable Jewish leaders included Rose Wortis, a legendary labor organizer in the needle trades, Rose Stokes, a radical journalist elected to the Workers Party's central executive committee, and Betty Gannett, who joined the party as a teenager in 1923 and was appointed national education director of its Young Communist League in 1929.

The majority of rank-and-file party members were garment workers or housewives. Many came to the party through the Jewish Federation, a Yiddish-language organization that originated in the Socialist Party and defected to the Communists in 1922.

The Jewish Federation's mission was to preserve and invigorate revolutionary "yiddishkeit" through community-based cultural projects, work that found a generally comfortable home in the Communist movement of the early 1920s.

Largest Communist Newspaper
in U.S. was the Yiddish-language *Morgen Freiheit*

The Yiddishists gave the party a vital link to, and influence among, the large Jewish immigrant Left. The *Morgen Freiheit*, the Communist Yiddish-language daily established in New York in 1922 soon became the largest Communist newspaper in America.

In Brooklyn's Brownsville district, Communist Jewish activists such as Clara Lemlich Shavleson and Kate Gitlow mobilized women in Jewish neighborhoods and gave birth to the United Council of Working Class Women (UCWW) in 1929.

Its membership was almost entirely Jewish until the mid-1930s. This departure from Yiddishist activism reflected a growing trend in Jewish communities. Increasingly, older immigrant Yiddishists were being outnumbered by younger, native-born leftists.

Many of these younger radicals aligned themselves with Communism during the Great Depression and World War II, the heyday of both the Communist Party and Jewish women's involvement in its work. The party swelled from just under ten thousand members in 1929 to about forty thousand in 1936 and to eighty-three thousand in 1943.

Female membership expanded from about 15 percent in the early 1930s to 30 or 40 percent at the end of the decade and to about 46 percent in 1943.

CP historians estimate, moreover, that almost half of the party's membership was Jewish in the 1930s and 1940s, and that approximately 100,000 Jews passed through the party in those decades of high member turnover.

It seems safe to say, then, that Jewish women were one of the CP's largest sectors during the Depression and war years; and for each who was a "card-carrying" Communist, there were several who took part in party-led mass organizations but did not belong to the party itself.

In addition to industrial workers and housewives, the new generation of Jewish women connected with the CP included a large number of college students, schoolteachers, office workers, and social service professionals.

There was also a small but significant cadre of artists and intellectuals, such as playwright Lillian Hellman and anthropologist Eslanda Robeson, a Sephardic Jew who wrote and lectured on "African affairs."

Jewish Communists did much of their organizing among Jews, often through multiethnic movements, Jewish fraternal networks, coalitions of women's clubs, and the Yidischer Kultur Farband, founded in 1937.

This work reflected the ethnic consciousness among Jewish Communists and heightened their attention to the party's position on Jewish issues. For example, both the older Yiddishists and the younger, Americanized generation were especially proud of the Soviet Union's laws against anti-Semitism.

Thousands of Communist Jews Deported from the U.S.

There were so many Jewish immigrants from eastern Europe and Russia in the party that U.S. Attorney General A. Mitchell Palmer, acting under the Sedition Act of 1918, began arresting these thousands of foreign-born party members and deporting them. The Communist Party was forced underground and took to the use of pseudonyms and secret meetings in an effort to evade the authorities.

The CPA re-emerged in 1921 using the legal front organization called the "Workers Party of America." An element of the party, however, remained permanently underground and came to be known as the "CPUSA secret apparatus."

Jay Lovestone/Liebstein

Factions quickly emerged once again, with the most prominent being led by the Jew Jay Lovestone (real name Jacob Liebstein), a Lithuanian Jew.

In 1921, Lovestone became editor of the Communist Party newspaper, *The Communist*, and sat on the editorial board of *The*

Liberator, the arts and letters publication of the Workers Party of America.

In 1927, Lovestone/Liebstein became the party's national secretary. He was eventually forced out of the Communist party in another factional dispute, and died in 1990.

The Jew Jay Liebstein (used the name Lovestone), just one of the thousands of Jews involved in the early U.S. Communist party.

Chapter 25
A Communist Defector
in America Spills the Beans

ONE of the major defectors from the Communist Party USA was the former editor of the *Daily Worker* and Politburo member

Louis Budenz. Of Hungarian and Irish origin, Budenz defected after the defeat of fascism. Budenz was a star witness on the organization and attitude of the Communist Party USA as well as its underground organization (the secret apparatus) and the illicit funding that it received from the USSR through the medium of the Comintern to enable its attempted conquest of North America.

Louis Budenz

Budenz published four books on the basis of his Communist experiences: *This is My Story;* [111] *Men without Faces: The Communist Conspiracy in the U.S.A.*[112]; *The Cry is Peace*[113]; and *The Techniques of Communism*[114].

It is from these works that the following list of Jewish Communist activists from the early years of the Communist Party of America is drawn:

1. Solomon Adler: Soviet agent in the US Treasury Department (Budenz, *Techniques*, p. 281). [115]

2. Israel Amter: Communist leader (Budenz, *Story*, p. 101)[116]; In charge of 'national groups'; i.e. 'civil rights', pro-negro and pro-Jewish, propaganda and organization (Budenz, *Story*, p. 205);[117] Leader of the Communist Party USA in New York State (Budenz, *Men*, p. 173).

3. John Arnold: Chief Editor of the Communist Party USA's Yiddish newspaper: *Daily Freiheit* (Budenz, *Cry*, p. 56).[118]

4. Sol Auerbach (better known as James Allen): Comintern representative in the Philippines (Budenz, *Cry*, p. 56); [119] Foreign Affairs editor of the Sunday edition of the *Daily Worker* (Budenz,

Story, p. 307; *Cry*, p. 56); [120]Conducted espionage against the US military (Budenz, *Story.*, p. 311).[121]

5. Rudy Baker (nee Rudolph Blum): Writer for the *New Masses* (Budenz, *Men*, p. 18); [122]Carried out espionage activities against US and Canadian governments (Budenz, *Men*, p. 18).[123]

6. Leonard Berkowitz: Communist Hollywood Film Script Writer (Budenz, *Cry*, p. 23);[124] Soviet agent in US Office of War Information (Budenz, *Cry*, p. 23; *Techniques*, p. 285).[125]

7. Lionel Berman: Writer for the *Daily Worker* (Budenz, *Men*, p. 219; *Techniques*, pp. 33-34).[126]

8. Alexander Bittelman: Long-time Communist leader and representative of the Comintern in North America (Budenz, *Men*, pp. 18; 78);[127] Chief Theoretician of the Communist Party USA (Budenz, *Cry*, p. 76; *Techniques*, p. 49).[128]

9. Alfred Blumberg: Former Professor at Johns Hopkins University (Budenz, *Cry*, p. 162);[129] Communist leader in Washington D.C. (Budenz, *Men*, pp. 105; 253)[130] and Maryland areas (Budenz, *Cry*, p. 162).[131]

10. David Bohm: Soviet agent inside the United States' atomic program (Budenz, *Cry*, p. 17).[132]

11. Joseph Brodsky: Communist Party USA's legal advisor and lawyer (Budenz, *Men*, pp. 44; 78);[133] Facilitated the Comintern's funding of the Communist Party USA (Budenz, *Men*, p. 108).[134]

12. Boris Bykov: Head of the GRU (Soviet Military Intelligence) in North America (till 1938) (Budenz, *Cry*, p. 61).[135]

13. Esther Cantor: Writer for the *Daily Worker* (Budenz, *Cry*, p. 84); In charge of distributing Communist propaganda to negroes; and inciting them against the government, in the US (Budenz, *Cry*, p. 84).[136]

14. Sam Carr (nee Schmil Kogan): Long-time member of the National Committee of the Communist Party of Canada (Budenz, *Story*, p. 280).[137]

15. Morris Childs (nee Moishe Chilovsky): Managed Communist Party USA's funding from the Comintern (Budenz, *Men*, p. 86);[138] Worked as a Soviet espionage agent in North and

Central America (Budenz, *Men*, pp. 86-87). Childs also worked as a FBI informant from 1952 onwards.

16. Joe Clark (nee Joseph Cohen): Professor at Brooklyn College (Budenz, *Cry*, p. 161); Writer for the *Daily Worker* and *New Masses* (Budenz, *Cry*, p. 161).

16. Judith Coplon: Soviet agent in the US Department of Justice (Budenz, *Cry*, p. 72).

17. Crystal Eastman: Wife of Communist leader: Max Eastman (Budenz, *Story*, p. 60); Edited the Communist *New Masses* magazine (Budenz, *Story*, p. 60).

18. Max Eastman: Edited the Communist *New Masses* magazine (Budenz, *Story*, p. 60).

19. Gerhart Eisler: Former leader of the German Communist Party [the KPD]); Representative of the Comintern in the United States (Budenz, *Story*, pp. 240-241).

20. Joseph Fields (nee Joseph Felshin): Staff writer for *The Communist* (Budenz, *Men*, p. 219); Wrote for the *Daily Worker* (Budenz, *Men*, p. 219).

21. Benjamin Gitlow: Leading Communist functionary until 1928 (Budenz, *Story*, pp. 102-103; *Men* p. 12;); Advised against helping striking and by then desperate miners (Budenz, *Story*, p. 93); Later became a leading exponent of 'anti-Communism' (Budenz, *Story*, p. 188; *Cry*, p. 117; *Techniques*, p. 310).

22. Arthur Gleason: Wrote for and was employed by left-wing magazine: *The Nation* (Budenz, *Story*, p. 61); Member of the Intercollegiate Socialist Society (Budenz, *Story*, p. 61); Founded the Communist magazine: *Labor Age* (Budenz, *Story*, p. 61).

23. Ben Gold: Head of the International Fur and Leather Goods Workers Union. (Budenz, *Men*, p. 190; *Techniques*, p. 193); Actively conspired to manipulate the American Federation of Labor while pretending not to be a Communist. (Budenz, *Men*, pp. 190; 202; *Cry*, pp. 75-76; *Techniques*, p. 188).

24. Jacob Gollosh: Born Yakov Naumovich Reizen; Chairman of the Communist Party USA's Control Commission (Budenz, *Men*, pp. 39; 78; *Cry*, p. 66); Headed the Communist holiday company: 'World Tourists' (Budenz, *Story*, p. 238; *Men*, p. 55);

Was a Soviet espionage agent (Budenz, *Story*, p. 238; *Techniques*, p. 123).[139]

25. Michael Greenberg: Soviet agent in the White House (Budenz, *Cry*, p. 68);[140] Worked with the pro-Communist Institute of Pacific Relations (Budenz, *Techniques*, p. 284).[141]

26. Abraham Heller: Managed the financial support given to the Communist Party USA by the Soviet Union (Budenz, *Story*, p. 132).[142]

27. Annalee Jacoby: Pro-Communist writer associated with the *Daily Worker* (Budenz, *Cry*, p. 46; *Techniques*, p. 228).[143]

28. Phillip Jaffe: Soviet espionage agent in China (Budenz, *Men*, pp. 53; 278;[144] *Techniques*, p. 281);[145] Used US government documents; given to him by Soviet agents, to help the Chinese Communist Party. (Budenz, *Cry*, p. 35;[146] *Techniques*, p. 286); Important figure in the pro-Communist Institute for Pacific Relations (Budenz, *Men*, pp. 264-265;[147] *Cry*, pp. 45; 50; 59; 63).[148]

29. Albert Kahn: Communist author. (Budenz, *Cry*, p. 99).[149]

30. Felix Kuzman: Soviet espionage and underground network courier (Budenz, *Men*, pp. 42; 74; 253);[150] Former member of the Abraham Lincoln Brigade (Budenz, *Men*, p. 81).[151]

31. Harold Laski: British Communist author (Budenz, *Story*, p. 100);[152] Confident of Karl Radek; a leading Jewish Bolshevik, who told him of his opposition to Stalin and support of Trotsky. (Budenz, *Story*, p. 138).[153]

32. Avram Landy: In charge of Communist propaganda amongst Slavic groups in the United States (Budenz, *Story*, p. 237).[154]

33. Adam Lapin: Washington D.C. and a foreign correspondent of the *Daily Worker* (Budenz, *Story*, p. 230;[155] *Men*; p. 269);[156]

34. Daniel de Leon: Set up and ran Communist and socialist trade unions to deliberately try and rival the American Federation of Labor (Budenz, *Story*, p. 44).[157]

35. Sam Liptzin: Writer for the Communist Party USA's Yiddish newspaper: *Freiheit*. (Budenz, *Men*, p. 70);[158]

36. Jay Lovestone: General Secretary of the Communist Party USA (until 1928) (Budenz, *Story*, p. 88).[159]

37. Jacob Mindel: Soviet espionage agent in North America (Budenz, *Men*, p. 98);[160] Trained female Communists to seduce US military officers to learn military secrets (Budenz, *Men*, p. 130;[161] *Techniques*, p. 116).[162]

38. George Mink: High-Ranking Officer in the Abraham Lincoln Brigade (Budenz, *Men*, p. 124);[163]

39. Steve Nelson (nee Steve Mesaros): Soviet espionage agent in North America (Budenz, *Men*, p. 34;[164] *Cry*, p. 17);[165] High-Ranking Officer in the Abraham Lincoln Brigade (Budenz, *Men*, pp. 36; 124);[166] Helped the Chinese and German Communist parties (Budenz, *Men*, p. 37).[167]

40. Moissaye Olgin: Communist leader (Budenz, *Men*, p. 42);[168] [169]Author of *Why Communism?* (Budenz, *Men*, p. 42; [170]*Techniques*, p. 22).[171]

41. Joseph Peters: Representative of the Comintern in the United States (Budenz, *Story*, pp. 138-139;[172] *Men*, p. 78).[173]

42. Joseph Pogany (former minister in the Bela Kuhn regime); Representative of the Comintern in the United States (till 1938) (Budenz, *Story*, p. 240;[174] *Techniques*, p. 26);[175] Conducted espionage activities against the US Government (Budenz, *Techniques*, p. 26).[176]

43. Abraham Lincoln Polonsky: Communist Hollywood Film and Radio Script Writer (Budenz, *Cry*, pp. 23-24);[177] Soviet agent in Office of Strategic Services (Budenz, *Cry*, p.24).[178]

44. Julia Stuart Poyntz: High-Ranking Communist Party USA Leader (Budenz, *Story*, p. 263);[179] Assassinated by the GRU (Soviet Military Intelligence) in 1938 for preparing to break away from the Communist Party USA (Budenz, *Story*, p. 263; *Cry*, p. 130).[180]

45. Morris Rappoport: Communist leader in Washington state (Budenz, *Men*, p. 105).[181]

46. Andrew Roth: Stole US Military documents for the Soviet Union (Budenz, *Cry*, p. 10).[182]

47. Harry Sacher: Communist Party USA Lawyer (Budenz, *Cry*, p. 82).[183]

48. Solomon Schwarz: Writer for the *Daily Worker* (Budenz, *Story*, p. 303).[184]

49. Nathan Gregory Silvermaster: Soviet spy in the US government (Budenz, *Men*, pp. 105-106).[185][186]

50. Jacob 'Jack' Stachel: Communist leader and representative to the Comintern (Budenz, *Story*, p. 127;[187] *Men*, p. 143; *Techniques*, p. 120);[188] Took his orders from Joseph Peters, Alexander Bittelman and Joseph Pogany. (Budenz, *Story*, pp. 188-189; 245; 251; 274; 335;[189] *Men*, pp. 18; 40; 51; 267; 269);[190] Endorsed lying to serve the Communist cause (Budenz, *Story*, p. 216).[191]

51. Joseph Starobin: Foreign Affairs editor of the 'Daily Worker' (Budenz, *Story*, p. 278; *Men*, p. 154).[192]

52. Sid Stein: Communist Party USA's Labor Commissar (Budenz, *Cry*, p. 84);[193]

53. Alexander Trachtenberg: Long-time member of the Communist Party USA's Central Committee (Budenz, *Story*, p. 230; *Men*, pp. 78;[194] 219; *Techniques*, p. 119);[195]

54. Joseph Woodrow Weinberg: Soviet espionage agent inside the United States' atomic program (Budenz, *Cry*, p. 17).[196]

55. Robert William Weiner: Treasurer of the Communist Party USA (Budenz, *Story*, p. 226; [197]*Men*, p. 78);[198] In charge of a large private Communist slush fund. (Budenz, '*Men*, pp. 107-108).[199]

56. Louis Weinstock: Communist union leader (Budenz, *Men*, pp. 96; 197).[200]

57. Max Weiss: Secretary of the Young Communist League (Budenz, *Men*, p. 46);[201]

58. Harry Dexter White (Weiss): Soviet agent in the US Treasury Department (Budenz, *Techniques*, p. 281).[202]

Chapter 26
Spies, Spies and more Spies in America

THE American Communist Party sponsored an elaborate intelligence network on behalf of the Soviet Union, involving over 500 members acting as agents. This massive spying network started from the very earliest times of the Soviet Union, and lasted right until the dissolution of the USSR. By then, Jews working as agents for the Israeli government had replaced the Jewish Communists as the most extensive spy network in America.

Stern

Both the American Communist Party and Israel could rely upon the loyalty of American Jewry to provide a constant source of Fifth Column recruits, while at the same time shouting down as "anti-Semites" anyone who dared point this fact out.

Manfred Stern:
Prominent Early Soviet Spy

Manfred Stern (aka Emilio Kléber, Lazar Stern, Moishe Stern, Mark Zilbert) was a Jewish member of the GRU, the Soviet military intelligence and one of the most prominent early Soviet spies in the U.S.

He also served as military advisor in China, and gained fame under his *nom de guerre* as General Kléber, leader of the International Brigade during the Spanish Civil War.

In 1929, Stern became the GRU's chief spy in the United States. Based in New York City and operating under the cover name of Mark Zilbert, he managed a network of sources and agents involved in the theft of military secrets. In one operation they stole the plans for a new American tank.

Another operation was foiled by a source who went to U.S. Naval Intelligence and continued to deliver faked documents to the Soviets. The apparatus kept a safe apartment on West 57th Street, owned by the Jewess Paula Levine.

Stern eventually fell out with his Communist bosses. Recalled to the Soviet Union, he was arrested and interned in a Gulag, where he died in 1954.

Alexander Petrovich Ulanovsky

Ulanovsky

The Jew Alexander Petrovich Ulanovsky (AKA Ulrich, William Joseph Berman, Bill Berman, Felik, Long Man, Nathan Sherman) was the chief illegal "resident" for Soviet Military Intelligence (GRU), in the United States from 1931 until 1934.

Ulanovsky came to America to take over the GRU apparatus assembled by his predecessor, Manfred Stern. He returned to Europe after the failure of several GRU operations, notably a bungled scheme to counterfeit U.S. currency.

Ulanovsky resurfaced in Copenhagen in 1935, operating under the alias Nathan Sherman, as the head of a Soviet espionage ring that collected military information on Nazi Germany.

The Danish police arrested Ulanovsky and two other American Jews, Leon Josephson and George Mink, following a search of their hotel room which turned up codes, money, and multiple passports. The motive for the search was a charge of rape against Mink by a chambermaid.

Ulanovsky told the Danish police that the three Jews were "anti-fascists" acting on their own (a common tactic, even today, see chapter on "The Communist Movement in Britain"), but the authorities had evidence that they were working for Soviet intelligence.

Ulanovsky was convicted of espionage, sentenced to eighteen months in prison and then deported to the Soviet Union.

The other two Jewish spies continued with their Communist activities once released: Josephson returned to America and worked as a lawyer representing Communist party members, while Mink went to Spain where he served as an NKVD assassin during the Civil War in that country.

In 1948, Ulanovsky's wife Nadezhda was arrested by the Soviets, and he was detained the following year following a falling out with their bosses. They were sent to the Gulag, and released in 1960. Ulanovsky died in 1970 and his wife died in Israel in 1983.

Elizabeth Zarubina/ Lisa Rozensweig

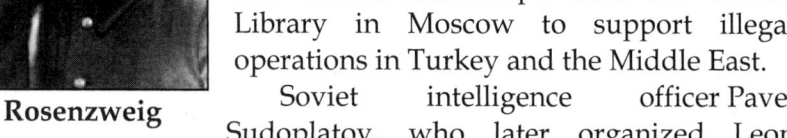

The Jewess Elizaveta 'Zoya' Yulyevna Zarubina was born Lisa Rozensweig, and joined the Soviet spy network in 1924, working in the Soviet embassy in Vienna.

In 1929, Rozensweig and fellow Jew agent Yakov Blumkin were posted as "illegals" in Turkey, where he sold Hasidic manuscripts from the Central Library in Moscow to support illegal operations in Turkey and the Middle East.

Rosenzweig

Soviet intelligence officer Pavel Sudoplatov, who later organized Leon Trotsky's murder, claimed in his autobiography that Blumkin gave part of the sale proceeds to Trotsky, who was then in exile in Turkey. According to his account, Rozensweig denounced Blumkin for this activity, and that was the reason he was recalled to Moscow and executed.

Shortly thereafter (1929), Rozensweig married the Jew Vasily Zarubin, and they traveled and spied together for many years, using the cover of a Czechoslovakian and USA business couple for work in Denmark, Germany, France and the United States.

According to the book *Special Tasks: The Memoirs of an Unwanted Witness – A Soviet Spymaster*, by Pavel Sudoplatov, Anatoli Sudoplatov, Jerrold L. Schecter, Leona P. Schecter, (Little Brown, Boston, 1994), p. 189. Rozensweig was "one of the most successful operators in stealing atomic bomb secrets from the United States".

Together with the chief Soviet spy in California and Jew Gregory Kheifetz (who served as the Soviet vice-consul in San

Francisco from 1941 to 1944, see above), she set up a ring of young Communist physicists around the Jew Robert Oppenheimer at Los Alamos to transmit nuclear weapon plans to Moscow. Rozenswieg avoided capture and died in Russia in 1987.

Koval

George Abramovich Koval

George Abramovich Koval was born in Sioux City, Iowa, USA, of Russian Jewish parents. Shortly after reaching adulthood he traveled with his parents to the Soviet Union to settle in the Jewish Autonomous Region near the Chinese border. There, Koval was recruited by the Soviet Main Intelligence Directorate, trained, and assigned the code name DELMAR.

He returned to the United States in 1940 and was drafted into the US Army in early 1943. Koval worked at atomic research laboratories and, according to the Russian government, relayed back to the Soviet Union information about the production processes and volumes of the polonium, plutonium, and uranium used in American atomic weaponry, and descriptions of the weapon production sites.

After the war, Koval left on a "European vacation" but went directly to the Soviet Union where he lived out the rest of his life, dying in Moscow in 2006.

His activities as a spy only emerged after the publication of a 2002 book, *The GRU and the Atomic Bomb,* which mentioned Koval by his code name and listed him as one of a handful of spies who evaded counter-intelligence groups.

On November 3, 2007, he received the posthumous title of Hero of the Russian Federation bestowed by Russian President Vladimir Putin.

When Koval was honored, the Russian presidential proclamation stated, "Mr. Koval, who operated under the pseudonym Delmar, provided information that helped speed up considerably the time it took for the Soviet Union to develop an atomic bomb of its own."

The Treason Trials

The U.S. Communist Party was involved in a series of highly publicized treason and conspiracy trials shortly after World War II, which were utterly without precedent in American history. These included:

* The "Amerasia Case,"

* The "Gerhart Eisler Case,"

* The "Judith Coplin Case,"

* The "Alger Hiss Case,"

* The "Hollywood Ten Case,"

* The "Fuchs-Gold Atom Spy Case,"

* The "Rosenberg-Sobell Case," and

* The case of "Eugene Dennis and the Convicted Eleven."

It was impossible, of course, to conceal altogether the Jewishness of the overwhelming majority of the defendants. But Jewish propagandists exhausted every trick in trying.

One Jewish publication — *Look* magazine — ran a picture story on the spy trials in which the defendants were variously described as "typical Americans" ... "American born" . . . and "as American as apple pie."

So there will be no further doubt regarding the racial identity of the American Communist party, we have accumulated photographs and data on virtually every Communist indicted or tried for Communistic activity since 1945. The reader may judge for himself.

The Amerasia Case

In early 1945 the FBI arrested six individuals — the majority of them Jews — for stealing 1700 highly confidential documents from State Department files. This became known as the Amerasia Case. Those arrested were:

1. **Phillip Jaffe,** a Russian Jew who came to the U.S. in 1905. He was editor of the magazine, *Amerasia,* and was the former editor of the Communist paper, *Labor Defense.* He was convicted and fined.

2. **Andrew Roth**, a Brooklyn-born Jew with a lieutenant's commission in Naval Intelligence.

3. **Mark Gayn**, a writer, born in Manchuria of Russian-Jewish parents. His real Jewish name was Julius Ginsberg.

4. **John Stewart Service**, a Gentile and high-ranking State Department official who gave Jaffe much of the stolen material.

Also arrested were Emmanuel Larsen and Kate Mitchel, nationality unknown and believed to be Jewish.

Only two of those arrested were actually brought to court, with the trial of the ringleader, Philip Jaffe, one of the strangest on record. Late one Friday afternoon he was rushed into court without any previous notice or publicity, and before anyone knew what was going on he pleaded guilty, and was sentenced and fined.

By paying the comparatively insignificant sum of $1,500.00 he was relieved from the danger of any future prosecution. Roth paid a $500.00 fine.

John Stewart Service was not prosecuted, nor was he discharged from his high State Department position. The State Department, despite the constant prodding of Senator McCarthy of Wisconsin, refused to accept the evidence against him. Four times he was called before the State Department's "loyalty board," and four times he was cleared.

This in spite of an FBI wire recording of his transactions with Jaffe! Not until the fifth loyalty hearing was it decided that there were "reasonable" grounds for suspecting his loyalty. This came six years after the original arrests. Somewhere, hidden hands were pulling wires.

Alger Hiss Case

The second treason case also involved the State Department. This was the trial of Alger Hiss, protégé of Supreme Court Justice Felix Frankfurter. Hiss, like Acheson, was a student under Frankfurter at Harvard.

Hiss was one of the most influential men in the State Department. At Yalta he had been a Roosevelt advisor; at San Francisco he helped draw up the United Nations charter. And he was an intimate friend of the secretary of state.

Hiss, although a Communist, was not convicted for being one. He perjured himself by denying his Communist activities, however, and it was on this charge that he was tried and convicted.

Felix Frankfurter
A Supreme Court Justice who had numerous protégés become prominent Communists

The Alger Hiss trial was also a unique one. Dean Acheson's wife campaigned to raise funds for his defense. Acheson himself declared: "I'll not turn my back on Alger Hiss."

Felix Frankfurter, an Austrian-born Jew who became an Associate Justice of the United States Supreme Court, friend and adviser of President Franklin Roosevelt, actually took the witness stand to testify as a character witness for his protégé. In spite of all this, Hiss was convicted and sent to the penitentiary.

Frankfurter's role in this treasonable drama is worth commenting on. Frankfurter, along with Lehman and Henry Morgenthau, was one of the most influential Jews in America at that time. In addition to Acheson and Hiss, he was responsible for the placing of an estimated 200 of his "protégés" in high places. These include:

1. Nathan Witt, former general secretary of the National Labor Relations Board;

2. Lee Pressman, chief legal counsel for the CIO;

3. John Abt, key attorney for the SEC, AAA, and WPA.

All are Marxist Jews; Pressman later admitted being a card carrying party member.

It was never proven that Frankfurter was a Communist Party member, but an amazing number of his protégés, including Alger Hiss, have turned out to be.

Judith Coplin

One of the most publicized treason trials was that of the Jewess Judith Coplin in June of 1949. She was caught red-handed passing classified documents from Justice Department files to a Russian agent, who was employed by the United Nations.

She was convicted of espionage and sentenced to 15 years in prison. Later the conviction was set aside by the Supreme Court on the grounds that the FBI had arrested her improperly and without a warrant.

Eisler celebrated on a stamp issued by the Communist East German government.

Gerhart Eisler

The highest ranking Communist ever brought to trial in the U.S. was Gerhart Eisler.

Between 1935 and February of 1947 he was the secret boss of the Communist Party in the U.S. In those years he commuted regularly between the U.S. and Russia, using the aliases Berger, Brown, Edwards, and others.

His right hand man, and the second ranking cominform (Communist Information Bureau) agent in the U.S. was "J. Peters," author of the "Peters' Manual." His real name was Goldberger, and like Eisler was a Jew.

Several of Eisler's family have also been prominent in the party. A brother, Hans, has built an outstanding reputation as a writer of revolutionary songs. He was employed as a songwriter in Hollywood. A sister, Ruth Fischer, was a Communist agent for a number of years.

Newsweek described Eisler in its February 23, 1948, issue as the "number one Red agent". When his last legal appeal had failed he jumped bail and secretly boarded the Polish liner *MS Batory* bound for London in May 1949. He was discovered by the crew only after the ship was at sea.

Once in England, authorities allowed him to leave for the German Democratic Republic, where Eisler became chief of East German radio and a leading propaganda voice for the Communist government. After his death during an official visit to Armenia, several schools and streets in East Germany were named in his honor.

The American Politburo

One of the top news stories of 1949 was the trial of Eugene Dennis and the Convicted Eleven. Collectively, this group comprised the National Secretariat of the American Communist Party; in other words, the American Politburo.

The much publicized trial was held in the court of Judge Harold Medina. Perhaps no other single event has served better to demonstrate the Jewishness of the American Communist party. Here were the top party executives driven out into the open for everybody to see. How many were Jewish? At least six. They are:

1. Jacob Stachel, a Russian-born Jew.

2. John Gates (Jew name Israel Regenstreif), editor-in-chief of the Daily Worker and a former officer in the Communist Brigade in Spain.

3. Gilbert Green (Greenberg).

4. Gus Hall (real name, Arvo Mike Halberg. It was claimed he was Jewish, Finnish or Lithuanian, or all three).

5. Irving Potash, a Russian-born Jew.

6. Carl Winter (Jew name Philip Carl Weissberg).

The racial identity of Eugene Dennis (Waldron), Robert Thompson, and John Williamson has not been determined.

Ten of the eleven were sentenced to 5 years in federal prison and fined $1,000,000 each. Thompson received a three year sentence.

The Silvermaster Group

The Silvermaster spy ring operated primarily in the U.S. Department of the Treasury but also had contacts in the Army Air Force and in the White House.

It was under the control of Nathan Gregory Silvermaster, a Jew from Odessa, Russia, who worked as an economist with the United States War Production Board (WPB) during World War II, Silvermaster was the head of a large ring of Communist spies in the U.S. government. All but three were Jews:

1. Nathan Gregory Silvermaster, Chief Planning Technician, Procurement Division, United States Department of the Treasury; Chief Economist, War Assets Administration; Director of the Labor Division, Farm Security Administration; Board of Economic Warfare; Reconstruction Finance Corporation Department of Commerce.

Silvermaster.

2. Helen Silvermaster, wife.

3. Anatole Boris Volkov, stepson.

4. Solomon Adler aka Schlomer Adler, U.S. Department of the Treasury.

5.Chandler, Norman Bursler, United States Department of Justice Anti-Trust Division.

6. Frank Coe, Assistant Director, Division of Monetary Research, Treasury Department; Special Assistant to the U.S. Ambassador in London; Assistant to the Executive Director, Board of Economic Warfare; Assistant Administrator, Foreign Economic Administration.

7. **Lauchlin Currie**, Administrative Assistant to President Roosevelt; Deputy Administrator of Foreign Economic Administration; Special Representative to China.

8. **Bela Gold**, Assistant Head of Program Surveys, Bureau of Agricultural Economics, United States Department of Agriculture; Senate Subcommittee on War Mobilization; Office of Economic Programs in Foreign Economic Administration.

9. **Sonia Steinman Gold**, Division of Monetary Research U.S. Treasury Department; U.S. House of Representatives Select Committee on Interstate Migration; U.S. Bureau of Employment Security.

10. **Irving Kaplan**, Foreign Funds Control and Division of Monetary Research, United States Department of the Treasury Foreign Economic Administration; chief advisor to the Military Government of Germany.

11. **George Silverman**, civilian Chief Production Specialist, Material Division, Army Air Force Air Staff, War Department, Pentagon.

12. **William Henry Taylor**, Assistant Director of the Middle East Division of Monetary Research, United States Department of Treasury.

Perlo.

13. **William "Lud" Ullman**, delegate to United Nations Charter meeting and Bretton Woods conference; Division of Monetary Research, Department of Treasury; Material and Services Division, Air Corps Headquarters, Pentagon.

14. **Harry Dexter White (Weiss)**, Assistant Secretary of the Treasury; Head of the International Monetary Fund.

The Perlo Group

The Perlo group is the name given to a group of spies that

provided information which was given to Soviet intelligence agencies during World War II. It had sources on the War Production Board, the Senate La Follette Subcommittee on Civil Liberties; and in the United States Department of Treasury.

The entire group was exposed to the FBI by the defection of the Gentile Communist Elizabeth Bentley.

The group was named after the New York-born Jew Victor Perlo, a Marxist economist, government functionary, and a longtime member of the governing National Committee of the Communist Party USA. All but two of the Perlo Group were Jews:

1. **Victor Perlo,** Chief of the Aviation Section of the War Production Board; head of branch in Research Section, Office of Price Administration Department of Commerce; Division of Monetary Research Department of Treasury; Brookings Institution.

2. **Edward Fitzgerald,** War Production Board.

3. **Harold Glasser**, Deputy Director, Division of Monetary Research, United States Department of the Treasury; United Nations Relief and Rehabilitation Administration; War Production Board; Advisor on North African Affairs Committee; United States Treasury Representative to the Allied High Commission in Italy.

4. **Charles Kramer**, Senate Subcommittee on War Mobilization; Office of Price Administration; National Labor Relations Board; Senate Subcommittee on Wartime Health and Education; Agricultural Adjustment Administration; Senate Subcommittee on Civil Liberties; Senate Labor and Public Welfare Committee; Democratic National Committee.

5. **Harry Magdoff**, Statistical Division of War Production Board and Office of Emergency Management; Bureau of Research and Statistics, WTB; Tools Division, War Production Board; Bureau of Foreign and Domestic Commerce, United States Department of Commerce.

6. **Allen Rosenberg**, Board of Economic Warfare; Chief of the Economic Institution Staff, Foreign Economic Administration; Senate Subcommittee on Civil Liberties; Senate Committee on

Education and Labor; Railroad Retirement Board; Counsel to the Secretary of the National Labor Relations Board.

7. Donald Wheeler, Office of Strategic Services Research and Analysis division.

The Smith Act Trials

The Smith Act trials of Communist Party leaders were a series of trials held from 1949 to 1958 in which leaders of the CPUSA were accused of violating the Smith Act, a 1940 statute that set penalties for advocating the violent overthrow of the government. The prosecution argued that the CPUSA's policies promoted violent revolution.

The 1951 prosecution followed the conviction of the "Eugene Dennis crew" of 1948, and resulted in the bringing to trial of a "second-string politburo" scheduled to assume control of the party apparatus. This new politburo consisted of 21 members, 14 of whom were Jewish.

On June 21, 1951, the Justice Department indicted the entire group for conspiracy against the United States government. Most of the Jews were convicted, but a number had their convictions squashed after lengthy appeals which resulted in a Supreme Court decision appeals and a ruling that membership of the Communist Party was not illegal.

1. Israel Amter, 70, a longtime party stalwart. He organized

Bachrach

the "Friends of the Soviet Union in the U.S.", a front organization which numbers Albert Einstein among its prominent members. Amter was later severed from the case due to illness and died in 1954.

2. Marian Maxwell Abt Bachrach, 52, public relations director and secretary of the party's "Defense Commission." She was a Chicago Jewess who wrote several tracts including "Amnesty! Proposal of an amnesty program to release the members of the Communist Party imprisoned under the provisions of the Smith Act." Conviction overturned on appeal.

3. Isidore Begun, 47, a Russian-Jew who formerly taught in New York City's public schools. He was a party writer and lecturer. Conviction overturned on appeal.

4. Alexander Bittelman, 61, a Russian-Jew, and reputed to be "one of the foremost theoreticians and dialecticians of the party." A founding member of the CPUSA, Bittelman was a long-time editor of The Communist, the monthly magazine of that organization. Bittelman was active in the Jewish Socialist Federation of the Socialist Party of America from 1915. In 1919, was editor of the Yiddish-language newspaper, *Der Kampf* (The Struggle). At the convention in Chicago which founded the CPUSA, Bittelman was part of the 9-member committee which wrote the program for the organization. He was a member of the governing Central Executive Committee of the Jewish Communist Federation from 1919–1920 and was elected a member of the Central Executive Committee of the CPUSA and its Executive Council in 1920. In July 1922 he was sent to Moscow as a representative of the CPUSA. He was convicted and served a three-year prison term, being freed in 1957. He died in April 1982.

5. George B. Charney, 46, a Russian-Jew. He was the trade union secretary of the N.Y. state Communist party. He was convicted and left the CPUSA after the fall of Stalin.

6. Elizabeth Gurley Flynn, 60, chairman of the party's "Women's Commission." A Gentile, she was born in Concord, N. H.

7. Betty Gannett, 44, national education director for the party. She was a Polish-Jewess. Conviction overturned on appeal.

8. Simon W. Gerson, 41, chairman of the party's "N. Y. State Legislative Bureau." In the 1950s, Gerson served as executive editor of the *Daily Worker* and in the 1960s assumed the same post with its successor, the Daily World. He also edited the English pages of the Communist Yiddish newspaper, *Morning Freiheit*, under the pen name, Will Simon.

While serving as legislative head of the New York Communist Party, Gerson was convicted but later acquitted under judicial order that membership in the Communist Party does not violate any laws. In 1976, Gerson became campaign manager for the Communist presidential ticket of Gus Hall and Jarvis Tyner and continued to serve as chair of the Party's political action commission for many years. He died in 2004, still a member of the national committee of the CPUSA.

9. Victor Jeremy Jerome, 54, chairman of the party's cultural commission. He was a Polish-Jew. Sentenced to three years at Lewisburg Penitentiary which he served between 1954 and 1957.

10. Arnold Samuel Johnson, temporary chairman of District 5 Western Pennsylvania. Born in Seattle, he was a gentile.

11. Claudia Jones, 36, secretary of the party's "National Women's Commission."

12. Albert Francis Lannon, 43, party's "National Maritime Coordinator" and president of the "Communist Political Association of Maryland and Washington, D. C." Nationality unknown.

Jew Communists Simon Gerson (left) and Isadore Begun outside the Federal Court in New York where they faced charges of conspiracy to the violent overthrow of the U.S. government.

13. Jacob Mindel, 69, an old-time party wheel horse. He was a Russian Jew. Conviction overturned on appeal.

14. Petty Perres, 54, national secretary of the party's Negro Commission.

15. Alexander Trachtenberg, head of International Publishers, Inc. Conviction overturned on appeal. He died in 1966, but International Publishers, Inc. still exists, is still affiliated with the CPUSA and maintains an office in New York City.

16. Louis Weinstock, 48, member of the party's "National Review Commission." A Hungarian Jew, Weinstock was imprisoned in 1955 for 27 months and upon his release in 1957, he received a hero's welcome at a Communist Party rally at Carnegie Hall. He died in 1994.

17. William Wolf Weinstone, 53, a charter member of the party and a former secretary of its Michigan branch. A Russian-Jew, Weinstone served as Executive Secretary of the unified Communist Party of America, the forerunner of the CPUSA from October 15, 1921 to February 22, 1922 and was an important figure in the party's activities among the auto workers of Detroit during the 1930s.

When the Communist Party was forced underground in 1920, Weinstone served as Executive Secretary of the secret party organization from October 15, 1921 to February 22, 1922, under the pseudonym "G. Lewis."

18. Fred Fine, 37, secretary of the party's "Public Affairs Commission." He was a Chicago Jew.

19. James Edward Jackson, 36, the party's "Southern Regional Director."

20. William Norman Marron, 49, executive secretary of the N. Y. State Communist Party. He was a Russian-Jew.

21. Sidney Steinberg, the party's "Assistant National Labor Secretary." He was a Lithuanian Jew.

These "second-tier defendants" were prosecuted in three waves: 1951, 1954, and 1956 and their trials were held in over a dozen cities, including Los Angeles, New York, Pittsburgh, Philadelphia, Cleveland, Seattle, Baltimore, Seattle, Detroit, St. Louis, Denver, Boston, Puerto Rico, and New Haven.

The defendants also used Jewish lawyers (five defense attorneys at the 1949 trial had been jailed for contempt of court, and two of them, Abraham Isserman and Harry Sacher, were disbarred from further legal practice).

Six of the West Coast Communists arrested were Jews:

1. Henry Steinberg, a Polish-Jew;

2. Rose Chernin (Kusnitz), a Russian-Jewess;

3. Frank Carlson, a Russian Jew;

4. Ben Dobbs, a New York Jew;

5. Frank Spector, a Russian-Jew;

6. Al Richmond, a Russian Jew.

Of the remaining nine, Dorothy Healey, Philip Connelly, and Otto Fox are gentile; Carl Rude Lambert is believed to be Jewish, and the identity of the others has not been determined.

Of the five arrested in the east, four were Jewish. They are:

1. Roy Wood, 36, a gentile and chairman of the Washington D.C., Communist Party;

2. Regina Frankfeld, 41, a party organizer in Cleveland;

3. George Meyers, 38, a party organizer;

4. Philip Frankfield, 44, an organizer;

5. Rose Blumberg, of Brooklyn.

By May 1956, another 131 Communists were indicted, of whom 98 were convicted, nine acquitted, while juries brought no verdict in the other cases.

Three Gentiles: Vanderbilt Field, Whittaker Chambers and Elizabeth Bentley

Some attention should be devoted to three gentiles who have figured prominently in several of the treason trials. The three are: Whittaker Chambers, Elizabeth Bentley, and Vanderbilt Field.

None of the three has been indicted or convicted of a crime, and none were party members. In fact, two became enemies of Communism. Nevertheless they deserve a place in any description of the American Communist party.

Because he is a Gentile and because he has a famous name, Vanderbilt Field is perhaps better known to the American public than any other member of the Communist conspiracy. This prominence is not accidental.

Jewish propagandists, whether Communist or not, invariably seek to conceal the Jewish nature of Communism by giving lavish publicity to gentiles such as Field. As a point of fact, Field did not belong to the party, nor was he among those arrested when the top leadership was being rounded up.

Field was secretary of the "Civil Rights Congress Bail Fund," which was entrusted with raising bail for party members in trouble. He was married to the Jewess, Anita Cohen, former wife of the convicted spy, Raymond Boyer.

One of the principal witnesses against Alger Hiss at his trial was Whittaker Chambers, who like Hiss was a Gentile. Chambers—of pumpkin letter fame—was formerly an editor of the *Daily Worker* and later an associate editor of *Time* magazine. A product of Columbia university Chambers began his underground work for the party in 1932. He later renounced Communism and joined the Catholic Church. Like Elizabeth Bentley, he gave invaluable aid to the FBI and the un-American activities committee in their efforts to track down key members of the Communist party. Chambers was married to a Jewess.

Elizabeth Bentley, a product of Vassar, is another former Communist who has done much to expose the Communist underground. For several years she served as a courier for a Communist espionage network. She was the mistress of the Jew, Jacob Golos, a trusted Soviet agent and her immediate superior. He died of a heart attack on Thanksgiving day, 1943.

It was after his death that Elizabeth Bentley turned against the party and started co-operating with the FBI and the un-American Activities Committee.

Morris Cohen/Peter Kroger

Morris Cohen was born in New York in 1910 of a Jewish

Communist Jew spies Morris and Lorna Cohen.

Russian father and a Jewish Lithuanian mother. In 1937, Cohen joined the Mackenzie-Papineau Battalion and fought as a foreign national volunteer in the Spanish Civil War on the Communist side. He returned to the U.S. in 1938, having been recruited to work as a spy for Soviet foreign intelligence.

In 1941, Cohen married Lona Cohen who was an activist in the Communist Party USA and a courier for Manhattan Project physicist, Soviet spy and "devout Jew" Theodore Hall, (see below). Cohen was also instrumental in relaying atomic bomb secrets to the Kremlin in the late 1940s.

"Thanks to Cohen, designers of the Soviet atomic bomb got piles of technical documentation straight from the secret laboratory in Los Alamos," the Soviet newspaper *Komsomolskaya Pravda* announced.

Cohen was drafted into the American army during World War Two, but resumed his intelligence work for the Soviet Union after the war. He and his wife worked closely with the infamous KGB Colonel. Rudolph Abel (who was later arrested and swopped for U2 pilot Gary Powers). Abel was another of the tribe, "fluent in Yiddish."[203]

In 1950, the Cohens went to live in the Soviet Union, but by 1954 they had been redeployed back to Britain under the names Peter and Helen Kroger. They posed as antique book dealers, and worked with a Communist espionage group known as the Portland Spy Ring that had penetrated the Royal Navy.

The Cohens were arrested in 1961 by British Intelligence, and served eight years in prison before being exchanged for a British intelligence agent being held in the Soviet Union. The Cohens were awarded the Order of the Red Banner and the Order of Friendship of Nations for their espionage work.

After the dissolution of the Soviet Union, they also were given the title of Hero of the Russian Federation by the Yeltsin government. They lived out their lives on KGB pensions until their deaths — Lana in 1992 and Morris in 1995 — without ever revealing the name of the "American" scientist who helped pass vital information about the United States atomic bomb project.

The Mocase Espionage Case

The Mocase espionage case made news in 1957, when five Jews were charged with being Soviet agents over the previous decade and a half. The Jewish spies were:

1. Boris Morros, American Communist Party member, Paramount Studios producer, Soviet agent, and ultimately a FBI double agent.

2. Jack Soble, sentenced to 7 years, brother of Robert Soblen;

3. Myra Soble, sentenced to 5½ years;

4. Robert Soblen, sentenced to life for spying at Sandia Lab, etc., but escaped to Israel, then committed suicide;

5. Mark Zborowski; received a four-year prison sentence in 1962.

Fred Rose and the Canadian Spy Ring

Canada has also had spy trouble. There as in the U.S., the Soviet Embassy served as headquarters for espionage activity. There, as in the U.S. the principal characters in the plot were Jews.

In early 1945 an employee of the Russian embassy in Ottawa packed hundreds of secret Russian documents into a suitcase and turned himself over to Canadian authorities. As a result, a spy ring was uncovered which included—among others—a member of the Canadian Parliament and a professor at McGill university.

Leader of the ring, and by far its most important member, was Fred Rose (Rosenberg) the only Communist in the Canadian Parliament. Rose, a Polish Jew, was the ringleader, the recruiter, and the courier for the ring.

On June 16, 1946, Rose was sentenced to prison for his activities. The following year (Dec. 6. 1947) Dr. Raymond Boyer, a professor at McGill university was sentenced to two years in prison for having given Rose information concerning the secret explosive, RDX. Boyer was married to the Jewess, Anita Cohen. Arraigned with Rose were Samuel Gerson (of Russian-Jewish parentage), and another Jew, David Shugar. Other Jews implicated in the Fred Rose spy ring included: J. Isidor Gottheil, Israel Halperin, and Sam Carr (Cohen).

Rose was released from prison in 1951 and in 1953 he went to settle in Communist Poland. There he worked for many years as English-language editor of *Poland*, a magazine designed to spread Communist propaganda in the West. While living in Poland, his Canadian citizenship was revoked in 1957, and he died in 1983.

Chapter 27
Atomic Treason

ON February 3rd, 1949, British intelligence agents arrested a diminutive German-born atomic scientist by the name of Klaus Fuchs. He was accused, and subsequently convicted, of passing atomic secrets to the Russians.

At the beginning of World War II Fuchs had been interned by the British as an enemy alien. He was subsequently released from British custody and admitted to the U.S. at the personal instigation of Albert Einstein.

As a scientist for the Manhattan Project, he had access to America's innermost atomic secrets between 1942 and 1945, and he is said to be one of the few men familiar with the overall construction of the A-bomb.

He served nine years in prison in England, and upon his release, emigrated to Communist East Germany where he was received with acclaim and served in the Institute for Nuclear Research in Rossendorf, near Dresden.

The Communist Jew spy Harry Gold is arrested. As courier for the spy ring, he quite literally delivered the atom bomb secrets to the Soviet Union.

The Fuchs-Gold Spy Ring

Acting on information obtained from Fuchs, the FBI began a series of investigations which resulted in the eventual arrest of nine other members of the ring. Of these nine, all of whom were later convicted, eight were Jewish. Here is a brief description of the entire ring:

1. Harry Gold (Jew name Goldodnitsky). A chemist, he was born in Switzerland of Russian-Jewish parents. He studied at

Drexel University, University of Pennsylvania, and Xavier University He was a courier for the Soviet espionage chief, S. M. Semenov, who used the Amtorg Trading Corporation as a base of operations.

Gold traveled all over the country collecting information from ring members strategically placed in defense and atomic energy installations. Arrested in May of 1950, he pleaded guilty of espionage and received 30 years in prison.

He was paroled in May 1965, after serving just over half of his sentence. Gold died in 1972 and is buried in the Har Nebo Cemetery Jewish cemetery in the Oxford Circle neighborhood of Philadelphia, Pennsylvania.

2. David Greenglass, the son of a Russian-Jewish father and a Polish-Jewish mother, was one of those who passed atomic information to Gold. Between 1943 and 1946 he was employed at the vital atomic installation at Los Alamos, New Mexico. He also gave Julius Rosenberg vital information concerning the "fuse" used to detonate the A-bomb. Significantly, the chief of the Los Alamos project at this time was the Jew, Robert Oppenheimer.

Greenglass was sentenced to 15 years in prison, served 10 years. After his release in 1960, he took up residence in New York City under an assumed name, where he was still living in 2012. In 2008, when the government sought to release transcripts of the Rosenbergs' grand jury proceedings, Greenglass objected to the release of his testimony. As a result, U.S. District Judge Alvin Hellerstein declined to release the testimony of Greenglass and other witnesses who declined to consent, or who could not be confirmed as dead, or located to obtain consent.

3. Abraham Brothman was another member of the ring. He headed the engineering firm of A. Brothman and Associates, Long Island, N.Y.

He supplied Gold with secret data on aviation gasoline, turbo aircraft engines, and synthetic rubber. So valuable was his contribution that a Russian official allegedly told him his efforts were worth two brigades to Soviet Russia. He was arrested on July 27th, 1950, for conspiracy against the U.S. and was convicted. He served two years in jail and died in 1980.

4. Miriam Moskowitz was also caught in the spy net. A graduate of the City College of NYC, she was arrested August 17, 1950 as part of the same apparatus. She was employed by the War Manpower Commission between 1942-44, and was later associated with the Brothman firm. She was convicted of conspiracy to obstruct justice and served two years in prison. As of 2012, she was still living in New Jersey.

5. Sidney Weinbaum, a product of Russia's "Charkoff" Institute of Technology, came to the U.S. in 1922. His real name was Israel Weinbaum. He was connected with the radiation laboratory at CalTech for four years, during which time he furnished the Soviet government with atomic secrets. His attendance of "Communist club" meetings and association with known Communists during his days as a student were held against him as proof of his perjury. In September of 1950 however, at the Federal District Court in Los Angeles, Weinbaum was convicted of perjury and sentenced to four years imprisonment.

6. Alfred Dean Slack, was the only gentile besides Fuchs to be apprehended. While employed at the Oak Ridge establishment he gave atomic information to Harry Gold. He is also believed to

Communist Jew spies Ethel and Julius Rosenberg, executed in 1953 for conspiracy to commit espionage during a time of war.

have given Gold intelligence about a new secret explosive while employed at the Holtson Ordnance Works at Kingsport, Tennessee.

Julius and Ethel Rosenberg

Three other members of the Fuchs-Gold ring were also arrested. However, unlike the first seven—who pleaded guilty—they chose to plead "not guilty."

As a result two of them— Julius and Ethel Rosenberg— received the death penalty and the third, Morton Sobell, received 30 years in prison.

1. Julius Rosenberg was born of Russian-Jewish parents. An electrical engineer and a graduate of the City College of New York City, he was instrumental in recruiting Greenglass into the spy ring. While employed at the Emerson Electric Company he stole the plans for the highly secret proximity fuse which was used against American planes in Korea. He also aided in the theft of atomic secrets: His job was to digest information from Greenglass, and then pass it on to Soviet agents. He was sentenced to death.

2. Ethel Rosenberg, wife of Julius, was convicted of the same charges at the same time. She was a sister of David Greenglass. David Greenglass's wife acted as a courier between Greenglass and the Rosenbergs, but for some reason was not put on trial. Ethel Rosenberg was sentenced to death and along with her husband, Julius, was executed on June 19, 1953 in Sing Sing prison—the first execution of civilians for espionage in United States history.

3. Morton Sobell was also a graduate of the City College of

New York City. He and Rosenberg were classmates together. Sobell passed electronic data to Rosenberg, including radar secrets. He fled to Mexico to escape arrest, was returned by Mexican authorities. He was convicted for conspiracy to commit espionage and was sentenced to 30 years in prison.

Communist Jew spies Joel Barr and Al Sarant

Other Jews in the Rosenberg Spy Ring

The other Jews arrested in the "Rosenberg Spy Ring" were as follows:

1. Joel Barr, met Julius Rosenberg at City College of New York, then spied with him and Al Sarant at Army Signal Corps lab in New Jersey; escaped prosecution by fleeing to Soviet bloc in 1950. Died 2007.

2. Max Elitcher, longtime friend of Rosenberg and Sobell from their days at CCNY before testifying against them.

3. Vivian Glassman, fiancée of Joel Barr.

4. Ruth Greenglass, escaped prosecution in exchange for her husband's testimony against his sister and brother-in-law, the Rosenbergs.

5. William Perl, active in Young Communist League at CCNY, then met Al Sarant at Columbia University; served 5 years for perjury.

5. Morton Sobell, involved with Barr, Perl and Julius Rosenberg at CCNY; sentenced to 30 years at Alcatraz.

6. Al Sarant, who worked on secret military radar at the United States Army Signal Corps laboratories at Fort Monmouth, New Jersey. Alexandre Feklisov, one of the KGB case officers who handled the Rosenberg spy apparatus described Sarant and Joel Barr as among the most productive members of the group. Sarant was recruited as a Soviet espionage agent by Barr.

The Venona project transcript records showed that Sarant and Barr delivered 17 authentic drawings relating to the APQ-7, an advanced and secret airborne radar system developed jointly by the Massachusetts Institute of Technology and Western Electric for the United States military.

In 1946 Sarant moved to Ithaca, New York where he worked at Cornell University in the physics laboratories. Sarant's next door neighbor was Philip Morrison, a former Manhattan Project scientist and personal friend who joined the Communist Party of the United States in 1939.

Two days after Julius Rosenberg's arrest on 17 July 1950, the FBI interviewed Sarant but did not arrest him, although it possessed decrypted KGB cables that clearly identified Sarant as a member of the Rosenberg ring. Three days later Sarant ran away with a neighbor's wife and fled to Mexico, They ultimately ended up living in the Soviet Union, where Sarant developed the Soviet bloc's first automated anti-aircraft weapon. Their technology was quickly deployed and was in use, with some minor modifications, into the 1980s.

In 1956 Sarant and Barr moved to Leningrad where they were placed in charge of a military electronics research institute. They have been credited with being the founders of the Soviet microelectronics industry, in part because Sarant and Barr conceived of, designed and won political backing for the creation of Zelenograd, the Soviet Union's Silicon Valley.

In 1969 Sarant received a state honor for the UM-1, a computer that was widely used in Soviet industry. He led the team that created the Uzel, the first digital computer installed in a Soviet submarine. The Uzel was integrated into the Kilo class submarines and as of 2007 was still in use in the Russian, Iranian, Chinese and Indian navies. Sarant died in 1979.

7. Andrew Roth, Office of Naval Intelligence liaison officer with United States Department of State.

8. Saville "Sarry" Sax. He was born in New York City in 1924, where he was introduced to Soviet agents by his mother, Bluma Sax (1895–1986) who worked for a Communist front organization called Russian War Relief.

Sax went by the cover name "Oldster," and periodically traveled to New Mexico to collect information from Hall/Holtzberg (see below). The true depths of Sax's treason only became known when the Venona transcripts were released to the public. Sax ended up teaching "values clarification" in New York, openly boasting of his role in the atomic spy ring and the fact that he had never been prosecuted, until his head in 1980.

Behind the Atom Treason

The question which instantly comes to mind is: how were Communist agents able to ferret out our valuable atom secrets when so much secrecy surrounded the entire project? Why was it that Russia had the full secret of atom-bomb manufacture before the American people even knew of the existence of atomic weapons?

These questions are especially puzzling when we consider the fantastic security measures taken to safeguard the secret. Well-known author Bob Considine once described a fire which burned down a large building housing an atomic installation. Although firemen could have easily saved the building, plant guards would not permit them to enter the restricted area because they didn't have authorized passes!

Not even members of the U.S. Congress were let in on the secret. Yet the Soviet agents were able to penetrate this security wall as though it weren't there. How did they do it?

First it should be remembered that a central figure in the atomic program was Albert Einstein, a foreign-born Jew with a record of 16 red fronts to his credit. It has never been proven that Einstein was an actual party member, but there can be absolutely no doubt as to where his sympathies lay. Nor can there be any doubt regarding the red tint of his friends.

A list of those around Einstein reads like a *Who's Who of Communism*. It was Einstein who was instrumental in having Fuchs brought to the United States.

Furthermore, it should be remembered that the chief of the Los Alamos installation between 1943-45, when most of the secrets were stolen, was the Jew, Robert Oppenheimer. Robert Oppenheimer had a brother, Frank, who was also an atomic scientist and who was a card carrying Communist. Frank Oppenheimer belonged to "Professional Unit No. 122 of the Communist Party," while on the staff at Cal-Tech.

As mentioned above, the Communist Jewess spy Elizabeth Zarubina/ Lisa Rozensweig set up a ring of young Communist physicists around Oppenheimer. The detailed information which they obtained could only have come from Oppenheimer. It was long suspected that Oppenheimer — who freely admitted to being a Communist sympathizer — was one of the "senior scientists" at Los Alamos who passed on the real nuclear secrets to the posse of Jews around him.

Finally, it should be noted that shortly after V-J day Harry Truman turned America's atomic energy program over to a board consisting of five men, three of whom were Jews. Not only that, but the Jewish chairman, David Lilienthal, had belonged to at least two Communist fronts previous to his appointment. This was the background to the atom treason.

Scientist X

There have been other instances of Jewish treason in the US atomic energy program. Witness the case of the much publicized "Scientist X" who from 1943 on passed vital atomic information to Soviet spy and Communist Party activist "Steve Nelson."

"Scientist X" proved to be a Jew by the name of Joseph W. Weinberg of the University of Minnesota. This fact was discovered when the Federal Bureau of Investigation had placed a listening device in Nelson's residence in October 1942 and overheard a man referred to as "Joe", whom the FBI suspected of being Joe Weinberg, describing to Nelson the significance and technical outlines of the secret nuclear research done at Berkeley. Future spying for the Soviet Union was implied.

This news led the United States Government to push Weinberg, and fellow Jewish Communist David Bohm out of the program.

"Steve Nelson" was not the agent's real name: he was a Belgrade-born Jew by the name of Stjepan Mesaros. His first arrest was for fraudulently having entered America by using the passport of one Joseph Fleishinger, a cousin. In 1923, by now using the Americanized name "Steve Nelson," he joined the youth section of the American Communist Party, the Young Workers League.

He went on to join the adult Workers (Communist) Party in 1925. He met his wife, the Jewess Margaret Yaeger in the Pittsburgh office of the party where she worked as a typist. In 1928, the Nelsons moved to New York City where Mesaros studied Marxism at   the Jewish-run   New   York   Workers School and then took full-time employment with the Communist Party.

Mesaros and his wife were sent to Moscow in 1931, he visited the International Lenin School for two years. He was a courier for the Communist International (Comintern), delivering documents and funds to Germany, Switzerland and China. They returned to the United States in 1933, but Mesaros then went to Spain to fight in the Abraham Lincoln Brigade on the side of the Communists.

In August 1950, after a raid on the Pittsburgh Party Headquarters, Mesaros and two local party leaders were arrested and charged under the 1919 Pennsylvania Sedition Act for attempting to overthrow the state and federal government.

Mesaros initially received a 20-year prison sentence, $10,000 in fines and $13,000 in prosecution costs. He was jailed in Pittsburgh for seven months and then released on bail pending his appeal. In 1953 he and five others were indicted under the Federal Smith Act. This time the fine was 5 years and $10,000. All six were granted bail. In 1956 in Pennsylvania v. Nelson, the United States Supreme Court overturned the Pennsylvania Sedition Act, saying that the Federal Smith Act superseded this and all similar state laws. By 1957 the government dropped all charges against the defendants and Mesaros died in 1993.

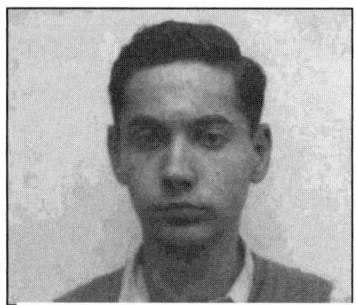

Hall-Holtzberg's photo-ID from Los Alamos.

Theodore Hall-Holtzberg and the Manhattan Project Spy Ring

The damage inflicted on America's nuclear secrets by the Rosenberg spy ring was significant. However, this paled in comparison to the pro-Communist treason committed by New York born-Jew Theodore Alvin Holtzberg (who changed his name to Theodore Hall).

After graduating from Harvard University at the age of 18, Holtzberg was hired to work on the secret U.S. atom bomb program, the Manhattan Project, where he was the youngest scientist at the Los Alamos base. While on a vacation in his hometown, New York, he entered the Soviet consulate and volunteered to pass information on the Manhattan Project to the Soviet government. The Soviets, were long accustomed to recruiting Jews for espionage work in the West. They made Holtzberg an offer, and soon he was passing vast quantities of information to the Soviet Union at the height of World War Two.

The information which Holtzberg passed on was of an extremely high level, and it is impossible that someone of his junior status could have had access to it. The only way he could have acquired the documents was if someone higher up was passing them to him. The Jew Oppenheimer was, as mentioned above, long suspected of being the senior scientist involved, although this has never been proven.

The full details of Holtzberg's treason was uncovered by means of a secret U.S. and U.K. intelligence project known as "Venona" which involved cryptanalysis of messages sent by intelligence agencies of the Soviet Union. It was not until 1995 that Venona project materials were released by the US government and the full extent of Holtzberg's treason became public knowledge.

According to the Venona decrypts, Holtzberg handed a detailed sketch of the "Fat Man" atomic bomb (used to bomb Japan) to a Soviet agent in New York, who transmitted the information to the NKVD in Moscow using a one-time pad cipher. Holtzberg's code-name was MLAD, a Slavic root meaning "young".

Until the release of the Venona decrypts, nearly all of the espionage regarding the Los Alamos nuclear weapons program was attributed to Klaus Fuchs. In reality, Holtzberg was questioned by the Federal Bureau of Investigation in March 1951 but wasn't charged. Alan H. Belmont, the number-three man in the FBI, decided that information coming out of the Venona project would be inadmissible in court, as hearsay evidence, and so its value in the case was not worth compromising the program.

Holtzberg was thus never prosecuted, and died in Britain in 1999 after confessing that he had had contact with the Soviets during his Manhattan Project time.

Chapter 28
The Tribal Shift: Spying Now for Israel

As Russians began the long process of taking back their government and deposing their Jewish elite, those actions coincided with a profound shift from Communism to Zionism on the part of Jews all over the world.

The 2009 arrest of two senior officials at the American Israel Public Affairs Committee (AIPAC), the most powerful pro-Israel lobby in Washington D.C., on spying charges for Israel, refocused attention on the reality of Israeli spying operations against America and the "dual loyalty" (actually the single loyalty) psychology upon which the Israeli state can rely from Jews all over the world.

Rosen and Weissman, AIPAC agents arrested on charges of spying for Israel. Despite their "mole," the Gentile Franklin, being found guilty and sentenced to jail, the two Jews had all charges against them mysteriously dismissed.

Steve Rosen, Keith Weissman and the AIPAC Case

The arrest of gentile Lawrence A. Franklin (an analyst of Iranian affairs who worked in the Pentagon) in 2004, revealed a network of Israeli spy networks that involved the passing of "classified information from the mole, to the men at AIPAC, and on to the Israelis," according to a CBS report.[204]

CBS sources said Franklin "described as a trusted analyst at the Pentagon," turned over a presidential directive on U.S. policy toward Iran while it was, "in the draft phase when U.S. policy-makers were still debating the policy." This put the Israelis, according to one source, "inside the decision-making loop" so they could "try to influence the outcome."

Franklin worked in the Pentagon Office of Special Plans, run by the Jew Richard Perle, who was caught giving classified information to Israel back in 1970 (see below). Perle was insisting that Iraq had "weapons of mass destruction" which required the United States to invade Iraq. There were no WMDs, of course, and Perle has blamed the "bad intelligence." Interestingly, much of the intelligence was generously provided by Israel.

Franklin pled guilty to several espionage-related charges and was sentenced in January 2006 to nearly 13 years of prison, which was "miraculously" reduced to ten months house arrest.

Franklin passed information to AIPAC policy director Steven Rosen and AIPAC senior Iran analyst Keith Weissman who were both indicted for illegally conspiring to gather and disclose classified national security information to Israel. The charges against those two Jews were mysteriously dropped.

In an interview with the Jewish *Forward* newspaper of July 10, 2009, Franklin described his interrogation as follows:

I was asked about every Jew I knew in OSD [Office of the Secretary of Defense], and that bothered me," Franklin said. His superiors at the time were both Jewish: Paul Wolfowitz, deputy secretary of defense, and Douglas Feith, undersecretary of defense for policy, whom Franklin believes was a target of the investigation. "One agent asked me, 'How can a Bronx Irish Catholic get mixed up with...' and I finished the phrase for him: 'with these Jews.'" Franklin answered, "Christ was Jewish, too, and all the apostles." "Later I felt dirty," he added.

The Franklin case was just one of many such incidents involving American Jews spying for Israel against America. Why would Israel, America's supposed "best ally" in the Middle East, want to launch aggressive spying actions against its "friend"?

The Franklin case was not the only such event, as the list below shows:

Jonathan Pollard.: The Most Damaging
Jewish Spy in American History

Jonathan Pollard is an American Jew born in Galveston Texas, who established a career as an intelligence analyst for the US Navy. From his position of trust within the US Navy, Pollard delivered over 800,000 pages of classified documents to Israel for which he was well paid. Included in those documents were the names of over 150 US agents in Europe and Mideast, who were traded for unknown compensation to Israel and eventually "eliminated."

Some of the more serious damage done by Pollard was to steal classified documents relating to the US Nuclear Deterrent relative to the USSR and send them to Israel. According to sources in the US State Department, Israel then turned around and traded those stolen nuclear secrets to the USSR in exchange for increased emigration quotas from the USSR to Israel.

Other information that found its way from the US to Israel to the USSR resulted in the loss of American agents operating inside Eastern Europe.

The most damaging Jew spy against America in its history Jonathon Pollard was sentenced to life imprisonment in 1987 for espionage. Right, a surveillance video from 1985 shows him stealing documents. While in prison, Pollard renounced his United States citizenship and became an Israeli national.

The official U.S. government response to an application which opposed a reduced sentence for Pollard, described the damage done to the United States as follows: "[It is] difficult to conceive of a greater harm to national security than that caused by... Pollard's treasonous behavior." The United States' nuclear deterrent cost an estimated five trillion taxpayer dollars during the 50s and 60s to build and maintain, and less than $100,000 for Pollard to undermine. Israel waited thirteen years to admit Pollard had been spying for them, and now lobbies for his release, having granted him Israeli citizenship.

1950s Jewish Spies for Israel against America

1950: John Davitt, former chief of the Justice Department's internal security section notes that the Israeli intelligence service is the second most active in the United States after the Soviets.

1954: A hidden microphone planted by the Israelis is discovered in the Office of the US Ambassador in Tel Aviv.

1956: Telephone taps are found connected to two telephones in the residence of the US military attaché in Tel Aviv.

The Lavon Affair

1954: "The Lavon Affair". Israeli agents recruit Egyptian citizens of Jewish descent to bomb Western targets in Egypt, and plant evidence to frame Arabs, in an attempt to incite an American war against Egypt. The early arrest of the Jewish agents exposed the plot, and the Israeli defense minister Pinchas Lavon resigned to try and avoid Israel being blamed. The plan was sanctioned at the highest levels of the Israeli government and had the personal approval of David Ben-Gurion.

Israel Steals Enriched Uranium from America

1965: Israel illegally obtains enriched uranium from NUMEC Corporation.[205]

The USS Liberty: A Terrorist Attack

1967: Israel attacks the *USS Liberty*, an intelligence gathering vessel flying a US flag, killing 34 and wounding 171 crew members. See *Assault on the Liberty*, by James M. Ennes, Jr. (Random House). In 2004, Captain Ward Boston, Senior Legal

Counsel for the Navy's Court of Inquiry into the attack swears under oath that President Lyndon Johnson ordered the investigation to conclude accident, even though the evidence indicates the attack was deliberate.

Given the use by Israel of unmarked boats and planes, and the machine-gunning of USS Liberty's lifeboats, the most likely explanation is that USS Liberty was to be sunk with all hands, with evidence left to frame Egypt for the sinking. This would have dragged the US into the war on Israel's side.

Both the U.S. Secretary of State and the Chairman of the Joint Chiefs of Staff were privy to classified information that shows Israel intentionally attacked the USS Liberty. Only the courage of the Liberty's captain enabled the ship to survive and thus foiled the Israeli plan.

1970s Jewish Spies for Israel against America

1970: While working for Senator Henry Jackson, the Israeli partisan, called "super Jew" by some, Richard Perle is caught by the FBI giving classified information to Israel. Nothing is done.

1978: Stephen Bryen, then a Senate Foreign Relations Committee staffer, is overheard in a DC hotel offering confidential documents to top Israeli military officials. Bryen obtains a lawyer, Nathan Lewin, and the case heads for the grand jury, but is mysteriously dropped. Bryen later goes to work for Richard Perle.

1979: Shin Bet [the Israeli internal security agency] tries to penetrate the US Consulate General in Jerusalem through a "Honey Trap", using a clerical employee who was having an affair with a Jerusalem girl.

1980s Jewish Spies for Israel against America

1985: The *New York Times* reports the FBI is aware of at least a dozen incidents in which American officials transferred classified information to the Israelis, quoting [former Assistant Director of the F.B.I.] Mr. [Raymond] Wannal. The Justice Department does not prosecute.

1985: Richard Smyth, the owner of MILCO, is indicted on charges of smuggling nuclear timing devices to Israel.[206]

1987: April 24 *Wall Street Journal* headline: "Role of Israel in Iran-Contra Scandal Won't be Explored in Detail by Panels."

1990s Jewish Spies for Israel against America

1992: The *Wall Street Journal* reports that Israeli agents tried to steal Recon Optical Inc.'s top-secret airborne spy-camera system.

1992: Stephen Bryen, caught offering confidential documents to Israel in 1978, is serving on board of the pro-Israeli Jewish Institute for National Security Affairs while continuing as a paid consultant — with security clearance — on exports of sensitive US technology.

1992: "The Samson Option," by Seymour M. Hersh reports, "Illicitly obtained intelligence was flying so voluminously from LAKAM into Israeli intelligence that a special code name, JUMBO, was added to the security markings already on the documents. There were strict orders, Ari Ben-Menashe recalled: "Anything marked JUMBO was not supposed to be discussed with your American counterparts."

1993: The Jewish Supremacist Anti-Defamation League (ADL) is caught operating a massive spying operation on critics of Israel, Arab-Americans, the San Francisco Labor Council, ILWU Local 10, Oakland Educational Association, NAACP, Irish Northern Aid, International Indian Treaty Council, the Asian Law Caucus and the San Francisco police. Data collected was sent to Israel and in some cases to South Africa. Pressure from Jewish organizations forces the city to drop the criminal case, but the ADL settles a civil lawsuit for an undisclosed sum of cash.

1995: The Defense Investigative Service circulates a memo warning US military contractors that "Israel aggressively collects [US] military and industrial technology." The report stated that Israel obtains information using "ethnic targeting, financial aggrandizement, and identification and exploitation of individual frailties" of US citizens.

1996: A General Accounting Office report "Defense Industrial Security: Weaknesses in US Security Arrangements With Foreign-Owned Defense Contractors" found that according to intelligence sources "Country A" (identified by intelligence sources as Israel, *Washington Times,* 2/22/96) "conducts the most aggressive espionage operation against the United States of any US ally."

The Jerusalem Post (8/30/96) quoted the report: "Classified military information and sensitive military technologies are high-priority targets for the intelligence agencies of this country."

The report described "An espionage operation run by the intelligence organization responsible for collecting scientific and technologic information for [Israel] paid a US government employee to obtain US classified military intelligence documents."

The Washington Report on Middle East Affairs (Shawn L. Twing, April 1996) noted that this was "a reference to the 1985 arrest of Jonathan Pollard, a civilian US naval intelligence analyst who provided Israel's LAKAM [Office of Special Tasks] espionage agency an estimated 800,000 pages of classified US intelligence information." The GAO report also noted that "Several citizens of [Israel] were caught in the United States stealing sensitive technology used in manufacturing artillery gun tubes."

1996: An Office of Naval Intelligence document, "Worldwide Challenges to Naval Strike Warfare" reported that "US technology has been acquired [by China] through Israel in the form of the Lavi fighter and possibly SAM [surface-to-air] missile technology." *Jane's Defense Weekly* (2/28/96) noted that "until now, the intelligence community has not openly confirmed the transfer of US technology [via Israel] to China." The report noted that this "represents a dramatic step forward for Chinese military aviation." (*Flight International*, 3/13/96)

1997: An Army mechanical engineer, David A. Tenenbaum, "inadvertently" gives classified military information on missile systems and armored vehicles to Israeli officials (*New York Times*, 2/20/97).

1997: *The Washington Post* reports US intelligence has intercepted a conversation in which two Israeli officials had discussed the possibility of getting a confidential letter that then-Secretary of State Warren Christopher had written to Palestinian leader Yasir Arafat. One of the Israelis, identified only as "Dov", had commented that they may get the letter from "Mega", the code name for Israel's top agent inside the United States.

1997: US ambassador to Israel, Martin Indyk, complains privately to the Israeli government about heavy-handed surveillance by Israeli intelligence agents.

1997: Israeli agents place a tap on Monica Lewinsky's phone at the Watergate and record phone sex sessions between her and President Bill Clinton. The Ken Starr report confirms that Clinton warned Lewinsky their conversations were being taped and ended the affair. At the same time, the FBI's hunt for "Mega" is called off.

Mass Arrests of Israeli Spies after 9-11

An investigation by the FBI in early 2000 led to the exposure of the largest foreign spy ring ever uncovered inside the United States - operated by Israel. Half of the suspected spies had been arrested before the events of September 11, 2001.

On 9-11, 5 Israelis were arrested shortly after the World Trade Towers in New York City collapsed. Supposedly employed by Urban Moving Systems, the Israelis were found with multiple passports and a lot of cash. At least two are positively identified as Mossad.

Witnesses testified that the Jews were seen at Liberty Park at the time of the first impact, and had set up a camera to film the events, which strongly suggested that they had foreknowledge of what was to come. They were interrogated, and then eventually sent back to Israel. The owner of the moving company used as a cover by the Mossad agents, later abandoned his "business" and fled to Israel.

The United States Government then classified all of the evidence related to the Israeli agents and their connections to 9-11. All of this was reported to the public via a four part story on *Fox News* by Carl Cameron. Pressure from Jewish groups, primarily AIPAC, forced Fox News to remove the story from their website.

Two hours prior to the 9-11 attacks, Odigo, an Israeli company with offices just a few blocks from the World Trade Center, received an advance warning via the internet. The manager of the New York Office provided the FBI with the IP address of the sender of the message, but nothing public was ever announced of an investigation, even if one did take place.

2000s Jewish Treason for Israel Against America

2001: It is discovered that US drug agents' communications have been penetrated. Suspicion falls on two companies, AMDOCS and Comverse Infosys, both owned by Israelis. AMDOCS generates billing data for most US phone companies and is able to provide detailed logs of who is talking to whom. Comverse Infosys builds the tapping equipment used by law enforcement to eavesdrop on all American telephone calls, but suspicion forms that Comverse, which gets half of its research and development budget from the Israeli government, has built a back door into the system that is being exploited by Israeli intelligence and that the information gleaned on US drug interdiction efforts is finding its way to drug smugglers.

2001: The FBI is investigating five Israeli moving companies as possible fronts for Israeli intelligence.

2001: The Jewish Defense League's Irv Rubin arrested for planning to bomb a US Congressman. He is killed in jail before he can be brought to trial.

2002: The DEA issues a report that Israeli spies, posing as art students, have been trying to penetrate US government offices.

2002: Police near the Whidbey Island Naval Air Station in southern Washington State stop a suspicious truck and detain two Israelis, one of whom is illegally in the United States. The two men were driving at high speed in a Ryder rental truck, which they claimed had been used to "deliver furniture." The next day, police discovered traces of TNT and RDX military-grade plastic explosives inside the passenger cabin and on the steering wheel of the vehicle. The FBI then announces that the tests that showed explosives were "false positives" by cigarette smoke, a claim test experts say is ridiculous. Based on an alibi provided by a woman, the case is closed and the Israelis are handed over to INS to be sent back to Israel. One week later, the woman who provided the alibi vanishes.[207]

2003: The Police Chief of Cloudcroft stops a truck speeding through a school zone. The drivers turn out to be Israelis with expired passports. Claiming to be movers, the truck contains junk furniture and several boxes. The Israelis are handed over to immigration. The contents of the boxers are not revealed to the public.[208]

Kadish

2004: Police near the Nuclear Fuel Services plant in Tennessee stop a truck after a three mile chase, during which the driver throws a bottle containing a strange liquid from the cab. The drivers turn out to be Israelis using fake identity documents. The FBI refuses to investigate and the Israelis are released.[209]

2004: Two Israelis try to enter Kings Bay Naval Submarine Base, home to eight Trident submarines. The truck tests positive for explosives.

2008: Ben-Ami Kadish, a former U.S. Army mechanical engineer, pled guilty to being an "unregistered agent for Israel," and admitted to disclosing classified U.S. documents to Israel in the 1980s.

Kadish had furnished classified American secrets to Yosef Yagur, the same Israeli agent who had received secret documents from Jonathan Pollard. In his judgment, Judge William H. Pauley III asked "Why it took the government 23 years to charge Mr. Kadish is shrouded in mystery." Kadish was fined (!) $50,000 and died a free man in 2012.

Jewish Extremist Pressure Groups I: AIPAC

The American Israel Public Affairs Committee (AIPAC) is the most public Jewish lobby in Washington D.C.. It has become obligatory for any would-be congressman, senator or even president to have to appear before the organization in public and avow their support to Israel. AIPAC actively organizes against any congressman who deviates from a pro-Israel line, and uses Jewish money and media control to subvert any election campaigns of candidates who oppose Zionist policies or Jewish control of the U.S. government. In this way, AIPAC has been able to ensure that all American governments and presidents are slavish supporters of Israel, even when that state acts in the most racist or extremist manner with regard to the Palestinians or African asylum seekers.

AIPAC is completely Jewish, and, as mentioned above, has been caught managing Jewish spy rings in the American government in the ""Lawrence Franklin" spy case. The indictment of the two AIPAC Jews, Steve Rosen and Keith Weissman, filed in Alexandria, Virginia on August 4, 2005, said that: "Between in or about April 1999 and continuing until on or about August 27, 2004, in the Eastern District of Virginia and elsewhere, defendants Lawrence Anthony Franklin, Steven J. Rosen, and Keith Weissman did unlawfully, knowingly and willfully conspire, confederate and agree together and with others, known and unknown to the Grand Jury, to commit the following offenses against the United States:

1) having lawful possession of, access to, and control over information relating to the national defense, did willfully communicate, deliver and transmit that information directly and

indirectly to a person or persons not entitled to receive it, having reason to believe that said information could be used to the injury of the United States and to the advantage of any foreign nation, a violation of Title 18, United States Code, Section 793(d); and

2) having unauthorized possession of, access to, and control over information relating to the national defense, did willfully communicate, deliver and transmit that information directly and indirectly to a person or persons not entitled to receive it, having reason to believe that said information could be used to the injury of the United States and to the advantage of any foreign nation, a violation of Title 18, United States Code, Section 793(e)."

Franklin was convicted while the two AIPAC Jews had the charges withdrawn against them because, Dana Boente, acting U.S. Attorney for the Eastern District of Virginia, announced in a statement that because of "the inevitable disclosure of classified information that would occur at any trial in this matter, we have asked the court to dismiss the indictment."

In other words, the charges were withdrawn because even more embarrassing – for Israel and AIPAC – information would have had to be disclosed to the public.

Jewish Extremist Pressure Groups II: The ADL

The Anti-Defamation League (ADL) was founded in October 1913 by the Jew Sigmund Livingston in honor of a Jewish murderer by the name of Leo Frank, who was convicted of murdering a young Gentile girl in Marietta, Georgia.

Having been created to defend the "honor" of a Jew murderer, the ADL then hypocritically went on to claim to oppose "all injustices" but remains a strong supporter of the Zionist state of Israel, which is without doubt one of the most prominent serial humans rights offenders in the modern world.

The ADL has become so slavishly pro-Israel that even well-known leftist activist Noam Chomsky has said that the organization has "lost entirely its focus on civil rights issues to become solely an advocate for Israeli policy" and that it "casts all left-wing opposition to Israeli interests as antisemitism."[210] The ADL has become little more than another underground Jewish spy network in the U.S., keeping track of and files on all those who it considers to be its enemies (all in breach of data protection legislation). This "information" is then passed on to other Jewish interest groups for their possible action.

Not all of the ADL's interventions have been successful. In 2001, a jury in a federal court case in Denver, Colorado, ordered the ADL to pay $10.5 million in damages to a local couple, William and Dorothy Quigley, whom it had publicly named as "vicious anti-Semites." In their lawsuit against the ADL and its local director, the Quigleys charged not only that the ADL had defamed them, but that the Jewish group was supportive of the illegal invasion of their privacy through its use of the improperly recorded telephone conversations. The payout was equivalent to a quarter of the ADL's annual budget.

In 1984, a Jew working undercover for the ADL, James Mitchell Rosenberg, was exposed as an agent provocateur, posing as a racist right wing paramilitary extremist. He appeared in this role as part of a TV documentary entitled "Armies of the Right" which premiered in 1981. Rosenberg was arrested that same year in New York for carrying an unregistered firearm in public view. In 1984, ADL fact-finding director Irwin Suall identified Rosenberg as an ADL operative in a court deposition.

Jewish Pressure Groups III:
The Southern Poverty Law Center

The Southern Poverty Law Center (SPLC), which masquerades as a "civil rights" organization, is in fact just another Jewish front organization. It was founded in Montgomery, Alabama, by Morris Dees and Joseph J. Levin–the former accused by his ex-wife in court of child molestation and extended sexual deviancy, and the latter a Jew.

In 2012, the SPLC president was the Jew J. Richard Cohen, and its main media representative was the Jew Mark Potok. The SPLC's other main "writers" are the Jewesses Heidi Beirich and Sonia Scherr, (the latter also uses the Gentile-sounding name "Claire Rollins"). The Jew journalist Alexander Zaitchik is also a former SPLC staff member and infrequent contributor. The majority of its "board of directors" is Jewish.

In 1994, the *Montgomery Advertiser* won a journalism award for a series of incisive and penetrating investigative articles exposing the unethical fundraising practices of the SPLC. A series of investigations by that newspaper revealed that with their made-up scare stories about "Ku Klux Klans" and other white demons about to plunge America into a race war, the SPLC has managed to rake in millions - far more than what they spend.

Here is what a former staffer said on this topic to the *Montgomery Advertiser*: "they're drowning in their own affluence," said Pamela Summers, a former SPLC legal fellow. "What they are doing in the legal department is not done for the best interest of everybody [but] is done as though the sole, overriding goal is to make money. I think people associate the SPLC with going to court. And that's why they get the money. And they don't go to court. There have only been a handful of court cases over the years, many of which remain unresolved."

The *Montgomery Advertiser* also interviewed former SPLC associate Courtney Mullin. Mullin declared that "they pretend to be on a side that has moral underpinnings (but) they do damage by their dishonesty. I mean the little old lady from North Carolina sends her $5 thinking that she's going to help, then it's just going to line the coffers of the Southern Poverty Law Center so they can have the most beautiful building in the world and have all this money in the bank. That's wrong."

Chapter 29
Communism in Hollywood

NO discussion of Communism would be complete without giving some attention to the Hollywood scene. Shortly after 1945, a number of investigations by the House Committee on Un-American Activities, and by California's "Tenney Committee," unearthed a veritable hotbed of Communism in the movie colony.

The Hollywood Ten

In 1950 the ten leading film writers of the Hollywood Film Colony, nine of whom are known Jews, were convicted for contempt of Congress and sentenced to prison. All had appeared before the House Committee on Un-American Activities in 1947, and all had refused to testify.

The Film Colony went all-out in its support. A group of film notables, including Lauren Bacall and Humphrey Bogart, chartered a special plane to Washington. Jewish publications everywhere raised the cry that the Un-American Activities Committee was victimizing a group of artists who, at the worst, were liberally inclined.

As events proved, the committee knew exactly what it was doing. Six of the "Hollywood Ten" were Communist Party members. The other four had flagrantly pro-Communist records.

Furthermore, as screen writers they were in a particularly advantageous position to insert subtle bits of red propaganda into pictures. Given here is a roll-call of the Hollywood Ten:

1. Alvah Bessie, a screenwriter. A Communist party member, he wrote for the party publication, *New Masses.*

2. Herbert Biberman, received a six month sentence and a $1,000.00 fine. A party member, he was the Yiddish husband of academy award winning actress Gale Sondergaard.

3. Lester Cole, also a party member.

4. Edward Dmytryk, who belonged to 15 fronts. Fined and sentenced.

5. Ring Lardner, Jr., a script writer and party member.

6. John Howard Lawson, a Broadway playwright and screen writer. Wrote "Professional," "Success Story." A party member.

7. Albert Maltz, wrote "Merry-go-Round," "Snake Pit." A party member.

8. Sam Ornitz, a screen writer.

9. Adrian Scott, nationality not verified.

10. Dalton Trumbo, a party member.

We have already made some mention of the convicted "Hollywood Ten" who received sentences for contempt of congress. There are hundreds of other high placed Jews with pro-Communist records in the film colony, including millionaire actors, directors, producers, writers, and executives.

The question immediately arises as to why so many of these wealthy and privileged Jews embrace Communism. The answer is, of course, that Communism is not an economic movement, but a racial movement. Communism cannot be understood, or dealt with, on any other basis.

An Easy Target

There is a question in the minds of many as to how and why the Communists took over Hollywood. To begin with, the

Hollywood motion picture industry is the most important vehicle of propaganda in the whole world today.

Hollywood exerts a greater influence over the America and the entire world than all other propaganda mediums combined. It was therefore a prime target for Communist infiltration. And since the film industry is overwhelmingly Jewish, Communist agents encountered a minimum of difficulty in setting up shop. To give the reader some idea as to the extent of the Jewish control over Hollywood here are the facts from Jewish writers working for Jewish run media organizations.

Los Angeles Times | OPINION

OPINION

How Jewish is Hollywood?

A poll finds more Americans disagree with the statement that 'Jews control Hollywood.' But here's one Jew who doesn't.

By Joel Stein
December 19, 2008

I have never been so upset by a poll in my life. Only 22% of Americans now believe "the movie and television industries are pretty much run by Jews," down from nearly 50% in 1964. The Anti-Defamation League, which released the poll results last month, sees in these numbers a victory against stereotyping. Actually, it just shows how dumb America has gotten. Jews totally run Hollywood.

How deeply Jewish is Hollywood? When the studio chiefs took out a full-page ad in the Los Angeles Times a few weeks ago to demand that the Screen Actors Guild settle its contract, the open letter was signed by: News Corp. President Peter Chernin (Jewish), Paramount Pictures Chairman Brad Grey (Jewish), Walt Disney Co. Chief Executive Robert Iger (Jewish), Sony Pictures Chairman Michael Lynton (surprise, Dutch Jew), Warner Bros. Chairman Barry Meyer (Jewish), CBS Corp. Chief Executive Leslie Moonves (so Jewish his great uncle was the first prime minister of Israel), MGM Chairman Harry Sloan (Jewish) and NBC Universal Chief Executive Jeff Zucker (mega-Jewish). If either of the Weinstein brothers had signed, this group would have not only the power to shut down all film production but to form a *minyan* with enough Fiji water on hand to fill a *mikvah*.

Recent columns

The person they were yelling at in that ad was SAG President Alan Rosenberg (take a guess). The scathing rebuttal to the ad was written by entertainment super-agent Ari Emanuel (Jew with Israeli parents) on the Huffington Post, which is owned by Arianna Huffington (not Jewish and *has never worked in Hollywood*.)

"Joel Stein -*LA Times* - Jews Run Hollywood"

The Hollywood film industry is almost exclusively a Jewish enterprise. According to an article in the *LA Times* of December 19, 2008, by Jewish journalist *Joel Stein*, "Jews totally run Hollywood."[211]

In a candid admission of Jewish power, Stein wrote:

"How deeply Jewish is Hollywood? When the studio chiefs took out a full-page ad in the *Los Angeles Times* a few weeks ago to demand that the Screen Actors Guild settle its contract, the open letter was signed by: News Corp. President Peter Chernin (Jewish), Paramount Pictures Chairman Brad Grey (Jewish), Walt Disney Co. Chief Executive Robert Iger (Jewish), Sony Pictures Chairman Michael Lynton (surprise, Dutch Jew), Warner Bros. Chairman Barry Meyer (Jewish), CBS Corp. Chief Executive Leslie Moonves (so Jewish his great uncle was the first prime minister of Israel), MGM Chairman Harry Sloan (Jewish) and NBC Universal Chief Executive Jeff Zucker (mega-Jewish). If either of the Weinstein brothers had signed, this group would have not only the power to shut down all film production but to form a minyan with enough Fiji water on hand to fill a mikvah.

The person they were yelling at in that ad was SAG President Allen Rosenberg (take a guess). The scathing rebuttal to the ad was written by entertainment super-agent Ari Emanuel (Jew with Israeli parents).

The Jews are so dominant, I had to scour the trades to come up with six Gentiles in high positions at entertainment companies. When I called them to talk about their incredible advancement, five of them refused to talk to me, apparently out of fear of insulting Jews. The sixth, AMC President Charlie Collier, turned out to be Jewish.

As a proud Jew, I want America to know about our accomplishment. Yes, we control Hollywood. Without us, you'd be flipping between "The 700 Club" and "Davey and Goliath" on TV all day.

So I've taken it upon myself to re-convince America that Jews run Hollywood by launching a public relations campaign, because that's what we do best. I'm weighing several slogans, including: "Hollywood: More Jewish than ever!"; "Hollywood: From the people who brought you the Bible"; and "Hollywood: If you enjoy TV and movies, then you probably like Jews after all."

I called ADL Chairman Abe Foxman, who was in Santiago, Chile, where, he told me to my dismay, he was not hunting Nazis. He dismissed my whole proposition, saying that the number of people who think Jews run Hollywood is still too high. The ADL poll, he pointed out, showed that 59% of Americans think Hollywood execs "do not share the religious and moral values of most Americans," and 43% think the entertainment industry is waging an organized campaign to "weaken the influence of religious values in this country."

That's a sinister canard, Foxman said. "It means they think Jews meet at Canter's Deli on Friday mornings to decide what's best for the Jews." Foxman's argument made me rethink: I have to eat at Canter's more often.

"That's a very dangerous phrase, 'Jews control Hollywood.' What is true is that there are a lot of Jews in Hollywood," he said. Instead of "control," Foxman would prefer people say that many executives in the industry "happen to be Jewish," as in "all eight major film studios are run by men who happen to be Jewish."

But Foxman said he is proud of the accomplishments of American Jews. "I think Jews are disproportionately represented in the creative industry. They're disproportionate as lawyers and probably medicine here as well," he said. He argues that this does not mean that Jews make pro-Jewish movies any more than they do pro-Jewish surgery. Though other countries, I've noticed, aren't so big on circumcision.

I appreciate Foxman's concerns. And maybe my life spent in a New Jersey-New York/Bay Area-L.A. pro-Semitic cocoon has left me naive. But I don't care if Americans think we're running the news media, Hollywood, Wall Street or the government. I just care that we get to keep running them."[212] ["How Jewish is Hollywood?" By Joel Stein. *Los Angeles Times*, December 19, 2008].

Hollywoodism: Boasting of a Jewish Takeover

A 1998 made-for-television film documentary aired on the Arts & Entertainment cable network boasted of the preeminent Jewish role in media and the shaping of our society to their purposes. It was made by Elliot Halpern & Simcha Jacobvici Productions, and written and directed by Simcha Jacobvici. It was called *Hollywoodism: Jews, Movies and the American Dream, and also titled Hollywood: An Empire of their Own.* The documentary shows how Jews overcame the Gentile filmmakers such as Thomas Edison and D.W. Griffith, took over the Hollywood film industry and gradually replaced their traditional American themes. Movies such as Griffith's "Birth of a Nation" which honored our traditional heritage became replaced with paeans to the Jewish agenda of immigration and multiracialism. They interview Jewish author

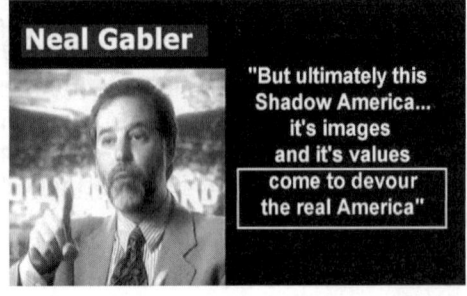

Neil Gabler, who frankly tells how they "devoured" the values of traditional America:

> "They created their own America, an America which is not the real America...But ultimately this shadow America becomes so popular and so widely disseminated that its images and its values come to devour the real America. And so the grand irony of all of Hollywood — is that Americans come to define themselves by the shadow of America that was created by the Eastern European Jewish immigrants who weren't permitted in the precincts of the real America."[213]

The film even quotes Gabler as saying that the leading Hollywood moguls were all Jewish persecuted refugees from

An example of Jewish Hollywood control is constant saturation of the Holocaust and nothing on the Jewish-led Red Terror

Tsarist Russia and their origins within just a few hundred kilometers of each other in Western Russia.

The narrator goes on to say that the Hollywood Jews became almost godlike in their power and set up a system to raise their prestige in the eyes of Americans:

Where there were new gods there must be new idols. So, the studio heads began a movie guild with the lofty title of the Academy of Motion Picture Arts and Sciences. It was Mayer's brilliant idea to create the Oscars where the movie moguls' guild honor themselves by giving each other awards. In this way, they went from being a group of immigrant Jews to award-winning American producers.[214]

Understanding their origins helps one to understand their sympathy to Communist ideologies and Jewish interests. Perhaps now you can understand why the Holocaust is a constant theme of Hollywood movie and TV productions but there is hardly a mention of the greatest numbers of humans slaughtered in history, far greater than any the official accepted numbers of the Holocaust. Of course, there is never an overt pointing out the fact that the Communist killing machine was dominated by Jews in Russia and throughout Eastern Europe.

Propaganda in the Movies

For many years, Jewish Hollywood limited its activities to the more subtle types of propaganda, but starting in the second half of the twentieth century, after their nation helped orchestrate the fratricidal Second World War, they then promoted the principles that dominated social Communism, sexual and social degeneracy, destruction of the family, promotion of drug and alcohol abuse, and every sort of human defilement possible. They then turned a new form of genocide on the "Russians" and "Ukrainians" of the Western World, the European elements of Europe, the U.S., Australia and New Zealand. They drove on toward their ultimate revenge, their long-held dreams of the destruction of their ancient enemies: the European peoples.

In America, first they replaced the European elites in academia, in media, in government, in finance, and then they opened the gates to the new Tower of Babel. Without the foundational floors of a harmonious people, the highest elements of an alienated people could not pose any real resistance to their Jewish racism and unrelenting supremacism.

In such an atmosphere they transformed the Holocaust into the ultimate crime while hiding their own enormous Holocaust against their European enemies. The Communist Holocaust was born in the bone and sinew of Moses Hess and Karl Marx, of Lenin, and Trotsky, and Yagoda, and Kaganovich and their steel (Stalin) Frankenstein that rose to their murderous bidding but then turned against his creator.

Chapter 30
A Tribal Media

Why is *The Secret Behind Communism* an unknown secret to most Americans and most of the world. The answer of course is that the same ethnocentric, misanthropic tribalists who created the Communist movement and who committed the greatest mass slaughter and torture in all of human history -- *are the same tribalists who dominate the global entertainment and news media.*

They know but we aren't supposed to know, or to care.

Here are some excerpts from the *Times of Israel,* another example of their power to say things that Gentiles don't dare say.

We Jews are a funny breed. ...We brag about Jewish authors, Jewish politicians, Jewish directors. Every time someone mentions any movie or book or piece of art, we inevitably say something like, "Did you know that he was Jewish?" That's just how we roll.

We're a driven group, and not just in regards to the art world. We have, for example, AIPAC, which was essentially constructed just to drive agenda in Washington DC. And it succeeds admirably. And we brag about it. Again, it's just what we do.

But the funny part is when any anti-Semite or anti-Israel person starts to spout stuff like, "The Jews control the media!" and "The Jews control Washington!"

Suddenly we're up in arms. We create huge campaigns to take these people down. We do what we can to put them out of work. We publish articles. We've created entire organizations that exist just to tell everyone that the Jews don't control nothin'. No, we don't control the media, we don't have any more sway in DC than anyone else. No, no, no, we swear: We're just like everybody else!

Does anyone else (who's not a bigot) see the irony of this?

Let's be honest with ourselves, here, fellow Jews. We do control the media. We've got so many dudes up in the executive offices in all the big movie production companies it's almost obscene. Just about every movie or TV show, whether it be "Tropic Thunder" or "Curb Your Enthusiasm," is rife with actors, directors, and writers who are Jewish. Did you know that all eight major film studios are run by Jews?

But that's not all. We also control the ads that go on those TV shows.

And let's not forget AIPAC, every anti-Semite's favorite punching bag. We're talking an organization that's practically the equivalent of the Elders of Zion. I'll never forget when I was involved in Israeli advocacy in college and being at one of the many AIPAC conventions. A man literally stood in front of us and told us that their whole goal was to only work with top-50 school graduate students because they would eventually be the people making changes in the government. Here I am, an idealistic little kid that goes to a bottom 50 school (ASU) who wants to do some grassroots advocacy, and these guys are literally talking about infiltrating the government. Intense.

...That the Mel Gibsons of the world are right in saying we're deliberately using our power to take over the world. That we've got some crazy conspiracy going down...

...The ADL chairman, Abe Foxman, was interviewed in a great article about the subject and he said that he "would prefer people say that many executives in the industry 'happen to be Jewish.'" This just about sums up the party line.

The truth is, the anti-Semites got it right. We Jews have something planted in each one of us that makes us completely different from every group in the world.215

Jewish journalists actually brag to themselves about the reason why *The Secret Behind Communism* is an unknown secret to most Americans and most of the world: their media control.

The reason the secret is maintained simply lies in the fact that Jews do dominate the media and believe that it is in their interest to keep general knowledge of their leading role in Communism covered up. Of course, there is tremendous pressure on any Jew or Gentile in the media who would expose the Jewish racism that enables their domination.

Chapter 31:

The Communist Origins of Neoconservatism

The "neo-conservative" movement—the lobby group directly responsible for the illegal, immoral and disastrous war in Iraq of 2003—is entirely misnamed. They are not "conservatives" in any sense of the word, and the entire ideology is essentially an extension of Jewish Trotskyism—as evidenced in their own words.

An article by the neoconservative "godfather" Irving Kristol in the *Weekly Standard* in 2003 summed up the situation:[216]

Irving Kristol, an open Trotskyite Communist, a founder of neoconservatism

"The historical task and political purpose of neo-conservatism would seem to be this: to convert the Republican party, and American conservatism in general, against their respective wills, into a new kind of conservative politics suitable to governing a modern democracy."

Kristol eschewed any attempt to justify U.S. support for Israel in terms of American national interest:

"Large nations, whose identity is ideological, like the Soviet Union of yesteryear and the United States of today, inevitably have ideological interests in addition to more material concerns... That is why we feel it necessary to defend Israel today, when its survival is threatened. No complicated geopolitical calculations of national interest are necessary."

Ideological Origins: Israel First

Neoconservatism's key founders trace their intellectual ancestry to the "New York Intellectuals," a group that originated as followers of Trotskyite theoretician Max Schactman in the 1930s and centered around influential journals like *Partisan*

Review and *Commentary* (which is published by the American Jewish Committee).

Key figures in leading the neocons away from calling themselves "leftists" and becoming "conservatives" were philosopher Sidney Hook and Elliot Cohen, editor of *Commentary.* The ideological kingpin of neoconservatism was Leo Strauss, a dedicated open Marxist devotee of Leon Trotsky (Lev Bronstein), the head of the Red Army who began the Red Terror in Russia.

Many of the leading neocons worked closely with Jewish activist organizations and it was only when the left began to be hostile towards the racist state of Israel, that these radical activists "abandoned" their Communist positions.

By the 1970s, the Jewish neocons had adopted an aggressive stance against the Soviet Union, whose anti-Zionist policy they interpreted as "anti-Semitism."

Jewish neocon Richard Perle, for example, later to become infamous as one of the major players in engineering the 2003 war against Iraq, was the prime organizer of Congressional support for the 1974 Jackson-Vanik Amendment. This legislation linked bilateral trade with the Soviet Union to special dispensation for Jews to emigrate from the USSR, primarily to America and Israel.

Leo Strauss - the ardent Communist follower of Trotsky who was the ideological founder of neoconservatism.

As the neoconservatives lost faith in radical leftism, several key neocons became attracted to the writings of Leo Strauss, a classicist and political philosopher at the University of Chicago. Strauss had a very strong Jewish identity and viewed his philosophy as a means of ensuring Jewish survival in the Diaspora. As he put it in a 1962 Hillel House lecture, later republished in *Leo Strauss: Political Philosopher and Jewish Thinker:*

"I believe I can say, without any exaggeration, that since a very, very early time the main theme of my reflections has been what is called the 'Jewish 'Question'." [217]

The Iraq War of 2003: A Jewish Neocon Conspiracy

The neocon's greatest coup to date has been the 2003 Iraq war. The Jewish neocons in the Bush administration who orchestrated that event show just how clearly the American government has fallen under the control of the Jewish elite.

The two Jewish former Trotskyites who orchestrated the catastrophic Iraq War for Israel's , not America's strategic interests

Leading government personalities included Deputy Secretary of Defense Paul Wolfowitz; Defense Policy Board Advisory Committee Chairman Richard Perle; Under Secretary of Defense for Policy Douglas Feith; Assistant to the Vice President for National Security Affairs and Chief of Staff to the Vice President of the United States Lewis "Scooter" Libby; Special Assistant to the President and Senior Director on the National Security Council for Near East and North African Affairs and Deputy National Security Advisor for Global Democracy Strategy Elliott Abrams; Middle East Adviser to the US Vice President and special assistant to John Bolton at the State Department David Wurmser; Undersecretary of State for arms control and international security John Bolton; and many others. All of these positions were instrumental in creating the tissue of lies about Iraqi "weapons of mass destruction" and bogus links to the attacks of September 11, 2001, which were used as justifications for the war.

Perle and Wursmer were also the authors of the strategy paper, *A Clean Break: A New Strategy for Securing the Realm* (commonly known as the "Clean Break" report), a policy document that was prepared in 1996 for the Israeli government which advocated a war against Iraq to protect Israel—this report's blueprint was used, almost to the letter, by the neocons in generating the war against Saddam Hussein.

The effects which these Trotskyite-origin "neocons" have had

on America—and indeed the world, through their criminal wars in the Middle East on behalf of the Zionist state—was summed up by famous Jewish journalist Carl Bernstein, in 2013.

Bernstein is perhaps the most respected and honored journalist in the United States. He was one of two reporters responsible for unearthing the Nixon Watergate scandal in 1973. Speaking on NBC television's "Morning Jo" program,—Bernstein stated explicitly that Jewish neocons were behind the Iraq war.

Bernstein's exact words were:

"This was an insane war that brought us low economically, morally. We went to war against a guy who had absolutely nothing to do with 9/11.

"It was a total pretext! It's inexplicable and there you go to Cheney, there you go to Bush, there you go to the Jewish neo-cons who wanted to remake the world. Maybe I can say that because I'm Jewish. . . . "

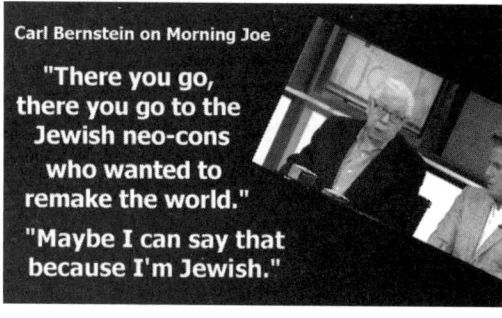

Carl Bernstein on Morning Joe

"There you go, there you go to the Jewish neo-cons who wanted to remake the world."

"Maybe I can say that because I'm Jewish."

It is good to know that there are indeed some honest Jews who dare to tell the truth about the real forces behind America's recent wars. However, he has not yet dared to speak about the collaboration of the Jewish dominated media with the Jewish neocons in hiding the Jewish origins of Communism and their continued domination of the Marxist left and Zionist right.

Chapter 32
The Communist Movement in Britain

THE Communist Party of Great Britain (CPGB) was founded in 1920 and officially affiliated with the Communist international Comintern. It was only dissolved in 1991 with the collapse of the Soviet Union. Several splinter groups have emerged in its wake.

British Jews "Disproportionately Represented in Communist Parties" Says Jewish Historian

Monty Goldman, veteran Communist **Jew leader in London who was the British Communist party's candidate for Mayor in 2012.**

According to the book by Jewish author Jonathan Frankel, *Studies in Contemporary Jewry, Volume XX: Dark Times, Dire Decisions: Jews and Communism* [Jonathan Frankel, (2005), Oxford University Press]: "Throughout the era of Communism, Jews were both influential and disproportionately represented in Communist parties. The Communist Party of Great Britain (CP) was no exception to this. By the 1960s two out of the three most important positions in the party were held by Jews.

"In the 1940s, nearly a third of all district party secretaries were Jewish. By the early 1950s, between 7 and 10 percent of the Communist party's activists (its cadres) were Jewish, even though Jews accounted for less than 1 percent of Britain's national population. Almost all Jewish Communists came from an Eastern European immigrant background."

Some of the more prominent Communist Jews involved with the CPGB included Zelda Kahan, Theodore Rothstein, Andrew Rothstein, Phil Piratin, Sam Aaronovitch, Sam Lesser, Hedi Stadlen, Sue Slipman, Dora Montefiore, Ivor Montagu, Anita Halpin, Monty Goldman and many, many more.

Some of these have also repackaged themselves and infiltrated social institutions. In general the party was made up of East End Jews and some gullible Gentiles from industrial cities.

The Communist Gerry Gable and Other Jewish Supremacist "Anti-Fascists"

One of its more infamous members was the hyper-Jew Gerry

Gable who presented himself to the compliant press as an "expert on the far right" in role as editor of the *Searchlight* "antifascist" magazine.

Searchlight is nothing but an extremist Communist Party front organization, and Gable stood as a formal Communist Party candidate in London as early as 1962. He has kept his Communist

Party affiliations and in 2008 was the guest speaker at a prominent Communist Party meeting in London.

Almost all of the contributors to this "antifascist" publication are Jews, with the longtime far-leftist American Jew Leonard Zeskind serving as their U.S. correspondent.

Other prominent UK-based Jews involved with Searchlight include Ketlan Ossowski, and John P. Goldstein, who uses the pen-name "John P." to try and hide his Jewishness.

Also closely allied to *Searchlight* is the equally Jewish Southern Poverty law Center in Montgomery, Alabama, USA (see Chapter 30).

Needless to say, none of the Jewish "anti-fascists" ever have

Gluckstein.

anything to say about the racist Zionist state of Israel, which outlaws marriages between Jews and non-Jews, and has racially-based immigration laws.

The Socialist Workers Party and Tony Cliff (Real Name Yigael Gluckstein)

Searchlight and Gable were closely involved with the setting up of the 'Unite Against Fascism' (UAF) organization. The UAF's other major component was the Socialist Workers Party (Britain) which was founded by the Israeli-born Communist Jew Tony Cliff, whose real name is Yigael Gluckstein (born in Israel).

Searchlight and Gable left the UAF after anti-Zionist Communists took control of its governing body. Gable is also a radical Zionist whose son served in the Israeli army, and thus objected to the anti-Israeli stance, and, complaining about anti-Semitism, left the UAF in a huff.

Chapter 33
South African Marxism: The Usual Suspects

THE South African Communist Party was founded in 1921 in Cape Town, and according to its launch manifesto, was constituted out of the following organizations:

> "The Communist Party of South Africa, which has been formed by the union of the former International Socialist League (S. A.), Social Democratic Federation of Capetown, Communist Party of Capetown, Jewish Socialist Society of Capetown, Jewish Socialist Society (Poalei Zion) of Johannesburg, Marxian Club of Durban, and other Socialist bodies and individuals, and which expects shortly to be affiliated to the World Communist International..." — [Manifesto of the Communist Party of South Africa, adopted at the inaugural conference of the Party, Cape Town, 30 July, 1921].

The Jewish preponderance in the party is obvious from that founding statement.

The South African Communist Party Created Out of Jewish Socialist Organizations

Almost all of the founding members were Jews, and for many years, almost all party officials were Jews, including the Chairman S.P. Bunting; the vice-Chairman E.S. "Solly" Sachs (also secretary of the Garment Workers Union); Molly (Zelikowitz) Wolton and Rebecca (Notlowitz) Bunting, both members of Executive Bureau; General Secretary and Editor: D. G. Wolton; General Secretary (in the 1930s) Lionel "Rusty" Bernstein; A.Z. Berman (who headed the Industrial Socialist League which was one of the formation organizations of the SACP); the Communist writer David Shub; Bennie Weinbren (who directed the Non-European Trade Union Federation); Issy Diamond; Abraham Levy; Hymie Levin; Issie Wolfson; Julius Lewin; Louis Joffe; Dr Max Joffe; Lazar Bach; Fanny Klenerman; Michael Harmel; Sam Kahn; Katy Kagan; Eli Weinberg; Yetta Barenblatt; Hymie Barsel; Leon and Norman Levy; Lionel Forman; Jacqueline and Rowley Arenstein; Errol and Dorothy

Shanley; Monty Berman; Bertram Hirson and Neville Rubin-among many others.

A South African Government Gazette Extraordinary (vol VI 16 Nov 1962 pp 2-28) listed "persons who have been office-bearers, officers, members or active supporters of the Communist Party of South Africa". The list included 66 "clearly identifiable as Jews", 61 "white non-Jews" and two uncertain.

According to the book *Traitors' End: The Rise and Fall of the Communist Movement in Southern Africa,*[218] Jews played a dominant role in Communism in South Africa:

> **"For the most part, the Jews had come to South Africa from Lithuania at the turn of the century... They had been popular at first, but by the mid-1930s this was no longer the case. The Jews had become heavily urbanized. In Johannesburg, they constituted 17 per cent of the population and were sufficiently conspicuous so that the metropolis was sometimes referred to, not as Jo'burg, but as Jewburg.**

> **"They aroused envy and some rancor during the years of depression because they controlled a large part of the business of Johannesburg and other cities... Anti-Semitism was fed by the economic discontent... A perhaps more important ingredient was the prominence of South African Jews in finance, mining and the other economic command posts of the nation, on the one hand, and in revolutionary and racial reform movements on the other.**

> **"From the outset, the Jews had been prominent in the Communist Party and its various fronts. They were equally conspicuous in the various movements that sought to break down the barriers separating the White from the non-White population. South African anti-Semitic propaganda depicted the Jew as a deracinated element who sought to destroy White civilization and nationalism with the twin weapons of** Communism **and international finance. Given the visible prominence of Jews in both areas, this doctrine fell on receptive ears."**

The Treason Trial of 1956

According to the book *Jews and Zionism: the South African Experience* (1910-67) [Dr. Gideon Shimoni, Oxford University Press, 1980], written by a Jewish author, the "extraordinary salience of Jewish individuals in the white opposition to the regime of apartheid" stands out.

Those involved in the Rivonia plot: From top left, going right: Mandela, Sisulu, Kathadra, Bernstein (Jew), Mhlaba, Goldberg (Jew), Mbeki, Kantor (Jew), Motsoledi, Mlangeni, Wolpe (Jew), Slovo (Jew), Hepple (Jew).

"Throughout this period Jewish names kept appearing in every facet of the struggle: amongst reformist liberals; in the radical Communist opposition; in the courts, whether as defendants or as counsel for the defense; in the lists of bannings and amongst those who fled the country to evade arrest. Their prominence was particularly marked in the course of the Treason Trial which occupied an important place in the news media throughout the second half of the 1950s.

"This trial began in December 1956, when 156 people were arrested on charges of treason in the form of a conspiracy to overthrow the state by violence and to replace it with a state based on Communism. Twenty-three of those arrested were Whites, more than half of them Jews. They included Yetta Barenblatt, Hymie Barsel, Lionel (Rusty) Bernstein, Leon Levy, Norman Levy, Sydney Shall, Joe Slovo, Ruth (First) Slovo, Sonia

Bunting, Lionel Forman, Isaac Horvitch, Ben Turok, Jacqueline Arenstein, Errol Shanley, Dorothy Shanley.

'In this extended five-year period between the emergence of violent opposition and its effective suppression, the prominent involvement of individual Jews was in the public eye more than ever before. This was even more so than in the dramatic circumstances of the 'Rivonia arrests'. "

The Rivonia Trial

The famous Rivonia Trial of the 1960s resulted from a raid on a farm near Johannesburg in which many of the top leadership of the Communist party were detained. Shimoni's book explained it this way:

"On 11 July 1963 the police raided the home of Arthur Goldreich in Rivonia near Johannesburg, where it captured, by surprise, the leadership cadre of the Umkonto we Sizwe underground. Seventeen people were arrested. Five of those arrested were Whites, all of them Jews," Shimoni continued. "They were: Arthur Goldreich, Lionel Bernstein, Hilliard Festenstein, Dennis Goldberg and Bob Hepple.. [There was an] overwhelming impression that Jews were in the forefront of the White radicals who were trying to overthrow the system."

Goldreich sits as police search the secret Communist headquarters.

The Rivonia plot included a plan called "Operation Mayibuye," which was described as follows: "Operation Mayibuye [a plan for guerrilla warfare, armed invasion of South Africa and Communist conquest of the country] was drafted by Arthur Goldreich, perhaps the most important of the men captured by the South African Police at Rivonia. Goldreich managed to bribe his way out of prison... During the trial, Goldreich was referred to by Nelson Mandela and other defendants as a military expert who served as an officer in the Israeli war for independence... Goldreich's plan was modelled on the guerrilla strategy of the Chinese Communists... Goldreich's notebook shows constant preoccupation with the practical details of revolutionary war. He goes into the types of explosives and fuses needed and their characteristics.[219] [*Traitors' End: The Rise and Fall of the Communist Movement in Southern Africa*, Nathaniel Weyl, Arlington House, USA, 1970, pp124, 127-8].

Goldreich and fellow Communist Jew Harold Wolpe, (who used South African Communist Party funds to buy the farm in Rivonia), also helped locate sabotage sites for Umkhonto we Sizwe, the military arm of the ANC, and draft a disciplinary code for guerrillas. Wolpe was arrested shortly after the Rivonia and taken to Marshall Square prison in the city, where Goldreich was already being held. There they managed to bribe a warder and escaped. Both fled to Israel, where Goldreich settled and where he died at the age of 82 in 2011.

In his autobiography, Nelson Mandela described Goldreich as having fought in the 1940s with the military wing of the Jewish National Movement in Palestine.

The Jewish Mr. Goldberg was a "technical officer" (that is, a bomb maker) in the ANC's armed wing arrested at Rivonia. He was sentenced in 1964 to four terms of life imprisonment. He was the only white member of Umkhonto we Sizwe to be arrested and sentenced in the Rivonia Trial to life imprisonment. He was released in 1985, after 22 years in prison. His first stop after being released was to visit his daughter in Israel, before going on to exile in London.

Rivonia was not the end of Jewish Communist involvement in the "armed struggle." According to Shimoni's book:

"When the secret African Resistance Movement (ARM) was crushed during 1964, it again became evident that many Jews were involved. One of its founders was identified as Monty Berman and others were Adrian Leftwich and Bertram (Baruch) Hirson. Among those who were associated with ARM were Neville Rubin and

Michael Schneider [and] others implicated were Frederick and Rhoda Prager, Raymond Eisenstein and Hugh Lewin." (pp. 232-3).

Other Communist Jews and the Subversion of South Africa

According to the book *Cutting Through the Mountain: Interviews with South African Activists* [Edited by Immanuel Suttner, Viking-Penguin, England and USA 1997],

"a disproportionate number of individual Jews played a part in transforming South Africa... There are two streams: those who fought 'within the system' as jurists, members of parliament, via the media, or in civil society, and those who entered 'illegal' organizations which were socialist, Communist **or mass-based in character." (p.2)**

The book 'welcomes (these Jews) back not only as worthy South Africans, socialists, Communists or liberals, but as worthy Jews' (p.3). Some of the 'remarkable people' (page vii) who are heroes of the book include:

Taffy Adler who was involved in the 1970s and '80s in the 'formation and consolidation of the black trade union movement'. His father was a Lithuanian Jew who emigrated to South Africa in 1926 and who was tremendously loyal to Stalin and Russian Communism' right up to the fall of the Soviet Union in 1989. His uncle, Michael Harmel, became general secretary of the South African Communist Party.

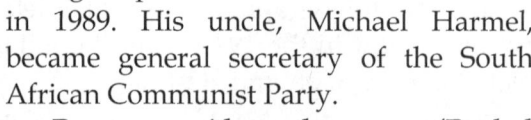

Ray Alexander (Rachel Alexandrowich) arrived in South Africa from Latvia and joined the SA Communist Party five days later. She played a leading role in the organization of trade unions. She was married to the Jew Jack Simons, a 'devoted Communist' and lecturer at the University of Cape Town.

Pauline Podbrey (Podbrez) born in Lithuania came to South Africa at the age of eleven. She joined the Communist Youth League, run by Max Joffe, and the related Labor League of Youth, run by Hilda Bernstein. Of the Communist Party she says 'the majority of the members were

Jewish...looking back on it now, it seems as if everybody was Jewish.' (Suttner, p.52).

Winnie and Nelson Mandela and Joe Slovo photographed at an ANC Communist Party rally in 1990. Joe Slovo was the "Brains" Behind the ANC.

Pictured here is Nelson Mandela, a former, self-proclaimed violent member of a Communist terrorist cell. It shows how important it is for one's image if he has worked for Jewish supported movements rather than against them.

(Note from the author) When I was 17 I joined a non-violent Klan group at my school. I condemned violence then as I still do. Not a single member of my organization was ever even accused of violence. Although I have certainly evolved in my views and moved on in my life, because I dare to oppose Jewish racism and supremacism, I am still condemned by the Ziomedia even though I made a clean break from my former affiliation almost 40 years ago. Contrast my non-violent past with Mandela posing under a symbol under which more people died than any other in history. Such are the double standards today in the Zio-media.

The most famous Communist in South Africa was Joe Slovo. Born in Lithuania to a devout Jewish family, he came to South Africa where he joined the Young Communist League at the age of sixteen. He became a central member of the Communist Party of South Africa and a 'hard-line Stalinist', becoming general secretary in 1986.

He concentrated on building up Umkhonto we Sizwe, the 'armed wing' of the ANC (African National Congress), becoming its chief of staff and head strategist in the campaign of bombings directed at civilian targets and other acts of terror. He only abandoned his commitment to Stalinism and Soviet-style Communism when the Soviet bloc started falling apart in the late 1980s and it became necessary to do so. A key strategist representing the ANC in the negotiations with F.W. De Klerk's government in the handover of power, he became a minister in Mandela's Cabinet when the ANC came to power in 1994. He died of cancer a few years later. South Africa's Chief Rabbi Cyril Harris officiated at the funeral of Joe Slovo, calling Slovo "a better Jew than most" (Fair Lady 22 May 2002 p. 37).

The Jewess Gill Marcus, the daughter of parents involved with the Communist Party, a long-time member of the Party and of the ANC, is now a Deputy Governor of the South African Reserve Bank after being a member of the first Mandela Cabinet.

Ronnie Kasrils: The Jewish Head of the ANC's Intelligence

The Jew Ronnie Kasrils became a central figure in the South African Communist Party and in its armed wing alongside Joe Slovo. He became head of military intelligence of the ANC's military wing. After the ANC came to power, he was appointed to the Ministry of Defense, and later became head of the South African government's secret service, the National Intelligence Service (NIS). When Kasrils returned to South Africa, he was lionized by a local Jewish establishment belatedly eager to associate itself with the struggle. His picture was put in the Jewish Museum in Cape Town and his name in the Book of Honor. The Jewish community basked in his reflected glory."[220]

Chapter 34
Spreading of Communism to China

Incredible as it sounds, Jews also played a leading role in the formation and tutoring of the Chinese Communist party which still rules that nation of 1.4 billion to the present-day.

The first large group of Jews who arrived in China did so under British protection following the First Opium War. Many of these Jews were of Indian or Iraqi origin, due to British colonialism in these regions, and they became the largest dealers in opium. The second community came in the first decades of the 20th century when many Jews arrived in Hong Kong and Shanghai during those cities' periods of economic expansion.

The Shanghai Ghetto

Another wave of Jews arrived in the late 1930s and 1940s, fleeing from the rise of Nazi Germany. Shanghai was notable for its volume of Jewish refugees, since it was one of the few places in the world where a visa was not required for entry. By 1941, nearly 20,000 Jews had found shelter there.

True to form, many of these Jews became highly active in the Chinese Communist Party. Here is a partial list:

1. Grigori Naumovich Voitinsky (1893–1956) was a Russian Jew and Comintern official sent to China in 1920 as an advisor to contact the prominent Chinese radicals such as Chen Duxiu, just before the formation of the Communist Party of China. The actual process of forming the infant Party can be mostly attributed to his influence.

In 1920, the Soviet Union established the Far Eastern Bureau in Siberia, a branch of the Third Communist International, or the Comintern. It was responsible for managing the establishment of a Communist party in China and other countries.

Soon after its establishment, the bureau's deputy manager Voitinsky arrived in Beijing and contacted the Communist vanguard Li Dazhao. Li arranged for Voitinsky to meet with another Communist leader, Chen Duxiu, in Shanghai.

In August 1920, Voitinsky, Chen Duxiu, Li Hanjun, Shen Xuanlu, Yu Xiusong, Shi Cuntong, and others began to establish the Comintern China Branch.

The *Shanghai Chronicle* was set up in 1919 in Shanghai by other Russian Communist Jews and received financial aid from the Soviet-Russian government in early 1920. Voitinsky and his colleagues came to China in the guise of editors and reporters for the newspaper, but also set up the Comintern's East Asia Secretariat in the newspaper office.

From then on, the *Shanghai Chronicle* became both a propaganda vehicle for the East Asia Secretariat and a cover for Bolshevik activity in China. Because the newspaper staff assisted Soviet Russian and Comintern personnel stationed under cover at the newspaper in activities to establish a Communist organization in China, the newspaper as a whole played a special role in the early Communist movement in China. Although the Shanghai Chronicle stopped publication at the end of 1922 because Russian aid came to an end, many staff members continued to work for Bolshevism.

**First Minister of Health in Mao Zedong
Government was an Austrian Jew**

2. Jakob Rosenfeld (1903-1952), more commonly known as *General Luo*, served as the Minister of Health in the

1947 Provisional   Communist   Military   Government   of China under Mao Zedong. Rosenfeld, a Jew born in Lemberg, the Austro-Hungarian Empire (today Lviv, Ukraine), fled to the Shanghai ghetto in 1939.

From 1941 he served the Chinese Communist force as a field doctor for the New Fourth Army, the Eighth Route Army and the Northeast People's Liberation Army during the outbreak of the Second Sino-Japanese war and Chinese civil war. He participated in the People's Liberation Army's march on Beijing and was rewarded with the senior government post in the post-war Communist Chinese government.

In 1950, Rosenfeld emigrated to Israel and died two years later. China has erected a statue in his honor, a hospital in Junan County, Shandong was named after him, and in 2006 a large exhibit was mounted in Beijing's National Museum of China in tribute to him. The museum exhibit in his honor was inaugurated by Chinese President Hu Jintao.

3. Stanislaw (Moishe) Flato (1910 – 1972) was a Polish Jew, born in Warsaw and who studied medicine in Paris. While in France, he joined the French Communist Party in 1932. He then volunteered for service on the Communist side in the Spanish Civil War, joining the Spanish Communist Party. He was interned upon his return to France in 1939 for his military and subversive activities, but released and then fled to China in August 1939.

He became a member of Communist Party of China, and served as a head of International Red Cross doctors at People's Liberation Army.

After World War II, Flato returned to Poland in September 1945 and joined the reconstituted Polish Communist Party with the new rank of Colonel. Flato served on the Polish army's General Staff from 1946 to 1952 and later became Chief Adviser at the Polish Embassy in Beijing, China, from 1957-1964. Thereafter he became deputy director at the Department for Asia in Ministry for Foreign Affairs of Poland. He died in 1972.

4. Eva Sandberg (1911 –2001) was a German Jewess who emigrated to The Soviet Union in the 1920s to join her coreligionists, In 1939 she married a visiting Chinese Communist, Xiao San. The same year, San was ordered by the Communist International to report for service to the revolutionary base at Yan'an in China, and Sandberg accompanied him.

After many adventures with the First (or Central) Red Army Xiao and Sandberg took over the editorial department at the Reds' Lu Xun Academy of Arts. Finally in 1959, with the Chinese Civil War over—and a Communist victory—Sandberg came into her own and began making films of the People's Republic for use by the Communist news agencies of Europe. She and San later fell out with the Chinese Communist leadership and were arrested. After years of internal exile, Sandberg died in Beijing in 2001.

5. Ruth F. Weiss, also known as Wèi Lùsh, (1908–2006) was an Austrian Jewess who fled to Shanghai in 1933. She worked as a journalist in that city, and later became a teacher at the Jewish School in Shanghai, at the School of the Chinese Committee of Intellectual Cooperation, and at the West China Union University. After working briefly as a secretary at the Canadian embassy in 1944, she became a correspondent at the United Nations Picture News Office in 1945 and joined the China Welfare Fund.

One year later she took up a post at the Radio Division of the United Nations Organization in New York. After she returned to China she became a lecturer for the Verlag für fremdsprachige Literatur (Publishing House for Foreign Literature) in Beijing from 1952 to 1965. In 1965 she worked as a journalist for "China im Bild"—all pro-Communist publications aimed at spreading Communism in the West.

Ruth Weiss was one of about one hundred foreign-born residents to receive Chinese citizenship in 1955. In 1983 she was named one of eleven foreign experts by the Communist Party of China that were part of the membership of the Chinese People's Political Consultative Conference. She died in Beijing in 2006.

6. Sidney Rittenberg (born 1921) is an American interpreter and scholar who lived in China from 1944 to 1979. He worked closely with PRC founder Mao Zedong, military leader Zhu De,

and key statesman Zhou Enlai, and other leaders of the Communist party during the war, and was the only American citizen to join the Chinese Communist Party (CCP). He was with these central Communist leaders at Yan'an and was able to experience much of the

Rittenberg and Mao Zedong.

life of Mao and his supporters.

7. Sidney Shapiro (born 1915) was a Polish-born Jew, born in Warsaw but raised in New York. He resides in Beijing, and is a member of the Chinese People's Political Consultative Council. Shapiro has held citizenship of the People's Republic of China since 1963, before the Cultural Revolution. He is a member of the People's Political Consultative Conference, a governmental assembly of the PRC which ostensibly provides a forum for input from non-Communist political organizations.

Main Communist Chinese English Language
News Source Run by the Jew Israel Epstein

8. Israel Epstein (1915 – 2005) was a journalist and author. He was one of the few foreign-born non-Chinese to become a member of the Communist Party of China. Israel Epstein began to work in journalism at age 15, when he wrote for the *Peking and Tientsin Times*, an English-language newspaper based in Tianjin.

In 1951, he became editor of the Chinese Communist propaganda newspaper, *China Reconstructs,* which was later renamed *China Today.* He remained editor-in-chief of *China Today* until his retirement at age 70, and then editor emeritus.

During his tenure at *China Today*, he became a Chinese citizen in 1957 and a member of the Communist Party of China in 1964. Israel Epstein was elected as a member of the Standing

Committee of the National Committee of the Chinese People's Political Consultative Conference, an advisory body, in 1983.

During his life, Israel Epstein was honored by Zhou Enlai, Mao Zedong, Deng Xiaoping, Jiang Zemin, and President Hu Jintao. His funeral was held at the Babaoshan Cemetery for Revolutionaries, in Shijingshan District, Beijing on June 3, 2005. The ceremony was attended by many officials, among them President Hu Jintao, Premier Wen Jiabao, as well as Politburo Standing Committee members Jia Qinglin and Li Changchun.

Chapter 35
The Key to Communism: Jewish Tribalism

In hundreds of pages and under the weight of massive historical evidence, it will be hard for any reader to deny *The Secret Behind Communism*. Ultimately, the Marxist ideology and movements originated and directed by Jewish tribalists were driven in large part by a greater Jewish agenda. In short, the Communist revolution could not have succeeded and the Communist Holocaust could not have occurred without both an elemental Jewish tribalism and the support of organized Jewry in Russia and around the world. The Jewish community worldwide saw promoting Communism as being in Jewish self-interest.

That being said, it would be an error to say that every Jewish Marxist was a Jewish racist. Indeed, some may have truly believed in the ideology they espoused. But it is hard to conceive of a level of self-deception so great that ideologues would murder millions of people if they really believed in the platitudes of human rights they espoused.

Only a tiny minority of Jews actively oppose Jewish tribalism. Even Jewish anti-Zionists will rarely criticize the Jewish tribalism and Jewish racism that is the source of Zionist influence and power.

The vast majority of Jewish Communist leaders had to be conscious of the overwhelming Jewish privilege in the Communist movement. One cannot ignore the revenge aspect of the Communist replacement of the Gentile elite with a Jewish elite.

How can anyone in the Communist Party dominated by the Jewish bourgeoisie truly believe they were really fighting for the proletariat? The Jewish favoritism and privilege associated with the Bolshevik revolution was never seriously challenged by ninety-nine percent of its Jewish participants.

Ultimately, the same is true of Jewish progressives in the United States who speak for diversity at our educational institutions, and then run Harvard and the Ivy League with massive ethnic discrimination in favor of less-qualified Jews over better qualified non-Jews. The discrimination is so draconian that Jews who are only 1.8 percent of the student age American population are the biggest plurality in the Harvard population.

In my book, *The Zionist Conspiracy,* I show that the Jewish domination of Harvard is not due to greater merit or ability, but achieved by naked racial discrimination against better-qualified European and Asian Americans. Jews are admitted at a rate more than 14 times, or 1,300 percent greater than their merit justifies.

Ultimately Jewish loss of power in the Soviet Union was brought about by Gentiles who finally rose against this tribal racism of the Jewish element. Aided in part by the Second World War and the elevation of Mother Russia as a means of rallying the Russian people against their ultimate enemy, National Socialism, Jews inadvertently sparked Russian patriotism that ultimately removed them from power.

Stalin, an utterly ruthless non-Jew, who was a cultural Judeophile in everything but descent, by the end of his life saw the Jews as the ultimate threat to both himself and the Russian people. A number of Jews have written well-argued books that Stalin was actually murdered by a coterie of highly placed Jews around him, including Kaganovich, in the "Doctors Plot."

There were certainly disagreements among the Jewish element in Russia just as there are divisions today among them on many levels. However, the first dedication of every organized element is their own people and perceived interests.

In Russia some of them wanted to be more openly Zionist and Jewish supremacist. Others saw Jewish destiny in their paramount role in Communist rule over Russia and ultimately over the planet.

The *International* was just that, an international Communist movement completely dominated by Jews, and as has been shown, they even dominated the spy rings that sought to overthrow the governments of the West.

At the time of the so-called Russian Revolution the Russian Tsarist government of Russia was considered the greatest enemy of Jews in Russia and worldwide. Not only was the Bolshevik

Revolution overwhelmingly led by Jews, the same was true for the entire international Communist movement.

As shown in these pages, the financiers of the Communist Movement were in fact Jewish capitalist bankers, such as Jacob Schiff, which again shows that Communism, to many of its most important Jewish supporters around the world, was not about economic justice, but about Jewish tribalist advantage.

The question naturally arises: why would one of the world's richest capitalists support a Communist revolution that is supposedly the ultimate enemy of capitalism?

The answer of course lies in Jewish ethnic tribalism. As I began this book, with the words that Solzhenitsyn personally told me, the Russian revolution was not Russian, but an alien invasion of Russia by a people that despised the Russian people for so-called anti-Semitism. The Jews who lived in Russia for centuries ultimately sided with Jewish Communist overlords who hatefully murdered millions of native Russians, those whom they saw as ethnic enemies.

In later years, before the fall and breakup of the Soviet Union, Jews lost their preeminent power in the nation. However, books such as the *Red Mafia* show that they had retained many positions in the Russian system and were still at the heart of huge corruption rackets there.

When Communism finally collapsed, those Jewish organized crime syndicates morphed into the most aggressive organized crime syndicates of all time, referred to as the "Russian Mafia" by the Jewish-dominated media. In fact, the so-called Russian Mafia is not Russian, it is a Jewish Mafia. In a word it is controlled from the top down by ethnic tribalist Jews. The overwhelmingly Jewish oligarchs, through murder, extortion, bribery, fraud and theft, stole much of the natural assets of the world's richest resource empire.

And to this day, Jewish tribal influence in media and government has sheltered and defended, sometimes even made into heroes, these Jewish gangsters who stole much of Russia. For example, the global media constantly treats Mikhail Khodorkovsky as a victim, rather than one of the worst predators and thieves in world history. And Europe, besieged with Jewish influence, gave shelter to Jewish gangsters, criminals and thieves such as Berezovsky, Gusinsky as well as many others.

Furthermore, it is clear that Jews remain the driving force behind left wing, Marxist style ideologies the world over, and that modern liberalism shares much of the same basic values as traditional socialism/Communism, particularly with regard to enforced social equality and the rise of all-powerful governments. Left wing Jews now work openly toward a world government along with their supposed ideological opponents: the Zionists.

Ideological Communism has morphed into a semi-capitalist, big-government entity today, but it relentlessly pursues the Jewish attack on almost every core value of society, the destruction of freedom of speech and thought, the elevation of degeneracy as ideal, the promotion of drug and alcohol abuse and the destruction of the core basis of society, the nuclear family.

Among Jews, there has, in recent times, been a massive conversion from Communism to Zionism. Just as Moses Hess evolved from a Communist to a dedicated Jewish supremacist Zionist. In the early years of the 21st Century, the vast majority of Jews now embrace Zionism as their destiny in comparison with those few that did in the early years of the 20th Century.

Interestingly, this conflict was revealed in Winston Churchill's amazing 1920 article on the struggle within International Jewry between Communist Jews and Zionist Jews. Ultimately, with the emergence of Russian nationalism, and the removal of much Jewish power in the Soviet Union under Stalin, Jews began to embrace a capitalist, Zionist model of achieving globalist economic and political supremacy.

Communism/Zionism & Moses Hess

Part of the reason for the delayed success of Zionism was that a Zionist State was just a dream when Communism first came on the scene. When Israel did come into existence right after the Second World War, Jewish tribalists were then much more attracted to a more blatantly Jewish form of supremacism than a more hidden, Jewish Marxist hegemony.

Once again we should understand the fact that Zionism and Communism have not only the same Jewish roots, but that even the ideological bases of both Zionism and Marxism have a common source. Shown here is an advertisement for a large International Jewish conference honoring Moses Hess as a "Revolutionary, Zionist, Communist." Perhaps nothing better illustrates the amazing connection between Communism and Zionism.[221]

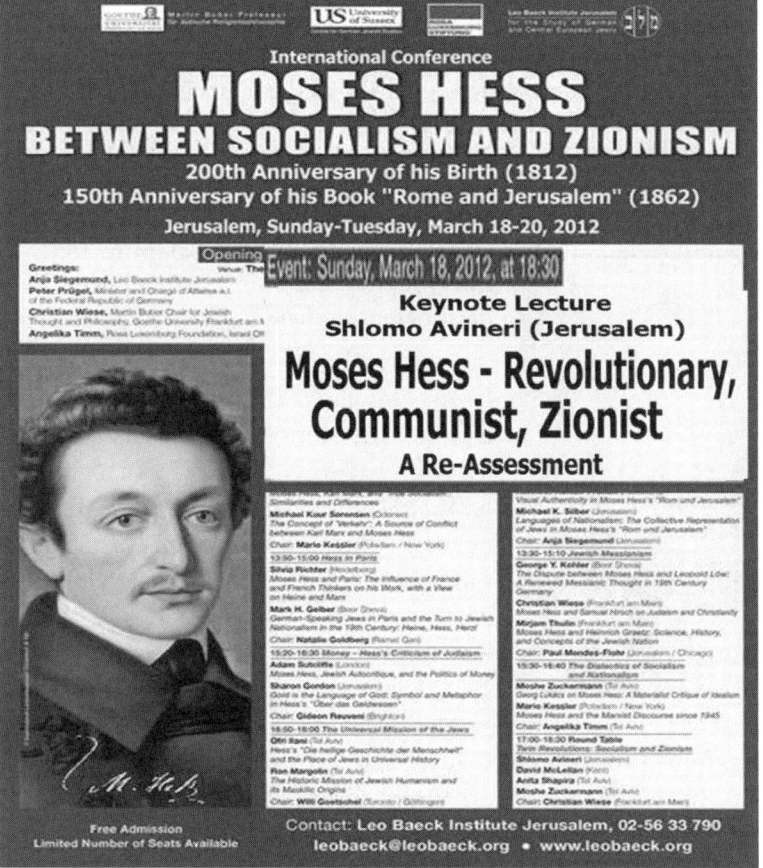

Advertisement for a very large conference in Israel in honor of Moses Hess. The lead lecture as shown clearly is by Shlomo Avineri on "Moses Hess - Revolutionary, Communist, Zionist"

Here is a description of Moses Hess in Wikipedia:

Hess originally advocated Jewish integration into the universalist socialist movement, and was a friend and collaborator of Karl Marx and Friedrich Engels. Hess converted Engels to Communism, and introduced Marx to social and economic problems.

He played an important role in transforming the Hegelian dialectical idealism theory of history into the dialectical materialism of Marxism, by conceiving of man as the initiator of history through his active consciousness.

Hess was probably responsible for several "Marxian" slogans and ideas, including religion as the "opiate of the people." Hess became reluctant to base all history on economic causes and class struggle, and he came to see the struggle of races, or nationalities, as the prime factor of history.

... From 1861 to 1863 he lived in Germany, where he became acquainted with the rising tide of German Anti-Semitism. It was then that he reverted to his Jewish name Moses in protest against assimilationism. He published Rome and Jerusalem in 1861. Hess

interprets history as a circle of race and national struggles.[222]

Interestingly, just as Hess morphed from Jewish Communist to Jewish Zionist, the same process was duplicated throughout the Jewish world both in Israel and the Diaspora.

As Communism fell out of favor with most Jews, at least in its basic vocabulary and syntax, Marxist Jews began a transition as they continued to dominate the Democratic Left. But, what is quite astonishing, they have also invented neoconservatism and ultimately have taken over the primary organizations and structures of so-called traditional conservatism.

Gentile conservatives for the most part are completely oblivious to the idea that the controllers of their movement, aside from a few diehards like Patrick Buchanan, now have an ideological foundation created by a cabal of former long-time Trotskyites. The patron saint of neoconservatism is Leo Strauss, a hyper-racist Jew who was a dedicated follower of Leon Trotsky, the former head of the Bolshevik Red Army. The same is true for Irving Kristol, and the real founders of neoconservatism.

Neoconservatism has essentially taken over traditional conservatism. Aside from some basic disagreements on certain tax issues, and on what Patrick Buchannan calls the culture war, both Jewish cohorts, on the older left and now on a new fake "right", have come down with an Israel-first commitment and a domestic policy that serves every aspect of the Jewish agenda.

Another interesting phenomenon is the fact that a number of Jews in the Soviet State, after years of service, clearly revealed that their ultimate identification and loyalty was to the Jewish people and Israel rather than to Russia.

As pointed out, Ilya Ehrenburg who was the chief propagandist of the Red army, a man who urged the mass murder of German and Eastern Europeans during the Second World War, ended up leaving his papers to the Yad Vashem museum in Israel, not to Mother Russia that gave him his fame and fortune.

Are All Jews Communists?

The answer to that question is obvious: no. While there is no doubt that the leading role players in Communist and far leftist organizations are Jews, it would be incorrect to claim that all Jews are Communists. Although the great mass of organized world Jewry supported the Jewish-led revolution in Russia, and gave their support to many Marxist-style movements, not all Jews did so. Today, Jews overwhelmingly embrace Zionism. The Council of Presidents of Major Jewish Organizations illustrates that fact.

However, there can be no doubt that broadly speaking, Jewish communities have displayed a far larger degree of sympathy for far leftist causes than any other ethnic group.

At the same time, Jews display a very high degree of ethno-centrism and desire to maintain Jewish identity (as exemplified in the state of Israel) which, if duplicated by any other nation or people, would be attacked by those same Jews as being "racist."

For example, in Israel it is illegal for a Jew to marry a non-Jew, and immigration is strictly restricted to those people who can prove racial Jewish descent. Any European nation attempting to adopt similar policies would be condemned outright by the Jewish-controlled media and by the Israeli government.

This staggering hypocrisy—of demanding ethno-nationalism for Jews but denying that right to everyone else—is part of the psychological underpinning which created Zionism and Marxism in the first place.

It is important to clearly understand that Jews dominate practically all movements against European peoples across the world. It is vital to understand why.

Why Do Jews Lead most anti-European Movements?

Answering the question is complicated. It is easy to make a list of Jews involved in Communism and subversion, but it is not so simple to explain why this phenomenon occurs.

America, in particular, opened its doors to Jews, allowing them to flee persecution for their behavior from many European countries. They were allowed to settle, flourish, and gain positions of great influence.

Yet American Jews are active in almost every single movement that seeks to destroy the foundations of the very same America that gave them sanctuary. From immigration issues through attempts to suppress freedom of speech, "hate crime bills", and control of American foreign policy (which makes America fight Israel's wars such as those in Iraq and their planned war against Iran), Jews and Jewish organizations have played a leading role behind the scenes—and sometimes at the front of them as well.

In addition they have driven an entertainment and print media that has demonized European Americans. It has encouraged non-Europeans to direct their anger at Europeans, and encouraged people of European descent to hate themselves.

When one understands Jewish racism and tribalism, the rationale for such strategies becomes obvious. In order for Jewish extremists to take over America they had to weaken the American majority, divide it, and through mass immigration overwhelm it.

Earl Raab, of the extremely Zionist Perlmutter Institute which is associated with the ADL, celebrates the coming minority status of European Americans in America. Once that has happened, he looks forward to "constitutional constraints" (restriction of freedom of speech):

> The Census Bureau has just reported that about half of the American population will soon be non-white or non-European. And they will all be American citizens. We have tipped beyond the point where a Nazi-Aryan party will be able to prevail in this country.

Earl Raab

> We have been nourishing the American climate of opposition to ethnic bigotry for about half a century. That climate has not yet been perfected, but the heterogeneous nature of our population tends to make it irreversible and makes our constitutional constraints against bigotry more practical than ever.[223]

> As Raab says, Zionist Jewish activists who have supported an exclusively Jewish-run national state have been nourishing massive nontraditional immigration into America, and they look forward to the time when the voting demographics of the United States reflect that transformation.

It seems that since Jews were accepted into the United States by the once-solid ninety-percent European American majority, it would be suicidal for them to attempt to weaken and harm such a group that had been so good to them.

It seems suicidal. If America is finally overrun by Third World immigration and turns into a larger version of the economic and social problems faced by Mexico, it seems Jewish power would decline. Take France as an example. After World War II, International Jewry has worked full time at suppressing any form of European nationalism, out of a fear that Hitler would again arise somewhere. This has led directly to the open borders immigration policy, which has dominated Europe since the 1960s.

Now that France has untold millions of non-White, North African Muslim immigrants, all there because of the Jewish-created hysteria of "non-racialism," the Jews in France are fleeing by the hundreds of thousands —to places like Florida — to escape what they call "anti-Semitism," but which is in fact a Muslim reaction to the excesses of the Zionist state of Israel.

Jewish behavior in Europe has led directly to the growth of a non-White population there, and now that this new population has exhibited signs of hostility to Jews, those same Jews are busy fleeing their own creation, much as in Mary Shelley's novel, *Frankenstein,* where a mad doctor creates a monster (similar to the Jewish Golem story) only to be destroyed by his own creation.

Judaism as an Evolutionary Strategy

Professor Kevin MacDonald, from the Department of Psychology, California State University Long Beach, has an explanation as to why Jews behave the way they do. He is an advocate of "evolutionary psychology," which seeks to explain the human mind and human behavior by examining them through evolutionary theory.

Professor MacDonald's theory is that evolutionary competition takes place not just between individuals and their differences hewn by genetic and social distinctions, but also between human groups.

In the course of Jewish history, MacDonald says, Jews have developed predispositions to verbal intelligence and intensity, altruism to kin, and a suit of other traits; and these traits further a "group evolutionary strategy," by which the Jewish population competes with non-Jewish populations.

This theory appears to be correct. The only element that is missing is the question of why Jews would develop such a specialized group evolutionary strategy in the first place. Why them, and not any other of the considerably vast range of racial groups on earth, not to mention the greater Semitic nation of families?

The answer lies in biology, and its direct offshoot, psychology. The study of psychology is, of course, actually just the study of the effects of biology associated with environment.

The first thing to understand about Jews is that they are a distinct biological entity to themselves. Genetic studies, some of which have been outlined earlier in this book, have demonstrated that Jews derive most of their ancestry from the Middle East and have little in common genetically with the Europeans among whom they live.

In other words, the genetic studies show very clearly that Jews are a distinct, largely homogenous, racially defined group, which has, despite great geographic dispersion, been able to maintain its biological group identity to an extreme degree.

This is a remarkable achievement. No other group has succeeded in retaining its unique identity in the face of geographic dispersion. However, in this ability to keep a distinct identity lies the explanation of Jewry's behavior.

Group Paranoia

Anyone who has studied the science of psychology knows that there are two symptoms of paranoia: delusions of grandeur, and delusions of persecution. The Jews are the only people on Earth who have made a religion out of these paranoiac symptoms.

On the one hand, the hard core of Judaism believes that they alone are God's chosen people and this closeness is based on blood rather than any particular belief, other than one: their own chosenness. On the other hand, their whole religious history is one of being persecuted, which can be seen even in their questionably historically accurate biblical stories. Passover, Purim, Chanukah, all are steeped in persecution myths, and in revenge and violence against their enemies.

Jews are a group that has made a religion out of paranoia, out of delusions of grandeur, and delusions of persecution. This group paranoia was probably started by a group of Jews in Palestine who suffered from this genetic proclivity. Those Jews who did not have this genetic tendency, who were not attracted to the belief system, and who found themselves more attracted to European aesthetics and behavior left the Jewish community, and the Jewish community scorned them. Jewish literature is full of the prevailing practice of devout Jews considering their own sons and daughters who intermarried as dead. They even do a ceremony called sitting "shiva."

"Sitting Shiva"

"Shiva (Hebrew: שבעה) (literally "seven") is the week-long mourning period in Judaism for first-degree relatives: father, mother, son, daughter, brother, sister, and spouse. The ritual is referred to as "sitting shiva."

As a result of the Jewish laws of biological descent (remember they still today believe that only someone born of a Jewish mother is actually a Jew), this Jewish group which had already excluded Jewish tribesmen who did not have these group genetic tendencies, became a closed gene pool.

This has led to what is known in genetics as a "founder gene" effect amongst Jews.

The "founder gene" effect is best demonstrated by a non-Jewish example. The disease known as "variegate porphyria," which is very common amongst white Afrikaners, for example, has been traced to a single Dutch person who settled in that country in 1688.

Despite being caused by one single person, variegate porphyria is the single most common genetic disorder amongst modern Afrikaners, and causes skin disorders and internal organ failure, which can include heart disease.

There are many other examples of founder gene effects, which directly cause a certain trait to become common amongst identifiable ethnic groups. Even facial shape can be affected by this founder gene effect, as anyone traveling in parts of Europe will be able to confirm.

This founder gene effect amongst Jews, confirmed by way of the discovery of a single founder gene for the Cohen subgroup of priestly-class Jews, combined with the "dropping out" of Jews who did not have this paranoia-gene, has created a self-feeding, closed genetic pool of people who, quite literally, suffer from a group paranoia, unseen and incomparable in history.

This closed gene pool and extensive inbreeding amongst Jews has some serious genetic side effects as well. It is well known that

Jews are one of the most inbred of all ethnic groups and manifest a large assortment of ailments attributable to that inbreeding.

A famous example is Tay-Sachs disease, and unusually high levels of imbecility among Jews, to the point where you will even find exclusively Jewish mental asylums.

Jewish Behavior the Result of Group Behavioral Psychology

This provides the best explanation for Jewish behavior. We are dealing with a group who, firstly, genuinely believe that they are chosen by God to be superior to everyone else—hence they call non-Jews cattle, or goyim, to be herded along like inferior creatures, and who, secondly, continually fear persecution which they know and understand, even if subconsciously, to be the inevitable result of their scandalous behavior toward the goyim, should their victims ever attain a degree of racial consciousness and understanding of what the Jews are doing.

This also explains Jewish consistency in their behavior, something that previously was thought to be the result of some grand conspiracy. There is no tightly directed conspiracy going back hundreds of thousands of years, it is a loose conspiracy in the classic sense of a group banding together for its own perceived interests.

An important thing to consider is the fact that Jews themselves are often divided as to their best strategy in advancing their ethnic supremacy. Hence, we had two different sectors of Jews sometimes working together and sometimes fighting: the Communists and the Zionists.

Both of these groups are extremely damaging to Gentiles among whom they live, and often to great numbers of Jews themselves. Because these interests may be detrimental to the majority of the population among whom they live, they must develop deceptive strategies for maintaining their influence and power.

Judaism is an intense racist philosophy that is far more than simply a religious view of God or even worshipping God. It is at heart the view that the Jewish people *are* God and that their ultimate loyalty is to the Jewish people itself.

A major syndicated article written by Jews revealed startlingly that about fifty-percent of Jews who are members of synagogues, and who are often even leaders in the synagogue who lead Jewish prayers, are in fact atheists.

Judaism without God? Yes, say American atheists

The *USA Today* article shown here appeared in the Jewish Newhouse-owned *The Times-Picayune* newspaper in New Orleans with the title: "Atheist and Jewish? For many, it's fine."

So fifty percent of religious Jews don't believe in God. The other fifty percent who do believe in God, don't mind that half of their fellow Jews in the synagogue are atheists who openly proclaim that they don't believe in God.

The only thing important to them is that they are fellow members of their tribe! Belief in God is secondary to them compared to Jewish tribalism.224 (from Kimberly Winston, Religion News Service, *USA Today*, 9/26/2011)

The article highlights the fact that many outspoken atheists are active, even leaders, in synagogues. It shows that Judaism does not demand belief in God, only adherence to Jewish laws. It shows how one-half of all "religious" Jews don't believe in God. And, it shows that these atheist Jews take part in Judaism not because of any belief in God, but as a connection to the Jewish people, one of blood rather than religious faith in God. Here are some quotes from the article:

> "Atheism and Judaism are not contradictory, so to have an atheist in a Jewish congregation isn't an issue or a challenge or a problem,...Unlike other religions, Judaism has often embraced its atheist strain."

"Atheism is entrenched in American Judaism. In researching their book American Grace, authors Robert Putnam and David Campbell found that half   [Approximately 50 Percent] of all American Jews doubt God's existence."

"They go because they want some kind of ethnic identity," Magid said. "They don't care about the prayers. It allows them to feel a sense of Jewishness, but has little to do with religion..."

That's what prompted Jennifer Cohen Oko, a Washington, D.C.-based writer, to join a Reform synagogue, her first. Neither Cohen nor her husband believe in God, but, like many Jews, they joined for their two children.

"I want my kids to understand they are Jewish, to be proud of being Jewish and to understand their heritage," Cohen said...

So we can say that the tribalist racism that has been the Jewish driving force behind Communism is a combination of elements. This racism includes social structure, workings of the Jewish religion, and psychology. These elements have an effect on Jewish reproductive selection, affecting Jewish traits. It is a symbiotic relationship, as Jewish genetic relatedness affects the religious and psychological structure of the Jewish community.

Unfortunately, all evidence points to steadily increasing Jewish extremism and racism in the modern world. Two factors are key in this radicalization:

1) In the modern world of interaction of Jews with the Gentile world, those Jews who find an inherent attraction to Gentile values, artistic and cultural expression, and aesthetics are far more likely to intermarry than the Jews in the closed, walled societies of the past. So those with more universalistic Gentile tendencies are removed from the Jewish gene pool. Their more moderate influence on policy and attitudes toward Gentiles are removed from the community.

2) The highest birthrates among Jews are found in the most radical, ethnocentric divisions of Judaism. For instance the Hasidic Jews have by far the highest birthrates and more "liberal" Jews have much lower ones.

The Jewish religion has elements within it which are driven by group genetics. These group genetics drive group psychology, which again in turn affects the Jewish gene pool.

The Jews, with their group paranoia have therefore become a self-fulfilling prophecy. They are indeed persecuted, not, as they tell everyone, because of the apparently continuous and mysterious existence of irrational anti-Semites, but because of the cause and effect: inevitable reactions to their own behavior. And the persecutions in turn reinforce and fuel their own misanthropic behavior.

All this being said, when one talks about a group, he is talking about common and prevailing tendencies and not characteristics necessarily applicable to every member of the group.

Individual genetic characteristics are often described as the result of a genetic dice cup. Sometimes children can be born with certain characteristics quite different from their parents. Certainly most Jews tend to naturally gravitate to intrinsic Jewishness, although not all of them do so. Also, there are what is called epigenetic aspects.

Many genes that affect psychology and even philological traits can be turned on or off by actions or a number of environmental factors.

It can be compared with a person who has a genetic predisposition to alcoholism. Usually it takes years for alcoholism to develop in even the predisposed. So, even someone predisposed to alcoholism will not develop it if he simply doesn't drink alcohol to begin with, the alcohol in effect turns on those genes responsible for alcoholism.

In truth, we should honor those Jews with both the inclination and courage to expose the tribalist racism so prevalent among Jews. One such person of Jewish heritage is Gilad Atzmon, who not only opposes Zionism, he recognizes the Jewish tribalism and mindset that has so damaged the world.

My book, *Jewish Supremacism* is dedicated to Israel Shahak, a Jewish human rights activist who dedicated his life fighting Jewish tribalism and extremism. His words are valuable for both Gentiles and Jews. He said it with simplicity and clearness:

> **"Anti-Semitism and Jewish chauvinism can only be fought simultaneously."**

Chapter 36
Final Words from
Nobel Laureate Aleksandr Solzhenitsyn

This book began with remarks from my personal discussions with Aleksandr Solzhenitsyn. He was a victim of Bolshevism and through his literary genius he laid bare the most horrific killing machine in all of world history.

Communism in all its forms, worldwide, has brutally oppressed and murdered far more people than the official, celebrity-endorsed numbers ascribed to Hitler's Germany. In fact, the Communist death toll exceeds the total of all oppressive regimes in the history of mankind.

Although an academic is reluctant to use the word evil, Communism, based on its horrific record, may be regarded as the greatest embodiment of evil in human history.

Many nations have waged wars and committed great crimes against civilian populations during those conflicts and conquests. But no regime has ever purposefully enslaved, tortured, imprisoned and murdered more of its own nation's population than the Bolshevik tyranny in Russia. Add to this Communism's subsequent incarnations of Marxist inhumanity.

Just to make it more possible to grasp the almost unimaginable magnitude of the Bolshevik genocide against humanity, it is accurate to say that Marxism's Russian, European and worldwide terrors led to the murder of more human beings than the total number of every man, woman and child in Great Britain today – about 60 million people!

Yet, there is no Ziomedia interest in remembering the innocent people murdered and crushed by Communism. The same Ziomedia endlessly obsesses with vivid dramatizations of Germany's National Socialist years as the sum of all evil. Yet, the far more numerous victims of Communism are completely ignored in comparison with those of the Holocaust.

The politically-correct official establishment total of six million in a Nazi Holocaust has been headlined for almost seventy years. The Jewish-executed Communist Holocausts of ten times that number are systematically Memory-Holed.

The Secret Behind Communism and its horrific mass murder is hardly a secret. The facts are there for all to see. But, the Jewish-dominated American and international media do not want you to be aware of it. The Ziomedia seeks, year after year, to avert the European anger that would erupt if our people were to ever fully feel the pain that lost millions of our own people have suffered at the hands of alien Communists.

It is thus fitting that this work ends where it began: with words committed to writing by the great Russian patriot and Nobel prize winner, from his book *Two Hundred Years Together, The Russian-Jewish History 1795-1916,*[225] and from other of his published articles and texts. *Two Hundred Years Together* is perhaps the Nobel prizewinner's most important book.

The book has not been published in English. It has not been reviewed in the major controlled media of the world. It has been in many ways made secret in the same way that its subject has been made secret.

The fact that this intensely-documented book, written near the end of the life of a Nobel Prizewinner in literature, one of the greatest writers of our time could not be translated and published in English by a major publisher, is a fact that screams a defining and fatal fact about the present world we live in. The Jewish tribal extremists have more power in the world today than they have ever had in history. And the evidence is

The final books of Nobel Prizewinner in literature, Aleksandr Solzhenitsyn, has not been made available to the English-speaking world. After reading *The Secret Behind Communism,* one understands exactly why.

convincing that they are driving the greatest conflict of the 21st century, the so-called "Clash of Civilizations."

The Suppression of Solzhenitsyn

It is time to share some of the information hidden by the suppression of this book. Here are some of Solzhenitsyn's documented revelations. Some of the text which follows was written by Wolfgang Strauss, to which we are indebted for some of the important quotations from this monumental work.

Solzhenitsyn points out that "Many more Jewish voices than Russian are heard in this book." The reason for this becomes obvious as one delves into the book. For example, even the "Russian" Social Democracy Party, from which the Bolsheviks were to emerge, was created out of personnel drawn from the *Allgemeine jüdische Arbeiterbund* in Lithuania, Poland, and Russia.

In his work, Solzhenitsyn writes of the "stranglers of Russia," the "hangmen of the dirty revolution" — and then goes on to describe them in detail: the "Bol'sheviki yevrey," or the "Jew Bolsheviks." In another place he uses the term "Bol'shevististkiye Juden" (Bolshevistic Jews).

Superordinate to these is the key expression -"Yevreyskiy vopros" (the Jewish Question). After 1918 the Communist censors in no way forbade this expression, even with regard to Jewish Bolsheviks the Jewish question was not a taboo.

On the contrary, the Jewish question became the central theme of the Party ideology, which had become a secular religion. Lenin himself set the example in 1924 with his famous instructive paper "On the Jewish Question in Russia," published by the Moscow Proletariat Publishing House (cited by Solzhenitsyn).

The overwhelming Jewish domination of the Communist movement was so obvious that it was arousing unrest among the ninety-eight percent non-Jewish population. Lenin points out the Jewish leadership and disproportionate percentage among the Communists but tries to downplay it, as it was becoming a problem for the ruling element of Communism.

Solzhenitsyn recalls that immediately before the Revolution, the Bolshevistic Jews Trotsky and Kamenev concluded a military alliance with three Jewish Social-Revolutionaries – Natanson, Steinberg, and Kamkov.

What Solzhenitsyn said is that Lenin's military putsch, from the purely military point of view, relied on a Jewish network. The collaboration between Trotsky and his coreligionists in the Left Social-Revolutionary parties assured Lenin's success in the Palace Revolt of October 1917.

Solzhenitsyn cites the Israeli historian Aron Abramovitch who in 1982 in Tel Aviv wrote:

> **"In October 1917 the Jewish contingent of soldiers played a decisive role in the preparation and execution of the armed Bolshevik uprising in Petrograd and other cities as well as in the following battles in the course of suppressing rebellions against the new Soviet power."**[226]

The famed Latvian Rifle Regiment of the 12th Army, Lenin's praetorian guard, had a Jewish commissar, Nachimson, in charge.

In 1924 the Jewish historian, Pasmanik, wrote:

> **"The emergence of Bolshevism was the result of special aspects of Russian history. However, Soviet Russia can thank the work of the Jewish commissars for the organization of Bolshevism."**[227]

Solzhenitsyn cites this key passage in his book, and puts the word "organization" in quotes in the book text.

The large number of eyewitness reports from the early period of Soviet rule is astounding. In the Council of People's Commissars, the writer Nashivin simply notes: "Jews, Jews, Jews." Nashivin avers that he was never an anti-Semite, but "the mass of Jews in the Kremlin literally knocks your eyes out."

In 1919 the famous writer Vladimir Korolenko, who was close to the Social Democrats and who had protested against the pogroms in Tsarist Russia, made the following entry in his diary:

> **"There are many Jews and Jewesses among the Bolsheviks. Their main characteristics – self-righteousness, aggressive tactlessness and presumptive arrogance – are painfully evident. Bolshevism is found contemptible in the Ukraine. The preponderance of Jewish physiognomies, especially in the Cheka,**

evokes an extremely virulent hatred of Jews among the people."228

Chapter 15 of Solzhenitsyn's book opens with the words: "Jews among the Bolsheviks is nothing new. Much has already been written about it."

This for Solzhenitsyn is further support for his cardinal thesis, namely, that Bolshevik Jews were the indispensable power brokers in the victory of Bolshevism, in the Russian Civil War, and in the early Soviet Regime.

> "Whoever holds the opinion that the revolution was not a Russian, but an alien-led revolution points to the Yiddish family names or pseudonyms to exonerate the Russian people for the revolution. On the other hand, those who try to minimize the over-proportional representation of Jews in the Bolshevik seizure of power may sometimes claim that they were not religious Jews, but rather, apostates, renegades, and atheists."

According to rabbinical law, whoever was born of a Jewish mother is a Jew. Orthodox Judaism requires more, i.e., recognition of the Hebraic Halacha scriptural laws and the observance of the religious laws of the Mishna, which form the basis of the Talmud. Solzhenitsyn then asks:

> "How strong were the influence, power, fascination, and adherence of secular Jews among the religious Jews and how many atheists were active among the Bolsheviks? Can a people really just renounce its renegades? Does such a renunciation make any sense?"

Solzhenitsyn's attempt to answer these questions on the basis of historical facts concentrates on several factors, namely, the behavior of Orthodox Jews after October 1917, the relative numbers of Bolshevik Jews before and after October, the ascendance of Bolshevistic Jews in the cadres of the Red Army and the Cheka, Lenin's Jewish strategy, and finally, Lenin's own heritage.

> "The Bolsheviks appealed to the Jews immediately after the seizure of power. And they came; they came in masses. Some served in the executive branch, others in the various governmental organs. They came primarily from among secular young Jews who in no way could be classified as atheists or even as enemies of God. This phenomenon bore a mass character."

By the end of 1917 Lenin had not yet left Smolny, when a Jewish Commissariat for Nationality Questions was already at work in Petrograd. In March 1919 the VIII Party Congress of the Communist Party (Bolsheviks) undertook to establish a "Jewish Soviet Russian Communist Bund."

In this matter Solzhenitsyn again relies on Jewish historians. Leonard Schapiro, living in London in 1961, wrote:

> **"Thousands of Jews streamed to the Bolsheviks whom they saw as the protectors of the international revolution."**[229]

M. Chaifetz also commented on the Jewish support of Bolshevism: "For a Jew, who came neither from among the aristocrats nor the clergy, Bolshevism represented a successful and promising new prospect to belong to a new clan." The Chaifetz article appeared in 1980 in an Israeli journal for the Jewish intelligentsia arriving from the USSR.

The influx of Jewish youths into the Bolshevik Party at first was a consequence of the pogroms in the territory held by the White Army in 1919, argues David Schub. Solzhenitsyn rejects Schub's argument as a myth: "Schub's argument is not valid because the massive entry of Jews into the Soviet apparatus occurred as early as 1917 and throughout all of 1918. Unquestionably, the Civil War situation in 1919 did hasten the amalgamation of Jewish cadres with the Bolsheviks."

Solzhenitsyn traces the rise in Judeophobia, among other things, back to the brutal Bolshevik suppression of peasant and citizen uprisings, the slaughter of priests and bishops, especially the village clergy, and finally, the extermination of the nobility, culminating in the murder of the Tsar and his family.

During the decisive years of the Civil War (1918-1920) the secret police (Cheka) was controlled by Bolshevik Jews. The commandants of the various prisons were usually Jews from Poland or Latvia.

Jews occupied the Party, Army, and Cheka command positions in Odessa. Jews constituted the majority in the Presidium of the Petrograd City Soviet. Lazar Kaganovich directed the Civil War terror in Nizhny Novgorod, while Rosalia

Salkind-Semlyachka commanded the mass executions by firing squads in the Kremlin.

In 1920 the farming areas of West Siberia were turned into a Vendée when Jewish grain-commissar Indenbaum through his confiscation campaigns caused mass starvation.

During the winter in the steppes, rebellious farmers were forced to dig their own graves. The Chekists doused the naked bodies with water; those that tried to flee were machine-gunned. The peasant uprising in Tyumen entered the history books as the "Iskhimski Rebellion".

By virtue of the sheer numbers liquidated and the radicalism and motivation of the perpetrators, the mass executions of Russian Orthodox priests assumed a genocidal character. The intellectual elite of Eastern Christendom in Russia was slaughtered.

In this destruction and extermination, Sverdlov, Dzerzhinski, and Trotsky were the most powerful executors. None of them were Russian. The executioners in Yekaterinburg and the Ural governments were not Russians.

The bloody careers of Goloshekin and Beloborodov, the Party terrorists and Ural mafia killers, are described in Solzhenitsyn's work.

On the eve of the XII Party Day 1923, the Politburo consisted of three Jews and three non-Jews. The ratio in the Komsomol Presidium was three to four. In the XI Party Day, 'Jew Bolsheviks' constituted 26% of the Central Committee membership. Because of this foreign invasion and anti-Slavic trends, prominent Russian Leninists decided upon an "anti-Jewish rebellion."

Solzhenitsyn's book dealt not only with Russia: in the period 1939-41, he points out, a large percentage of Jewry in eastern Poland, Galicia, and in the Baltic States collaborated with the Red Army, Stalin's secret police, and Bolshevism in general. He writes:

> **"In eastern Poland, which had been incorporated in the Soviet Union in September 1939, the Jews, especially the younger generation, welcomed the invading Red Army with frenetic jubilation. Whether in Poland, Bessarabia, Lithuania, or**

Bukowina, the Jews were the main support of Soviet power. The newspapers report that the Jews are enthusiastically supporting the establishment of Communist rule."[230]

Shortly before the opening of the XIII Party Day, veteran Russian revolutionaries Frunze, Nogin, and Troyanovsky called for the expulsion of the 'Jewish leaders' from the Politburo. The opponents of the purge reacted quickly. In no time, Nogin died after an operation on his esophagus, after which Frunze went under the knife.

In Solzhenitsyn's opinion, the main reason for this outbreak of new anti-Semitism was to be found in the hostility towards Russians inherent in the extreme Jewish internationalism.

Unlike the Jewish intelligentsia who greeted the revolution of 1918 with great passion, the Russian proletariat was not fascinated by the idea of a Russian-led internationalism. After 1918 the Jews spoke consistently of "their country."

To support his thesis Solzhenitsyn cites the most important Russian, non-Jewish Bolshevik leader, Nikolai Bukharin. He was crucial in the early days in getting the support of Russians to the new regime. Ultimately, after courageously exposing Jewish tribalism in the Communist leadership, he was executed after the last Moscow show trial in 1938.

In the second half of the 1920s a debate raged between the right wing and left wing of the Communist Party. "Right wing Communists" may sound oxymoronic to American ears, but these were the labels used. The right wanted to continue policies favoring agriculture and light industry, while the left wanted to extract as much as possible from the peasants in order to build the heavy industries necessary for war. Tellingly, the sides in the debate were drawn largely along ethnic lines.

Former Princeton Professor Stephen F. Cohen is an American Jewish academic who specializes in this period of Russian history. This is how he described the opposing sides in his biography of non-Jewish Bolshevik revolutionary Nikolai Bukharin:

"Three other features distinguished the Politburo Right. In contrast to the predominantly Jewish Left and the increasingly Transcaucasian complexion of Stalin's group, all of its major and second-rank leaders were Russians....But the seemingly probable was not always the case. During the ascendancy of the Politburo Right, for example, non-Russian nationalities enjoyed their greatest freedom under Soviet rule. The second feature was particularly striking in contrast to Stalin: Bukharin, Rykov, and Tomskii had reputations as popular Bolshevik leaders."

"[T]he Politburo Right's third political distinction: the great support their leadership obtained in Commissariats (particularly Agriculture, Finance, Labor, and Trade) and other state organs (the Supreme Economic Council, the State Bank, and Gosplan [the state economic planning agency]) responsible for preparing and administering economic policy. These institutions, by nature sympathetic to the return to orthodox economic practices, and with their importance revived by NEP, were staffed largely by former anti-Bolshevik intellectuals, so called nonparty specialists. In particular, both former Mensheviks working in the Supreme Economic Council and Gosplan and Socialist Revolutionaries in the Commissariat of Agriculture strongly preferred Bukharin and Rykov as party leaders to either Stalin or the Left."[231] – from Stephen F. Cohen: *Bukharin and the Bolshevik Revolution: A Political Biography, 1888-1938* (Oxford, Oxford University Press, 1980), pp. 232-233.

Cohen reveals that Nicholai Bukharin and the more Russian elements of the Communist Party were opposed to the mass murders of the Jewish elements that drove them on.

The greatest tragedy of Soviet history, and perhaps the entire history of the 20th Century, is that this predominantly Jewish Left won its struggle against the ethnic Russian right, which had much more support from the people and also from the intellectuals and nonparty specialists responsible for the economic restoration.

Not only was the Bolshevik Revolution largely a Jewish affair, but the greatest crime committed by the Bolsheviks was engineered and carried out by the Jewish faction over the opposition of the ethnic Russian faction. Jewish ethnic hatred and extremism played the crucial role in the greatest mass murder of all time.

At the Leningrad Party Conference in early 1927 Bukharin had criticized the 'capitalistic' nature of the Jewish mid-level bourgeoisie who had come to power and had taken the place of the Russian bourgeoisie in the main cities of the USSR, and "whom we, comrades, must sharply condemn." Former chief Bolshevik theorist Bukharin concluded by saying that the Jews themselves were responsible for the new anti-Semitism.

There were also reasons for the outburst of proletariat anti-Semitism in two other sensitive areas. The Russian working class young people were getting nowhere in their quest for advancement on the educational front.

In 1926, 26% of university students were Jews who had enjoyed a bourgeois background, Solzhenitsyn pointed out.

Mostly Jews, between 30 and 50%, occupied the main positions in the domestic and foreign trade commissariats. Their empire included rural and urban store chains, restaurants, business canteens, prison and barracks galleys, cooperatives, and consumer goods production.

Management of the Gosplan (State Plan) and the five-year plans was exercised by Rosenholz, Rukhimovich, Epstein, Frumkin, and Selemki; they controlled the nation's food supply.

Despite the enormous bloodletting in 1936-38, millions of Jews still served the Stalinist regime with cadaver-like loyalty; they remained enthusiastic, unshakable, almost blind defenders of the cause of Socialism. Solzhenitsyn writes:

> **"Cadaver-like obedience in the GPU, the Red Army, the diplomatic service, and on the ideological front. The passionate participation of young Jews in these branches was in no way dampened by the bloody events of 1936-38."**[232]

From the very beginning the secret police were under the control of the 'Bolshevik Jews.' Solzhenitsyn revealed their names in the most interesting chapter of his book called "The Nineteen Twenties."

Solzhenitsyn gives us the biographies of the mass murderers at their desks in the Cheka, the OGPU, and the GPU. But they were not just sitting at their desks. Uritzki, Unschlicht, Katznelson, Bermann, Agranov, Spiegelglas, Schwarz, Asbel, Chaifetz, Pauker, Maier, Yagoda, personally participated in the tortures, hangings, crucifixions, and incinerations.

Years later, when the Gulag Archipelago was being expanded, they were again to be found in the front line of executioners. Israel Pliner was the slave master of the Moscow-Volga-Canal; Lazar Kogan, Zinovey Katznelson, and Boris Bermann directed the forced labor genocide at the White Sea Canal project.

Solzhenitsyn comments: "One cannot deny that history elected very many Jews to be the executors of Russia's fate."

Commissioned by the NKVD, the Jewish designer of execution systems, Grigori Mayranovsky, invented the gas chair.

When, in 1951, Mayranovsky, as the former head of the NKVD Laboratory Institute, was himself incarcerated, he wrote to Beria: "Please do not forget that by my hand hundreds of enemy- pigs of the Soviet State found their deserved end."

The mobile gassing truck was invented and tested by Isay Davidovich Berg, head of the NKVD Economics Division in the Moscow region.

In 1937, a second acceleration in the Great Purge, prisoners were sentenced to death in conveyor-belt fashion, packed into trucks, taken to the places of execution, shot in the back of the neck, and buried.

In the economic sense, Isay Berg found this method of liquidation inefficient, time-consuming and cost-intensive. He, therefore, in 1937 designed the mobile asphyxiation chamber, the gassing truck (Russian: dushegubka), as Solzhenitsyn describes in detail.

The doomed were loaded into a tightly sealed, completely airtight Russian Ford; during the drive the deadly exhaust from a gasoline engine was directed into the section containing those sentenced to death. Upon reaching the mass gravesite, the truck dumped the corpses into the burial ditch.

Solzhenitsyn lists the names of about fifty mass murderers of prisoners in his book. Their names betray their ethnic origin. Moise Framing, Mordichai Chorus, Josef Khodorovsky, Isaak Solz, Naum Zorkin, Moise Kalmanovich, Samuel Agurski, Lazar Aronstam, Israel Weizer, Aron Weinstein, Isaak Grindberg, Sholom Dvoylazki, Max Daitsh, Yesif Dreiser, Samuel Saks, Jona Jakir, Moise Kharitonov, Frid Markus, Solomon Kruglikov, Israel Razgon, Benjamin Sverdlov, Leo Kritzman...

Also in this section Solzhenitsyn reveals the names of the butchers who bossed the secret police. They once headed the notorious Lubyanka torture prison and torture complex, now

Dr. David Duke lectures at the Mayakovsky Museum next to the infamous Lubyanka Prison

they themselves succumbed in the chambers of Lubyanka: pistol-flaunting Matvey Berman, Josef Blatt, Abraham Belenki, Isaak Shapiro, Serge Shpigelglas, Israel Leblevski, Pinkus Simanovski, Abraham Slutski, Benjamin Gerson, Zinovi Katsnelson, Natan Margolin – an almost endless list of 'Jew Bolsheviks.'

Solzhenitsyn asks who were their victims? The overwhelming majority were Russians. Those shot in cellars, those burnt to death in the cloisters, those drowned in river boats, those hanged in the forest; officers, peasants, aristocrats, proletariats, the anti-anti-Semitic bourgeois intellectuals – Russians mostly, but others as well. The "hangmen of the Revolution," guilty of crimes they try to justify with internationalism, transformed their "dirty revolution" into what Solzhenitsyn calls an "antislav" revolution. The Nobel Laureate Solzhenitsyn emphasizes that the Cheka-Lubyanka-Gulag holocaustic perpetrators could not possibly be a Slavic people (The people of Russia and Eastern Europe) (p. 93)[233]

Solzhenitsyn in *Two Hundred Years Together* and the massive work of scholarship *The Gulag Archipelago* volumes I, II, and III begs the question of why the greatest crime against humanity in all history is unimportant to ninety-nine percent of global media. By contrast, the Jewish suffering in the Second World War is saturated by media and thus something felt emotionally by the vast majority of the modern world.

Truly moral people oppose the murder, or any kind of harm against a population. Jewish people suffered terribly during the war, and the cause of their suffering is rightfully condemned. Yet, giving our hearts to Jewish victims does not absolve us to ignore non-Jewish ones, including those of far greater numbers.

Blame must fall on the perpetrators of the Red Terror just as the Ziomedia heaps blame on those accused of crimes against Jews, for if we don't identify the malevolent force that committed the biggest slaughter in history, we are in danger of reliving it.

In fact, the supremacist, tribalist forces that created The Red Terror's annihilation of human life and freedom, has more power in the globalist world now than it did then.

There is no more important task for everyone who supports human life and rights than to learn *The Secret Behind Communism.*

In doing so, we can help prevent a tribalist world tyranny that will eclipse the horrors of even Soviet Bolshevism.

This is surely vital for us, but another purely human motivation must be to answer our hearts. We must safeguard the memory of the millions of men, women and children who suffered this evil horror, but who are tragically forgotten.

We must share *The Secret Behind Communism* for their sake, as well as for the sake of our children.

Every people on Earth is haunted by its collective memory.

We must remember. If we forget, we will lose our way.

In our remembrance of those who suffered, and in defense of all that is just and noble, we must prevail.

We must defend the victims, as well as defend ourselves, our children and our yet unborn.

To this task we commit our lives, inspired by the eternal spirit of Aleksandr Solzhenitsyn.

Index

Endnotes

1Duke, Dr. D. "A Life-Changing Conversation in Moscow" Duke Report 2002

2 Solzhenitsyn, A. (1974). *The Gulag archipelago, 1918-1956 : an experiment in literary investigation, I-II.* Tran. Thomas P. Whitney. London : Collins : Harvill Press. p.79.

3 Server Plocker, *Stalin's Jews,* YnetNews.com, published: 12.21.06

4 "Soviet Genocide in Ukraine. By Raphael *Lemkin* (1953)

5 V. Danilov et al., Sovetskaia derevnia glazami OGPU_NKVD. T. 3, kn. 2. Moscow 2004. P. 572 With thanks to Professor Roman Serbyn whose research provided this quote.

6 Rose Kleiner, "Archives to throw new light on Ehrenburg," *Canadian Jewish News* (Toronto), March 17, 1988, p. 9.

7 Ibid.

8 Alfred de Zayas, *Nemesis at Potsdam* (London: Roudedge & Kegan Paul, 2nd edition, 1979), pp. 6546, 201; Erich Kern (ed.), Verheimlichte Dokumente (Munich: FZ- Verlag, 1988), pp. 260-61, 353-55.

9 *Who's Who In World Jewry.* (1965). New York : Pitman Publishing. Corp.

10 *Who's Who In American Jewry.* (1927-). New York : The Jewish Biographical Bureau, Inc.

11 Goldwater, B. M. (1960). *The Conscience Of A Conservative.* Shepherdsville, Kentucky: Victor Publishing Co.

12 Stormer, J. (1964). *None Dare Call It Treason.* Florissant, Missouri: Liberty Bell Press.

13 Schwarz, F. C. (1960). *You Can Trust The Communists.* Englewood Cliffs, New Jersey: Prentice-Hall.

14 Churchill, W. (1920). Zionism versus Bolshevism: A Struggle for the Soul of the Jewish People. *Illustrated Sunday Herald.* February 8.

15 Churchill, W. (1920). Zionism versus Bolshevism: A Struggle for the Soul of the Jewish People.

16 U.S. National Archives. (1919). Record Group 120: Records of the American Expeditionary Forces, June 9.

17 Wilton, R. (1920). *Last Days of the Romanovs.* New York: George H. Doran Co. p.148.

18 U.S. National Archives. (1919). Record Group 120: Records of the American Expeditionary Forces, June 9.

19 Francis, D. R. (1921). *Russia From the American Embassy.* New York: C. Scribner's & Sons. p.214.

20 National Archives, Dept. of State Decimal File, 1910-1929, file 861.00/5067

21 Nettl, J. P. (1967). *The Soviet Achievement.* New York: Harcourt, Brace & World.

22 *Encyclopedia Judaica.* p. 791-792.

23 Trotsky, L. (1968). *Stalin: An Appraisal of the Man and His Influence.* ed. trans. Charles Malamuth. London, MacGibbon & Kee.

24 Shub, David. (1961). *Novyi Zhurnal* no. 63.

25 Shub, D. (1966). *Lenin: a Biography*. Harmondsworth, Penguin.

26 *Review de Fonds Social Juif*. (1970). no. 161.

27 Ben-Shlomo, B. Z. (1991). Reporting on Lenin's Jewish Roots. *Jewish Chronicle*. July 26. p.2.

28 Hoffman, Michael. (1997). Campaign for Radical Truth in History. P.O. Box 849. Coeur d' Alene, ID 83816. Ehrenburg won the Order of Lenin and the Stalin Prize and willed his papers to the Israeli Yad Vashem Holocaust Museum.

29 Goldberg, Anatol. (1984). *Ilya Ehrenburg : Revolutionary, novelist, poet, war correspondent, propagandist : the extraordinary epic of a Russian survivor*. New York : Viking.

30 Solzhenitsyn, A. (1974). *The Gulag Archipelago, 1918-1956 : An Experiment in Literary investigation*, I-II. Tran. Thomas P. Whitney. London : Collins: Harvill Press. p.79.

31 Aronson, G. (1949). *Soviet Russia and the Jews*. New York: American Jewish League Against Communism.

32 *The Jewish Voice*. (1942). New York. January.

33 *The Congress Bulletin*. (1940).(New York). American Jewish Congress, January 5.

34 George Bernard Shaw, quoted in *The Jewish Guardian* (1931). said: "I have seen the statement which Stalin gave recently to the Jewish Telegraphic Agency on Anti-Semitism and in which the Soviet leader said that under the Soviet laws militant Anti-Semitism is punishable by death."

35 Joseph Stalin (Note to the Jewish Telegraphic Agency). 12th January 1931, Collected Works, vol. 13.

36 Gregor Aronson. (1949). *Soviet Russia and the Jews*. New York: American Jewish League Against Communism.

37 *Encyclopaedia Britannica*. (1947). Vol. 2. p.76.

38 Latimer, E.W. (1895). *Russia and Turkey in the 19th Century*. A. C. McLury & Co. p. 332.

39 *Jewish Communal Register of New York City*. (1918). p.1018-1019

40 *New York Journal American* (1949). February 3.

41 Andelman, M.S. (1974). *To Eliminate the Opiate*. New York-Tel Aviv: Zahavia. Ltd. 26

42 Nedava, J. (1971). *Trotsky and the Jews*. Philadelphia. Jewish Publication Society.

43 Marx, Karl, (1936). *Das Kapital*. English. New York: The Modern library.

44 Marx, Karl, (1932). *Capital, the Communist manifesto and other writings*. New York: The Modern library.

45 *Chicago Jewish Sentinel*. (1975). Inside Judaica. October 30.

46 *Barnes Review*. (1996). The Racism of Marx and Engles. Oct. vol. 2. 10. p. 3.

47 *The Encyclopedia of Zionism in Israel*. (1971). New York: Herzl Press/McGraw-Hill. p.496-497.

[48] Wilton, R. (1920). *Last Days of the Romanovs*. New York: George H. Doran Co. 148.

[49] Rapoport, Louis. (1990). *Stalin's War Against The Jews*. Free Press/Simon & Schuster.

[50] Curtis, William Elroy. (1907). *National Geographic Magazine*. The Revolution in Russia. May. p.313.

[51] Orwell, George. (1948). 1984.

[52] page 76, volume 2, 1947.

[53] *Russia and Turkey in the 19th Century,* by E. W. Latimer, page 332. A. C. McClury & Co., 1895.

[54] *Three Who Made a Revolution,* page 360, by Bertram Wolfe, Dial Press, New York, 1948

[55] *Russia,* page 41, by Bernard Pares, New American Library, New York, revised 1949.

[56] page 285, vol. 9, New York, 1939.

[57] p. 228, vol. 9.

[58] *Donald Thompson in Russia,* page 54, by Donald Thompson, Century Co.. New York, 1918.

[59] *Russian Bolshevik Revolution,* page 58, by Edward Alsworth Ross, Century Company. New York. 1921

[60] *Russian Bolshevik Revolution,* ibid., p. 45, 67

[61] *Stalin: An Appraisal of the Man and His Influence,* by Lev Trotsky (translated by Charles Malamuth), Harper Bros., New York & London, 1941.

[62] Leon Trotsky, *Stalin,* page 48, 220-221.

[63] *ibid* page 48, 222-223.

[64] *ibid,* page 48, 217.

[65] Jewish Encyclopedia, 1943 vol. 10, pg. 312. A line it quotes probably from a newspaper account.

[66] Ecyclopedia Judaica

[67] Ibid.

[68] Ibid.

[69] Ibid.

[70] Churchill, W. (1920). Zionism versus Bolshevism: A Struggle for the Soul of the Jewish People. *Illustrated Sunday Herald.* February 8.

[71] Ibid.

[72] U.S. National Archives. (1919). Record Group 120: Records of the American Expeditionary Forces, June 9.

[73] Ibid.

[74] *Lenin,* page 156 (ibid page 34).

[75] John Toland in his book *Hitler* (p. 76)

[76] John Toland, *Adolf Hitler,* Doubleday & Company, Inc., Garden City, New York. (p. 76)

[77] *Encyclopedia Britannica,* page 517, vol. 13-1946

[78] Dodd, Mead, Co., page 587

79 Hanebrink, Paul A. (2006). *In defense of Christian Hungary: religion, nationalism, and antisemitism.* Ithaca, NY: Cornell University Press. pp. 84–86

80 *The Tragedy of Hungary,* An Appeal for World Peace, Birinyi, Louis, Cleveland, 1924.

81 Trotsky, L. (1968). *Stalin: An Appraisal of the Man and His Influence.* ed. trans. Charles Malamuth. London, MacGibbon & Kee.

82 *The Wolf of the Kremlin,* Stuart Kahan, William Morrow & Co; 1987.

83 V. Danilov et al., Sovetskaia derevnia glazami OGPU_NKVD. T. 3, kn. 2. Moscow 2004. P. 572 With thanks to Professor Roman Serbyn whose research provided this quote.

84 "Soviet Genocide in Ukraine. By Raphael *Lemkin* (1953)

85 Lubomyr Luciuk, "Lemkin: Holodomor 'classic' genocide" Kyiv Post Nov. 19,2009

86 Alfred de Zayas, *Nemesis at Potsdam* (London: Roudedge & Kegan Paul, 2nd edition, 1979), pp. 6546, 201; Erich Kern (ed.), Verheimlichte Dokumente (Munich: FZ- Verlag, 1988), pp. 260-61, 353-55.

87 "Stalin's Jews," Ynet News, 12.21.2006

88 Ibid.

89 Jewish Run Concentration Camps in the Soviet Union,1937

90 The Jewish Century by Yuri Slezkine (Princeton, NJ: Princeton University Press, 2004

91 Ibid.

92 Be*hind the Iron Curtain,* by John Gunther, Harper Brothers, New York.

93 William Tonesk, Interview published in the *New York Polish Daily* of June 9, 1987

94 *Kracow Tygodnik Powszechnw,* March 20, 1988

95 The Jewish Century by Yuri Slezkine (Princeton, NJ: Princeton University Press, 2004

96 p. 306 The Jewish Century by Yuri Slezkine (Princeton, NJ: Princeton University Press, 2004

97 ibid., p. 308

98 ibid., pp. 313–314

99 ibid., p. 314

100 ibid., p. 310

101 ibid., p. 330

102 ibid., p. 333

103 ibid., p. 342

104 ibid., p. 362

105 ibid., p. 345

106 ibid., p. 360

107 Shelfer, G, At Putin's side, an army of Jewish billionaires, *Jerusalem Post,* 06/26/2012.

108 *Nasha Strana, no. 2850.* Buenos-Aires, 23 August 2008.

109 *The Jewish People, Past and Present,* Central Yiddish Culture Organization (CYCO) New York.

110 *Reviews in American History,* Volume 38, Number 2, June 2010 p. 359

111 Budenz, Louis ,*This is My Story* 1947, McGraw-Hill: New York.

112 Budenz, Louis, *Men without Faces: The Communist Conspiracy in the U.S.A* 1948, Harper: New York.

113 Budenz, Louis, *The Cry is Peace 1952*, Henry Regnery: Chicago.

114 Budenz, Louis, The Techniques of Communism, 1954, Henry Regnery: Chicago.

Budenz, Louis ,*This is My Story* 1947, McGraw-Hill: New York.

Budenz, Louis, *Men without Faces: The Communist Conspiracy in the U.S.A* 1948, Harper: New York.

Budenz, Louis, *The Cry is Peace 1952*, Henry Regnery: Chicago.

Budenz, Louis, *The Techniques of Communism*, 1954, Henry Regnery: Chicago.

115 Ibid.

116 Budenz, Louis ,*This is My Story* 1947, McGraw-Hill: New York.

117 Ibid.

118 Budenz, Louis, *The Cry is Peace 1952*, Henry Regnery: Chicago.

119 Ibid.

120 Ibid.

121 Budenz, Louis ,*This is My Story* 1947, McGraw-Hill: New York.

122 Budenz, Louis, *Men without Faces: The Communist Conspiracy in the U.S.A* 1948, Harper: New York.

123 Ibid.

124 Budenz, Louis, *The Cry is Peace 1952*, Henry Regnery: Chicago.

125 Budenz, Louis, *The Techniques of Communism*, 1954, Henry Regnery: Chicago.

126 Ibid.

127 Budenz, Louis, *Men without Faces: The Communist Conspiracy in the U.S.A* 1948, New York.

128 Budenz, Louis, *The Techniques of Communism*, 1954, Henry Regnery: Chicago.

129 Budenz, Louis, *The Cry is Peace 1952*, Henry Regnery: Chicago.

130 Budenz, Louis, *Men without Faces: The Communist Conspiracy in the U.S.A* 1948, Harper: New York.

131 Budenz, Louis, *The Cry is Peace 1952*, Henry Regnery: Chicago.

132 Ibid.

133 Budenz, Louis, *Men without Faces: The Communist Conspiracy in the U.S.A* 1948, Harper: New York.

134 Ibid.

135 Budenz, Louis, *The Cry is Peace 1952*, Henry Regnery: Chicago.

136 Ibid.

137 Budenz, Louis ,*This is My Story* 1947, McGraw-Hill: New York.

138 Budenz, Louis, *Men without Faces: The Communist Conspiracy in the U.S.A* 1948, Harper: New York.

139 Budenz, Louis, *The Techniques of Communism*, 1954, Henry Regnery: Chicago.

140 Budenz, Louis, *The Cry is Peace 1952*, Henry Regnery: Chicago.

141 Budenz, Louis, *The Techniques of Communism*, 1954, Henry Regnery: Chicago.

142 Budenz, Louis ,*This is My Story* 1947, McGraw-Hill: New York.

143 Budenz, Louis, *The Techniques of Communism*, 1954, Henry Regnery: Chicago.

144 Budenz, Louis, *Men without Faces: The Communist Conspiracy in the U.S.A* 1948, Harper: New York.

145 Budenz, Louis, *The Techniques of Communism*, 1954, Henry Regnery: Chicago.

146 Budenz, Louis, *The Cry is Peace 1952*, Henry Regnery: Chicago.

147 Budenz, Louis, *Men without Faces: The Communist Conspiracy in the U.S.A* 1948, Harper: New York.

148 Budenz, Louis, *The Cry is Peace 1952*, Henry Regnery: Chicago.

149 Ibid.

150 Budenz, Louis, *Men without Faces: The Communist Conspiracy in the U.S.A* 1948, Harper: New York.

151 Ibid.

152 Budenz, Louis ,*This is My Story* 1947, McGraw-Hill: New York.

153 Ibid.

154 Ibid.

155 Ibid.

156 Budenz, Louis, *Men without Faces: The Communist Conspiracy in the U.S.A* 1948, Harper: New York.

157 Budenz, Louis ,*This is My Story* 1947, McGraw-Hill: New York.

158 Budenz, Louis, *Men without Faces: The Communist Conspiracy in the U.S.A* 1948, Harper: New York.

159 Budenz, Louis ,*This is My Story* 1947, McGraw-Hill: New York.

160 Budenz, Louis, *Men without Faces: The Communist Conspiracy in the U.S.A* 1948, Harper: New York

161 Ibid.

162 Budenz, Louis, *The Techniques of Communism*, 1954, Henry Regnery: Chicago.

163 Budenz, Louis, *Men without Faces: The Communist Conspiracy in the U.S.A* 1948, Harper: New York.

164 Ibid.

165 Budenz, Louis, *The Cry is Peace* 1952, Henry Regnery: Chicago.

166 Budenz, Louis, *Men without Faces: The Communist Conspiracy in the U.S.A* 1948, Harper: New York.

167 Ibid.

168 Ibid.

169 Ibid.

170 Ibid.

171 Budenz, Louis, *The Techniques of Communism*, 1954, Henry Regnery: Chicago.

172 Budenz, Louis ,*This is My Story* 1947, McGraw-Hill: New York.

173 Budenz, Louis, *Men without Faces: The Communist Conspiracy in the U.S.A* 1948, Harper: New York.

174 Budenz, Louis ,*This is My Story* 1947, McGraw-Hill: New York.

175 Budenz, Louis, *The Techniques of Communism*, 1954, Henry Regnery: Chicago.

176 Ibid.

177 Budenz, Louis, *The Cry is Peace* 1952, Henry Regnery: Chicago.

178 Ibid.

179 Budenz, Louis ,*This is My Story* 1947, McGraw-Hill: New York.

180 Budenz, Louis, *The Cry is Peace* 1952, Henry Regnery: Chicago.

181 Budenz, Louis, *Men without Faces: The Communist Conspiracy in the U.S.A* 1948, Harper: New York.

182 Budenz, Louis, *The Cry is Peace* 1952, Henry Regnery: Chicago.

183 Ibid.

184 Budenz, Louis ,*This is My Story* 1947, McGraw-Hill: New York.

185 Budenz, Louis, *Men without Faces: The Communist Conspiracy in the U.S.A* 1948, Harper: New York.

186

187 Budenz, Louis ,*This is My Story* 1947, McGraw-Hill: New York.

188 Budenz, Louis, *The Techniques of Communism*, 1954, Henry Regnery: Chicago.

189 Budenz, Louis ,*This is My Story* 1947, McGraw-Hill: New York.

190 Budenz, Louis, *Men without Faces: The Communist Conspiracy in the U.S.A* 1948, Harper: New York.

191 Budenz, Louis ,*This is My Story* 1947, McGraw-Hill: New York.

192 Budenz, Louis, *Men without Faces: The Communist Conspiracy in the U.S.A* 1948, Harper: New York.

193 Budenz, Louis, *The Cry is Peace* 1952, Henry Regnery: Chicago.

194 Budenz, Louis, *Men without Faces: The Communist Conspiracy in the U.S.A* 1948, Harper: New York.

195 Budenz, Louis, *The Techniques of Communism*, 1954, Henry Regnery: Chicago.

196 Budenz, Louis, *The Cry is Peace* 1952, Henry Regnery: Chicago.

197 Budenz, Louis ,*This is My Story* 1947, McGraw-Hill: New York.

198 Budenz, Louis, *Men without Faces: The Communist Conspiracy in the U.S.A* 1948, Harper: New York.

199 Ibid.

200 Ibid.

201 Ibid.

202 Budenz, Louis, *The Techniques of Communism*, 1954, Henry Regnery: Chicago

203 Hearn, Chester G. (2006). *Spies & Espionage: A Directory*. Thunder Bay Press. San Diego, California.

204 Israeli Diplomat, Spy Suspect Met, *CBS News,* Feb. 11 2009.

205 *Washington Post*, 6/5/86, Charles R. Babcock, "US an Intelligence Target of the Israelis, Officials Say."

206 *Washington Post*, 10/31/86

207 Police Seize Rental Truck With TNT Traces, *Fox News*, May 13, 2002.

208 Cloudcroft Chief Stops Israelis With Suspicious Cargo, *Alamogordo Daily News,* May 19, 2003.

209 Chase suspects held without bond, *Asheville Citizen-Times,* Tuesday, May 11, 2004.

210 *Necessary Illusions,* Noam Chomsky. 1989.

211 "How Jewish is Hollywood?" By Joel Stein. Los Angeles Times, December 19, 2008

212 Ibid.

213 Simcha Jacobvici, *Hollywoodism: Jews, Movies and the American Dream*, and also titled *Hollywood: An Empire of their Own*.

214 Ibid

215 Friedman, Manny, *Times of Israel*, "Jews Do Control the Media"

216 The Neoconservative Persuasion, *Weekly Standard*, August 25, 2003.

217 Deutsch, K.L., and Nicgorski W., *Leo Strauss: Political Philosopher and Jewish Thinker*, Rowman & Littlefield Publishers 1994

218 Nathaniel Weyl, Arlington House, USA, 1970.

219 *Traitors' End: The Rise and Fall of the Communist Movement in Southern Africa*, Nathaniel Weyl, Arlington House, USA, 1970, pp124, 127-8.

220 *Fair Lady* 22 May 2002 p. 37.

221 Leo Beck Institute, Jerusalem 20

222 Moses Hess, Wikipedia

223 Jewish Bulletin. (1993). Feb. 19.

224 http://usatoday30.usatoday.com/news/religion/story/2011-09-26/jew-atheist-god/50553958/1

225 Solzhenitsyn, Aleksandr, *Two Hundred Years Together* Vagrius (Russia) (2008)

226 Ibid.

227 Ibid.

228 Ibid.

229 Ibid.

230 Ibid.

231 Stephen F. Cohen, *Bukharin and the Bolshevik Revolution: A Political Biography*, 1888-1938 (Oxford, Oxford University Press, 1980), pp. 232-233.

232 Solzhenitsyn, Aleksandr, *Two Hundred Years Together* Vagrius (Russia) (2008)

233 Ibid.

A Personal Message from Dr. David Duke

Thank you for reading my book with an open mind and for thinking deeply about the challenging things I write. I hope I have helped awaken you and your loved ones to the Zio-Globalist threat to our freedom, our heritage, our values, health, and indeed, our children's future.

I am writing, speaking and working for you and your family. I stand up to the threats and the smears of the Zionists. I say things that you would love to say to the world but that you may feel you can't. But you can! Together, we can work for the day when we can speak our minds and hearts, free and unfettered.

I want to speak for you! Actually, our success depends really on your support. I decided long ago to take a difficult path of completely giving my life to this mission. I am not asking you to take on the toughest challenges of my lifelong work -- although you may be inspired to join me in my calling. However, at the very least, I hope that you will make this work a big part of your life.

But, I do feel justified in straightforwardly asking you to give a part of your life to this work, meaning a decent portion of your time and income devoted to changing the world in which our children will live.

Here are some ways you can help my work:

- **You can send money. Sounds funny to blurt it right out like that but it's true because I can't do it alone. Your generous gifts fund this work.**

- **You can leave a legacy that will live on long after you, by including my work in your will or bequest, or as an insurance beneficiary,**

- **You can buy more copies of this book for friends and family, and for all those you want to wake up!**

- **You can subscribe to DavidDuke.com, and also to my mailed printed newsletter.**

- **You can read more and deepen your knowledge .**

- **You can listen to my daily radio show, stay up on the world and also learn to make a difference in your own life -- the revolution within! Details are at DavidDuke.com**

To contact me directly: Email me at

www.DavidDuke.com (*I will read it!*)

I welcome your comments on this book and thank you for your respect for me and your support of my work! Thanks!

Now that you've enjoyed this great book...
You will also love Dr. David Duke's other works:

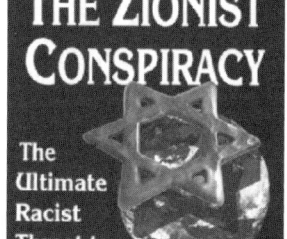